EUROPE'S
LAST
CHANCE

EUROPE'S LAST CHANCE

Why the European States
Must Form a More Perfect Union

Guy Verhofstadt

BASIC
BOOKS
NEW YORK

DESIGNED BY LINDA MARK

Library of Congress Cataloging-in-Publication Data

Names: Verhofstadt, Guy, 1953– author.
Title: Europe's last chance : why the European states must form a more perfect
    union / Guy Verhofstadt.
Description: New York : Basic Books, 2016.
Identifiers: LCCN 2016037184 (print) I LCCN 2016044014 (ebook) I
    ISBN 9780465096855 (hardback) I ISBN 9780465096862 (ebook)
Subjects: LCSH: European cooperation. I European Union countries—Politics
    and government—21st century. I BISAC: HISTORY / Europe / General. I
BIOGRAPHY & AUTOBIOGRAPHY / Presidents & Heads of State. I
    HISTORY / United States / General.
Classification: LCC JN30 .V4656 2016 (print) I LCC JN30 (ebook) I DDC
    341.242/2—dc23
LC record available at https://lccn.loc.gov/2016037184

10 9 8 7 6 5 4 3 2 1

To Heinrich von Brentano and Paul-Henri Spaak

CONTENTS

PART III: **DECAY**

PART IV: **PANIC**

PART V: **REBIRTH**

INTRODUCTION

Europe weathered crises before, but today the European Union (EU) is stretched beyond measure: Great Britain's decision to exit the EU; devastating terrorist attacks in Paris; desperate refugees flooding into nations unable—or unwilling—to shelter them humanely; intricate currency issues shaking the foundation of a common market; belligerents like Russia and the Islamic State in Iraq and Syria (ISIS) promising fearful assaults. Never—not in all my years as Belgium's prime minister and later on as a leader within the European Parliament—have I seen Europe standing so close to the brink.

Many see this crisis as proof that the European Union is broken beyond repair. Indeed, some may deem Great Britain's vote foolish, but it was a response to very real threats. And yet, clearly no one country can address all of these threats alone. In the weeks immediately following the Brexit vote, we were already witnessing Great Britain's struggle with its "independence."

Without a powerful new vision for the continent *as a whole* working together, Europe will very soon be lost to itself—and to its principal ally, the United States, whose need for support in a multipolar world has never been greater. For we Europeans, and for our American friends, this really is our last chance.

* * *

A UNITED STATES structured on the European model would be laughable. Imagine a US federation in which each state governor had veto power to block any decision from Congress or the president, an America where the governor of the smallest state could torpedo nationwide immigration reform or federal fiscal reform. Imagine a United States conceived as an asymmetric federation in which states could opt out of the Federal Bureau of Investigation (FBI), the Border Patrol, the Coast Guard, or the dollar, in which the states could say, We claim our right to join any of these federal institutions later, but for the moment we will simply observe and see how the rest of you cope. The world might believe the Americans had gone rogue, that it was impossible to safeguard a continent and build a world economy on the shaky foundations of voluntary participation.

Nevertheless, Europe finds itself in exactly that position today. There is no cooperation between the twenty-eight "member states" of the European Union—soon to be twenty-seven once the Brexit is set in motion. We have twenty-eight national intelligence services, which, each on their own, combat organized crime and terrorism. Yet the tragic 2015 events in Paris made it heartbreakingly clear that this fragmented strategy has failed. Following attack after attack, we learned that at least one of our national intelligence services had known of the terrorists but had been unable to pursue them across intra-European borders. Information exchange between our twenty-eight national intelligence services only happens erratically, on a voluntary basis, seriously weakening each country's security.

The security services mandated to protect European citizens still respect old borders; terrorists and criminals assuredly do not.

It is time to speak the unthinkable. The 2015 Paris attacks culmi-nated a decade of *preventable* terrorism in Europe. After the attacks in 2004 in Madrid, in 2005 in London, and in 2014 in Brussels, European leaders *finally* came up with the idea of a unified European record of passenger names to determine who flies in and out of the union. But this system is "European" in name only, because, in the name of sovereignty, it consists of twenty-eight unconnected national databases. But what is sovereignty when you cannot keep your citizens safe? Although we have free movement of people within Europe, we still don't have a common system to secure our European space. The Europe we have instead is *less* than the sum of its parts.

And this state of affairs stems not just from terrorism. Twenty-eight member states hold veto power over almost every decision, from whether to rescue Greece's plummeting economy to how to deal with the mass influx of refugees from Syria, Afghanistan, and Iraq. Despite the conti-nental importance of such decisions, it takes only one small party—like the extreme right True Finns, a junior partner in Finland's coalition gov-ernment, representing only half a million voters—to threaten the Greek deal and thus the future of the entire eurozone. It takes only a handful of prime ministers—from countries the size of New Hampshire—to block an agreement on the refugee crisis, stymying a desperately needed solu-tion for the thousands of people arriving on European soil every day, looking for shelter and protection.

The Brexit vote provides only one example of how European nations fold back on themselves and increasingly look inward instead of to the outside world. While the world catches fire and our economy remains bogged down, we fan the flames by plunging ourselves into an institu-tional crisis. Member states' hubris is the delusion that they can only regain sovereignty by splitting off from the European project and facing the great challenges on their own.

It is no exaggeration that, at this point, old nationalisms pose more danger to Europe than new threats. We might meet and overcome each of these fresh challenges—if only we could learn to pull together.

*　*　*

THOSE WHO DOUBT that a continental democracy is possible—or, indeed, desirable—need only look to the United States. Unless Europe learns to emulate its American cousin, it is surely doomed.

Many Americans think Washington, DC, is broken. These citizens believe federal politics can no longer deliver because of polarization and gridlock. Well, the situation in the American capital is nothing compared with the European quagmire. Many Americans criticize their government's response to the financial crisis, whereas from our perspective in Europe—where the crisis has never ended—America's actions were shockingly successful. Eight years later, Europe is the only continent on the globe that has still not recovered from the economic meltdown. We "grow" at a pace to slow to create new jobs. We are economically weak. We have a common currency supported by a microscopic treasury that covers barely 1 percent of European gross domestic product. These concerns only exacerbate the existential catastrophe: ultimately, there is a real chance that the EU could break up.

Obviously, this state of affairs isn't good for Europe. But it is no better for America. In a new and dangerous multipolar world—full of religious terrorism, humanitarian crises, escalating climate change, revanchist Russia, and rising China—America has learned the painful lesson that it can no longer stand alone.

If you subscribe to the view that America plays a unique role in defending democracy and human rights—like President Woodrow Wilson, who famously believed that the United States served as a blueprint for world peace—then losing Europe would entail the loss of one of the greatest pillars of Western civilization and democratic government.

But a weak European Union is equally problematic if you're a hard-nosed pragmatist who believes the world is chaotic, violent, and structured around continuously changing alliances. The ultimate foreign policy realist, former secretary of state Henry Kissinger, idealized the "Westphalian order" (which structured seventeenth-century Europe around a couple of big powers) "as the path breaker of a new concept of international order," believing that the division of nations promotes diversity and strengthens peace. Even in that case, a pragmatic America will have no easy time with a fragmented Europe presenting itself in the form of twenty-eight different interlocutors. It would mean dealing with a never-ending election cycle in twenty-eight countries instead of working with one head of state who held the same position for four years. We've already seen how Great Britain's exit has only further complicated America's delicate strategic plans. In Kissinger's world, a disunited Europe in military and foreign affairs is an unstable and unpredictable factor.

With Vladimir Putin seizing land in Ukraine and Georgia, an increasingly aggressive China projecting new power in the Old World, and terrific fear that ISIS will use the continent as its next battlefield, the United States needs a weak Europe like a hole in the head.

No matter how idealistic, gloomy, or pragmatic your worldview, the United States benefits from a strong and united Europe. It can never be in Washington's interest to confront a patchwork of twenty-seven or more European nation-states. Such is not a worthy alliance.

* * *

BUT IT DOESN'T have to be like that. The European Union could have developed differently and still has the opportunity to do so.

In the 1930s and 1940s, the United States was the only sizeable democracy in the world. While large parts of Europe lived under the oppression of dictators—such as Francisco Franco in Spain, António de Oliveira Salazar in Portugal, Adolf Hitler in Germany, and Benito Mussolini in Italy—the United States overcame its economic crisis not by renouncing democracy but by doubling down on its democratic promise through the New Deal. The nation emerged from the crisis stronger not by conceding to populism but by adhering to its liberal values, and thus it remained a shining beacon of democracy throughout the twentieth century.

Europe took longer to arrive at a similar point. But when it did, the continent was ready to stand up for its historic values and transformative promise. In 1953, six countries—Belgium, the Netherlands, Luxembourg, France, Italy, and West Germany—agreed to form a tight federation. The representatives of the six states wrote and even agreed to an elegant yet concise constitution—a rarely seen consensus in European history, one whose promise we have yet to achieve.

Barely a decade after the most catastrophic war in European history, former adversaries took the extraordinary step of agreeing to joint democratic governance and a shared military. Yet this common defense notion deterred most French representatives and was the main reason the whole project was voted down 319–264. Due to this political accident, the federal constitution for Europe didn't get ratified in the French National Assembly. The newly elected French prime minister, Pierre Mendès France, regarded the European constitution as an unimportant project of his predecessor, not worth defending. Because of this hiccup—this inattentiveness—the European constitution, and with it the entire political project, stumbled.

Finally, in 1957, the same six European nations approved a rump version of the 1953 constitution. The new project limited itself to an economic cooperation effort, focused mainly on a common market in transport and atomic energy. The so-called Treaty of Rome (1957)—the foundation for our own current European Union—was not the big success our history books proclaim. It merely recycled plans for a European federation aborted four years before.

This failed attempt laid the foundations for so many of our current ills in the European Union. With only an economic union, citizens feel the EU only when it touches their pocketbooks. Without a political union, citizens have no way to affect union-level policy; nor does the union itself have the tools to address such issues. Brexit, Grexit, the refugee crisis, the economic meltdown, cowardice before foreign foes: all these terrible outcomes are bound up in our missed opportunity to abandon artificial nationalism in exchange for a coherent and effective government of all Europeans.

Amazingly, America once faced nearly identical obstacles to its prosperity, security, and unity. The years after the Revolutionary War were hard, exacerbated by the terribly ineffective Articles of Confederation, which loosely bound the states together. In 1786—only three years after winning independence from the British Empire—the thirteen states concluded that the confederation was very inefficient at collecting taxes and defending itself against enemies, foreign and domestic. A convention called in Annapolis was far from successful: only five states bothered to send delegates. A new attempt, one year later, in Philadelphia was an improvement, with twelve of the thirteen states attending and fifty-five out of seventy-four delegates actually showing up. From such inauspicious beginnings arose the Constitutional Convention, which would redefine—and, indeed, save—the new nation.

The original plan was to update the existing confederation, but idealistic statesmen who dreamed of molding a mighty new government from the fractured individual states soon hijacked the convention: we know them as the Federalists under the leadership of James Madison. Only thirty-nine delegates signed a new compromise text, today's US Constitution, a much less impressive buy-in than the near-unanimity the Europeans achieved in 1953. Yet this "Philadelphia moment" still shines brightly across all of subsequent American history.

The text was far from perfect. Benjamin Franklin, as many others, wasn't exactly happy with the ultimate compromise: "I confess that there are several parts of this Constitution which I do not at present approve." To nobody's surprise, four states refused to ratify the document. Rhode Island resisted the longest, but despite all the opposition, the "thirteen colonies" finally agreed to make the giant leap together—to overcome their differences with the goal of forging a more perfect union.

Europe had its own "Philadelphia moment" but failed to carry the baton over the finish line. We should have used the historic momentum in 1953 just as the Americans did in 1787. We should have pushed harder, against France's initial resistance, for a strong federation. All of the projects we still debate today—a common emigration or economic policy, a joint military command or pan-European elections—we could have implemented decades ago. The world would have been better for it.

With some impressive exceptions—such as the creation of a common market in 1992 and the launch of the euro in 2001—we still drag ourselves from microdecision to microdecision, never rising to the great challenge of 1953. But it is never too late to take up the baton again.

* * *

As the former prime minister of a small country of 11 million people who speak three different languages, I have seen firsthand how easy it can be to accentuate differences and pit people against each other. Even at this small scale, the schisms between neighbors can seem insurmountable, and brokering deals can take every ounce of political savvy one possesses.

And yet, all that I've seen in my own small but proud nation, and across the continent as a whole, convinces me more than ever that the cure for Europe's ills is not less union but more. I met Putin when he was a Europe-friendly reformer and again after he had become the terrifying autocrat we know today. I flew into Libya after the fall of Muammar Gaddafi—with an EU mission in an effort to bring stability to our disintegrating neighbor—and landed in Athens at the height of the Greek fiscal crisis that promised to tear the EU apart from within. I've stood in the European Parliament as a candidate for president of Europe, and I've also stood with protestors against Putin in Moscow's Pushkin Square and against oligarchy and despotism in Kiev's Maidan Square. I advocated very vocally in the European Parliament for Great Britain to stay within the union.

Detractors wish to paint each of these crises as emblematic of a broader breakdown of the European project. Instead I see a great mass of people and institutions desperate to stay together. After decades in service to the European people, I can honestly say that, at every turn, the greatest threat to the safety and prosperity of Europe is a failure to finish the great project begun in 1953, to unite the seemingly disparate nations of the continent together into one grand federal project.

Accomplishing this grand objective will not be easy. But it represents Europe's only chance to protect the diversity of its culture and the proud history of its civilization. Otherwise, at best, we sink into parochial oblivion as America, China, and Russia take the lead; at worse, we become a battleground for the next generation of extremism, racism, and violence.

❊ ❊ ❊

THE PAGES AHEAD will do many things: show how the delusion of nationalism still holds sway in Europe and threatens to fragment the union beyond repair; highlight the difficulties of governing a continent undermined by its very own national governments; reveal how America, despite its own considerable share of problems, ultimately overcame the financial crisis, while Europe sat idle; and offer a concrete path forward in which the member states *must* put aside their differences and accept an American-style federal government.

Again and again, I provide examples of European squabbles over the most trivial of details as the foundation of our society crumbles from within and erodes from without. But each setback offers an opportunity for us to see that this crisis is *man-made.* With fresh ideas and the proper resolve, we can set Europe—and the world—on the right path again.

Europe must stand united if it wants to survive in today's world. Only in this way can the "old" continent reestablish itself as a worthy ally of the United States. Only if Europe and the United States can count on each other's strengths can we make the world a safer and more prosperous place.

PART I

AT THE BRINK

CHAPTER ONE

DIVIDED WE FALL

O N Tuesday, December 29, 2015, I drove in the late after-
noon along the A-13 highway from the direction of Rouen. As dark-
ness fell, I entered the ever-animated city of Paris, the pleasure-loving
capital of France, the world's mecca of fun and entertainment. Before,
people rushed to do their last holiday shopping, intoxicated with flamboyant wrapping paper and curled ribbon. As ever, we were taking our leave
of the dying year by giving presents. This time, however, we were saying
good-bye *sans regrets*, *sans remords*. Only a few weeks had passed since the
most recent string of devastating tragedies in this wonderful city.

The past twelve months had been too cruel, too frightening, and
above all too unreal: *Charlie Hebdo*. The Bataclan. January 7. November
13. Televised videos and images of beheadings had assaulted our eyes
almost on a weekly basis. No one knew when this madness would end or
when the next bloody attack would take place.

Paris was deserted. Here and there one saw a handful of tourists: Russians, Chinese, Japanese. One heard the rowdy chat of a few Americans.

But hardly any French people were about. It seemed as if the Parisians had fled their beautiful city. There were no traffic jams; taxis roamed the streets, green lights on their roofs. And most of the cafés seemed empty too, but for a few stray tourists.

I had decided on an impulse to ring in the new year in Paris. I did not want to let the terrorists have things their way. I wanted to resolutely oppose the atmosphere of panic that the French media—intentionally or otherwise—had created. Above all I wanted to lend my symbolic support to the people of Paris, who had suffered so much in 2015.

I must admit, however, that I myself was not in a much better state. I still felt quite shaken by those attacks, still devastated, even more so than after the terror of September 11. A fervent supporter of the United States, I still remember the horror of those attacks aimed at the American people and their president: the Twin Towers, the Pentagon, the White House. But November 13 in Paris was completely different. That evening, terrorists attacked and murdered rock music, football, and Parisian night life—in other words, our way of life.

RULE OF LAW?

A few days later, sitting in a taxi on the evening of December 31, I listened to French president François Hollande deliver his New Year's address in beautifully articulated French sentences designed to rally his compatriots. But his "fellow citizens" were thoroughly frightened, preferring to stay at home or, at most, to venture out to dinner with relatives or a few friends. The terrorists were winning: society was in disarray, and under the state of emergency then in force, the police could detain you, no questions asked, and put you behind bars for days, with no right of appeal and no defense. What had become of the rule of law? Which of our freedoms still applied?

Habeas corpus is more or less the foundation of our European society, our gift to the rest of the world, much as the ancient Greeks gave us democracy and the Arabs gave us algebra. This legacy is now in jeopardy, being pushed aside without political opposition. On that night in Paris, it seemed as if only comedians and clowns on New Year's shows were expressing dissent.

Politicians apparently have no problem with the changes that have occurred in the wake of terrorist attacks on European soil. They are caught in the stranglehold of a uniform mentality focused on what populists are calling the "new security culture," a hierarchy of values that subordinates virtually all of our rights and freedoms to one overriding concern, "public safety," as if we can buy and guarantee security by sending heavily armed soldiers to patrol the streets, passing new security laws, and setting up giant databases.

The great thinkers buried here in the Pantheon knew better. The inscription on Voltaire's grave reads, "He fought the nonbelievers and fanatics; he inspired tolerance; he claimed the rights of man against the feudal servitude." In much the same spirit, the battle against terrorism and fanaticism will be won in people's *minds*—not by restricting our liberties.

But perhaps I have little right to say this. As head of the Belgian government in December 2007, I myself declared Anti-Terrorism Alert Level 4, restricted access to the Christmas market, and canceled the traditional New Year's Eve fireworks in the Brussels main square. I did this in response to clear indications of planned attacks. Nizar Trabelsi, a former professional footballer who had reinvented himself as a terrorist, intended to escape from prison to create havoc with arms and explosives in the center of Brussels.

To be honest, I would likely respond in the same way today. When you are responsible for a country, you do not have much scope for considering whether liberal values or public safety should prevail. In that situation, all that counts is the well-being of the populace, which you must protect at all costs. Consequently, I do have some sympathy for President Hollande, who responded to an unprecedented attack in the heart of his country by declaring a state of emergency and perhaps allowing it to continue for longer than was strictly necessary.

But are all these emergency measures actually an effective way of combating terrorism itself? Or are they merely intended to calm the people and pull the wool over their eyes? In order to answer this question, we need to establish exactly what has gone wrong. How did we fail to see the attacks coming sooner and to prevent them? Was it because for years we neglected to cultivate a "security culture"?

However plausible it may sound, that theory does not stand up to the facts. All terrorists who have succeeded in launching effective attacks within European territory in the past ten years were already known to at least one intelligence or security service in one of our member states. So our governments and their administrative apparatuses did not lack information. They either did not share the information they had with the country where the attack later took place or they did so too late. It is hard to see how Great Britain will be any safer, having now lessened its chances of receiving even partial intelligence from other European countries.

Without a federal European government, there is no comprehensive system for storing and consulting intelligence. The terrorists, however, are not hampered by national borders.

＊ ＊ ＊

THIS ANALYSIS RESTS on a long list of facts. Jamal Zougam, who carried out the 2004 train bombing in Madrid, had come to the attention of the French, British, and Moroccan intelligence services three years previously. That Zougam had already appeared in court in France in connection with the 9/11 attacks did not guarantee his subsequent monitoring in Spain as well. If it had, the 2004 attack could perhaps have been prevented. A year later, on July 7, Mohammad Sidique Kahn blew up the Edgware Road metro station in London. He too was known to security services. Nicolas Sarkozy, then France's minister of the interior, indicated that, as long ago as 2002, the French security services had placed members of the London terrorist cell under "partial arrest." If we can believe Sarkozy, these criminals too had been known in advance and monitored by at least one security service, and they too had slipped through the net with dramatic consequences.

The British parliamentary committee of inquiry that sought to shed more light on the case never received an answer to the questions it put to the French authorities. In 2014, Mehdi Nemmouche, armed with a Kalashnikov rifle, shot a number of innocent people at the Jewish Museum of Belgium in Brussels. The French authorities had entered his name into the Schengen Information System II, after the Germans informed them that he had returned from Syria in March. But again, there was no follow-up.

The same pattern crops up in connection with the January 2015 attacks on *Charlie Hebdo* and the Jewish supermarket in Paris. The Kouachi brothers managed to carry out their assaults despite being known to several intelligence and security services. Cherif Kouachi had been intercepted in 2005 before he could travel to Syria and then on to Iraq to fight against the United States. Three years later, he was convicted of involvement in a network conspiring to send yet more Muslim fighters to Iraq. Both brothers had been recorded in US databases as suspected terrorists and listed on the US no-fly list, a crucial item of information undoubtedly passed on to British intelligence. The other *Charlie Hebdo* terrorist, Amedy Koulibaly, had been sentenced to five years' imprisonment in 2010 for his involvement in a series of attacks carried out by Smaïn Aït Ali Belkacem in Paris in 1995. This information never made its way to the right people in time.

In the case of the November 13, 2015, attacks on the Bataclan, the Stade de France, and several restaurants in Paris, several European national security services had again possessed in advance crucial intelligence related to the perpetrators. In the week before the attacks, the German police had discovered heavy weapons and ammunition in a car in Bavaria, concealed in a "professionally made" compartment. The destination on the car's satellite navigation system was set to "Paris," a piece of information not communicated to the French intelligence and security services. Nor did those services know that Abdelhamid Abbaaoud, the Belgian head of a Franco-Belgian terrorist cell, had returned from Syria until a foreign intelligence service finally tipped them off that he had been spotted in Greece. The Belgian state security service, on the other hand, knew that another perpetrator, Bilal Hadfi, had returned from Syria.

The pieces of this puzzle were highly dispersed, and communication between national intelligence services—insofar as it existed—was sorely inadequate. As a result, on the morning after the attacks, French police checked Salah Abdeslam, one of the men who had opened fire on café customers in Paris, at a roadblock near Cambrai. In Belgium, Abdeslam was a known terrorist suspect and convicted criminal. However, not having this information, the French police did not regard him as suspicious and, disastrously, permitted him to continue on his way.

We can draw from this and a whole series of other incidents an unequivocal conclusion: rather than monitoring all our citizens even more closely, we should follow up on existing intelligence better and, above all, share it with one another. Sporadic exchanges of information between national intelligence and security services within Europe are completely inadequate and obsolete for the purpose of combatting terrorism and organized crime. We can no longer rely on an "intelligence and security culture" that depends on the goodwill of national institutions, some of which have traditionally cooperated closely, as they continue to do, while others have virtually no contact due to mutual distrust.

And as each of the terrorist attacks of the past ten years makes clear, there exist severe problems even between the intelligence services of the so-called large member states. Borders do not constrain terrorists—either within the EU or elsewhere—and it is therefore no longer practical for them to separate our intelligence and security services.

SAFEGUARDING ALL OF EUROPE

We must cease to regard security as a national matter, as our ministers of the interior and their bosses, the leaders of the EU member states, do. Installing an antiterrorism coordinator alone will not defeat ISIS or al-Qaeda.

It makes no sense to create a single "Schengen" area—in which everybody can move freely—without organizing shared control of the external borders. It is equally absurd to create that common area without also building a common antiterrorism capacity. The attacks in Madrid, London, Brussels, and Paris demonstrate that we cannot continue to fragment our security policy.

I do not mean that we should abolish our national security services. On the contrary, when it comes to fighting terrorism, we must establish a single European intelligence and security capacity that operates in addition to, and in support of, national security services. It is not enough for European leaders to shed tears about terrorism if, when the chips are down, they are not prepared to surrender sovereignty to Europe in the field of security.

Here the United States serves as a good basis for comparison. In the late nineteenth century, the National Chiefs of Police Union established the National Bureau of Criminal Identification, which passed information about criminals to the various police and security services in the field. After the assassination of President William McKinley in 1901, however, people became increasingly convinced that anarchist terrorists wished to destabilize the American state, and the national bureau received more and more resources and powers. After changing its name a few times, in the mid-1930s it became the world-famous Federal Bureau of Investigation (FBI).

What began as a tiny office with a few dozen officers, who did no more than pass information on to the various states, grew into a federal organization employing 35,000 people, with a budget of more than $8 billion, with powers to investigate two hundred categories of federal crimes throughout the United States. Together with the Central Intelligence Agency (CIA) and the Department of Homeland Security (DHS), the FBI today ensures that in the United States cross-border crimes and terrorism hardly stand a chance.

Here in Europe, despite all the attacks, we still have not reached that stage. Indeed, we cannot take even a modest first step toward a European FBI by introducing compulsory intelligence sharing, which could strike a decisive blow against terrorism and prevent fresh attacks. The latest wheeze in the fight against terrorism is no exception: the Passenger Name Record (PNR) system, designed to keep information (name, address, credit card details, family relationships, and dietary preferences, thus, in many cases, religion) about everybody traveling on scheduled flights to, from, and within Europe—an enormous invasion of the privacy of all European citizens that yields no demonstrable benefits.

To begin with, the vast majority of people travel within Europe by road or rail. PNR is a useful instrument primarily to track suspicious long-term travel patterns, such as those of drug dealers. As a way of tracking Syrian combatants or adherents of the Islamic State, PNR is useless—particularly because the member states decided to establish not a single European PNR database but twenty-eight national ones.

The assertion that PNR will protect us against terrorists is a cruel deception. Ministers of the interior took great pains to prevent establishment of a single European database. And even exchanges among the twenty-eight national databases will in fact not be compulsory, because they will not happen automatically. A country's service will have to request data separately in each case from its foreign counterparts—by e-mail or telephone—once again raising the danger that crucial intelligence will languish. A terrorist suspect will still have no problem driving from Belgium or the Netherlands to Frankfurt in order to fly away, again without any serious difficulties, to Ankara or Antalya. It is now virtually certain that Salah Abdeslam used a similar escape route. PNR is a pointless system, reflecting merely the national opposition to a full-fledged European FBI or DHS.

PNR reveals the true concern of our heads of state and government: preserving the sacred cow of national sovereignty. But what use is national sovereignty if it does not guarantee citizens even the most basic form of security?

* * *

IN 2001, WHILE still reeling from 9/11, European politicians had firmly resolved to take a different approach. And our security since would have been far better for it.

I remember well the debates within the European Council, which I chaired, in the months shortly after 9/11. We took a first step with the introduction of the European Arrest Warrant (EAW). We had observed that many terrorists and criminals managed to evade impending arrest simply by traveling to another jurisdiction. The EAW would definitively put a stop to that. At that time, too, the "sovereignty" argument received great play. Then, too, leaders from many member states climbed onto their high horses. And then, too, they resorted to the tried-and-true method of not torpedoing the plan themselves in the European Council but leaving the dirty work to their representatives in the Council of Ministers of Justice, who raised the most senseless practical objections in order to destroy the whole project.

I had to convene the European Council no fewer than three times in order to confirm the decision on the introduction of the European Arrest Warrant—until even the ministers of justice finally realized that there was no going back and that any further opposition would be a waste of time. Italian head of government Silvio Berlusconi was the last holdout, even though his own administration and the whole of the Italian Ministry of Foreign Affairs were in favor.

I never understood his attitude properly, but rumor had it that he feared Spanish examining magistrate Baltasar Garzón Real might use the new instrument against him personally. Thanks partly to help from Italy's minister for foreign affairs, Renato Ruggiero, a believer in Europe, we managed to persuade the Italian government to support the proposal. Berlusconi insisted on a ten-year transitional period for his country, then dismissed Ruggiero for his treachery and assumed his post, serving simultaneously as Italy's prime minister and its minister for foreign affairs—a true disaster for Europe and, of course, for Italy.

Difficult though its genesis was, EAW was a European solution, one that made Europe more secure: launched on January 1, 2004, it immediately made its impact felt on the ground. The EAW represented the opposite of the PNR, a sham solution that will have little or no effect precisely because it is not a European solution.

MORE UNION, NOT LESS

As a result of the wave of terrorist attacks, there is now a growing chorus to abandon Schengen and the European project. This time, fault lies not with nationalists, populists, or Euroskeptics but with our very own generation of national political leaders. As in any field, by continuing to opt for half-baked measures and solutions, they are encouraging people to think that we would be better off if we reinstated national borders—that the nation-state can do what Europe cannot.

In fact the opposite is true. By reducing "Europe" to a "coordinator of national administrative bodies" or by "coordinating national policy strategies better," we shall never succeed in making our continent more secure or protecting it better. We must tackle this challenge at the European level with European policies and specific European instruments. If we are unwilling or unable to take that path, we will prove the Euroskeptics and critics of Europe right. In that case it would be better to pull the plug on the project.

In this globalized and interconnected world, logic might seem to dictate renationalizing everything: perhaps it would be safer for member states to withdraw behind their own national borders, politically and economically. At this point, not only nationalists and Euroskeptics but also leaders of traditional political parties have made that choice and given up on Europe. Nicolas Sarkozy, for example, in a recent speech before the Flemish Chamber of Commerce in Antwerp, Belgium, pontificated, "Schengen is dead. Schengen has never truly worked and never will, because we do not have a European migration policy."

Such a stance, of course, turns Europe's project on its head. We must formulate a common migration policy precisely in order to save Schengen and preserve freedom of movement. Sarkozy is right about one thing, however: it is not possible to have the one without the other.

A free trade area with free movement of persons can of course only survive if jointly guarded and—in terms of migration—jointly managed. And that calls for a single set of rules on migration and asylum rather than twenty-eight different ones. Anyone not prepared to go down that road is indeed signing the death warrant of a single free European area.

It therefore comes as no surprise that Sarkozy's firm assertion on that evening in Antwerp received no applause; instead the audience—full of businessmen and -women running small and medium-sized enterprises—looked frightened. The last thing that they want is reintroduction of the customs checks and border queues of the past. The Brexit discussion has similarly revealed contradictory desires. Many "Brexiters" want to remain part of the European internal market without having to accept the free movement of people. But free movement is the cornerstone of the European common market. You simply cannot have the cake and eat it too.

* * *

SECURITY IS JUST one aspect of the challenge presented by terrorism. Equally important, if not more so, is the lack of a common foreign and defense capability to eradicate the breeding grounds of that terrorism around the world.

It is bitter news, but the terrorism in Europe—now being nurtured in Syria—is largely our own fault. At the very least, we could have prevented it by acting correctly. Time and time again, we neglected to support the democratic, secular opposition to Syrian dictator Bashar al-Assad and thereby created a vacuum that sucked in the most extremist forces of Sunni jihad.

The jihad that raged through Europe in 2015 indicates a crisis not only in the European project but, to an even greater extent, in our European civilization. European values no longer inspire people, although they still possess the potential to do so, because the world perceives a cowardly, divided, and decrepit Europe that can no longer muster the courage to stand up for its ideals. Europe must unite to fight terrorism, even if that means surrendering national sovereignty. Because what we surrender nationally in terms of self-government we shall regain in the form of effective action at the European level.

Only by adopting the wider view can we defend and disseminate our own European values credibly. Only if we adopt a strong united front can we tackle with confidence and determination other problems at the root of the terrorist threat at home: racism, inequality in the labor market, and discrimination in the rental market and, regrettably, in many other areas of society too.

These problems give rise to the most worrying facet of the terrorist attacks in Europe: they have been committed by young people who grew up among us, whose families have lived in Europe for two, three, and in some cases four generations. Until a few months before they left for Syria, these young people were drinking beer in Europe's cafés and smoking weed with their friends, but in political Islam they found a cruel way to express their discontent with their treatment by society. Great Britain will be no safer with its newly "guarded" borders. So long as our continent spends its political capital in discussing the institutional aspects of our security services, there won't be a lot of time and resources left to address the social ills that constitute the breeding ground of terrorism, and we will therefore largely continue to fail to get our society back on track.

The EU member states are not succeeding in keeping their citizens safe, whatever their origin, rank, or status. And so long as we have to keep going on about the structures of security services or about a defense community, we shall have no time or attention to spare for the far more complex phenomenon of social disaffection underlying terrorism, a phenomenon that raises the crucial question of how we can ensure that young people with a migrant background embrace our society and values instead of attacking them. That is the real challenge facing us, one that Europeans can only solve together.

CHAPTER TWO

UNITED WE STAND

THE ONLY SOLUTION FOR EUROPE IS TO REFORM THE EUROPEAN Union in the model of the American federal government. A "United States of Europe" will be better able to stop the next terrorist attack, to respond to the next economic downturn, to listen to the voices of the people before it's too late. Fragmented as it is, Europe today can barely tread water as it fails to respond to the refugee crisis, the sputtering economy, and the rise of terrorism and xenophobic politics. Devastating internal divisions that limit our ability to respond effectively undermine even the seeming unity of scorned Europeans after the Brexit vote.

Many say that the European Union is at the breaking point, and they are right. Yet the solution is not less union but more. Europe desperately requires a new, federal government modeled on the United States, one that protects the remarkable diversity of its countries even as it doubles down on their values and strengths to stand tall in a changing world.

❋ ❋ ❋

WE CANNOT CONTINUE to stand separately and muddle along like this while globalization mercilessly batters our member states' national sovereignty. Whether in relation to the banking crisis, global warming, international fraud, or organized crime, anyone seeking an effective solution to these issues inevitably concludes that one exists only at the European level. Thus we must opt for stronger European institutions and a federal European state.

In fact, globalization necessitates the advent of this sort of federal Europe. And globalization is only going to gather speed. After a dramatic drop-off in 2009, world trade is back at precrisis levels. In the political arena, too, we are seeing increasing international cooperation, with governments seeking solutions for more and more military and economic conflicts via informal international forums like the Group of Eight (G8) and the Group of Twenty. That the sanction causing Vladimir Putin the biggest headache was Russia's exclusion from the G8 demonstrates how important this kind of international gathering has become.

These dual tendencies—globalization and international cooperation—are two sides of the same coin. Concepts like national territory are becoming increasingly eroded and less and less relevant politically and economically. Far-reaching structural cooperation between countries, by contrast, is becoming increasingly important. One sees how even "newly independent" Great Britain suddenly finds itself needing to "opt in" to many different international alliances and arrangements to maintain its prosperity—a fine example of the dangers inherent in thoughtlessly "going it alone."

So the notion of a decision to promote the deeper integration of the European Union is actually already out of date. As a consequence of the world we live in, integrating is no longer an option; it is a necessity.

OLD NATIONALISM, OLD IGNORANCE

Although, from a rational point of view, a European federation is the only option, a strong countermovement has been on the rise for some time now: Euroskepticism. The latest variant of the populism and tribalism marching across our continent, this movement argues for a return to the nation-state as a solution to our political and economic problems.

Great Britain clearly held the latest high mass of tribalism with its referendum to leave the European Union. Euroskeptics do not just want their countries to leave the union; they want to see the whole project dismantled and push their cause with hollow rhetoric about the supposed "loss of national identity." They attempt to frighten people about the ongoing unification of the European continent. They maintain that the retreat of each country behind national borders will solve the majority of our problems, which they posit the European Union not only fails to solve but actually makes worse. In their view the European Union is a scapegoat, not a solution.

Euroskeptics eagerly exploit all kinds of fallacies and emotional arguments. To counter the current economic uncertainty—which they attribute entirely to globalization and to Europe—they offer the false reassurance of national democracy, painting the nation-state as a safe haven against the vagaries of the modern world. They elevate traditions and symbols such as national flags and anthems to objects of sacred adoration once again. Whereas a few years ago national institutions—such as the United Kingdom's National Health Service, a crucial though fraudulent tool in convincing voters to opt for "leave"—were depicted as decaying and outdated bureaucracies, they now sit once again on a pedestal as beacons of welfare and stability, as national bulwarks that will protect citizens from nefarious foreign influences. Toxic influences emanate from a "federal" Europe that does more than any other supranational body to emasculate and undermine our national identities: our languages, our cultures, our ways of life.

Yet a federal Europe actually offers us the best guarantee of cultural diversity. European values include the protection of multilingualism against the instinct of many nation-states to favor one dominant culture or national language. This is even more the case when it comes to protection of the wide variety of cultural, religious, and ethnic "minorities" who live on our continent and find themselves facing pressure to assimilate. A federal Europe is thus not a threat but, in fact, a safeguard against the imposition of a single cultural or religious norm.

If you look at the map of Europe, you will see that its linguistic and national boundaries are practically identical. For centuries the norm, linguistic diversity is now the exception as a result of two hundred years of nationalistic delusions. Outsiders looking in on our debates about European identity witness a strange scene: a continent unique in that it is no longer growing—either geopolitically or economically—but where once again discussions about language, culture, flags, anthems, and other national symbols rage. As we know, it is not these elements, but democratic accountability and the effectiveness of social and political institutions, that determine the prosperity and well-being of a people.

WHAT MIGHT HAVE BEEN

Many Americans won't know it, but once there was another option. On September 10, 1952, six foreign ministers met in Luxembourg. On behalf of France, Germany, Belgium, the Netherlands, Italy, and the host country, they signed the first European constitution, which seventy delegates of the six countries approved six months later at what became known as the "Ad Hoc Assembly." The following year, on August 30, 1954, the French Assemblée Nationale voted 319–264 not to ratify a significant part of the deal, the proposed European defense community.

Since then, the text of this constitution has been largely forgotten, although it is remarkable in several respects—first and foremost in its length: in marked contrast to the hundreds of pages of treaty texts that now lay the ground rules for the European Union, the first European constitution was barely thirty pages long. And uncluttered by today's political jargon, it was also a very simple read. It comprised only 117 articles, with no litany of exceptions and nuances.

Even more remarkable, however, is the content. The text approached Europe not as some kind of anomaly in need of ad hoc construction but as an ordinary state. Instead of talking of an "ever closer Union"—whatever that means—its intention was clear: the formation of a European federation and the advent of a new, supranational sovereignty in Europe, legitimized and underpinned by democratic institutions. A quarter century before the first elections to the European Parliament (1979), this first constitution already envisaged directly elected representatives of the people at the European level. It represents a breathtaking vision and a colossal missed opportunity.

The European citizens did not partake directly in the European project for another twenty-five years, and so, thirty-five years later, we are still suffering from a big hangover in the form of a democratic deficit whereby Parliament struggles against other, *nondemocratic* institutions. The European Parliament still has no say whatsoever over the union's foreign policy. And it remains deprived of the right to raise revenue by levying taxes—a terrible offense to the only democratically elected assembly for all of Europe.

The author of this first, mold-breaking European constitution was Heinrich von Brentano, a German politician and lawyer of Italian-German background, who was also intimately involved in the creation of the constitution—or *Grundgesetz*—of the Federal Republic of Germany. The similarities between the two texts are thus no coincidence. Like every constitution, it began with a preamble, in this case setting out the vision and purpose of the federation as "a living, united free Europe" that contributed to culture and peace, secured prosperity, and safeguarded "the dignity, freedom and fundamental equality of men of every condition, race or creed." The opening section contained much more than vague aspirations and empty promises. Article 4, for example, stipulated that the union "shall have juridical personality" and that "in international relationships [it] shall enjoy the juridical personality necessary to the exercise of its functions and the attainment of its ends." The federation thus would have had at its disposal all the resources it needed—including a shared defense program—to exercise a full-fledged foreign policy.

In relation to home affairs, too, the federation would have received the greatest possible authority to safeguard the fundamental rights of its citizens directly. In the territories of the member states, the constitution stipulated, the federation "may acquire . . . movable and immovable assets and may sue." The document even provided a procedure whereby member states could implement measures to maintain "constitutional

order and democratic institutions within their territory." The European
Parliament would have further defined and refined the precise conditions—based on the premise that the various national constitutions
would have to demonstrate scrupulous respect for European values.
Thus the constitution left no room for a Silvio Berlusconi to enact laws
to suit his own ends or for a Viktor Orbán to attempt to introduce the
death penalty. Our values would have formed the core of our politics.

＊ ＊ ＊

THE BRENTANO CONSTITUTION also proposed simple and transparent
institutions light years away from what we know today. European politics might be notoriously opaque to Americans, but the large majority
of the Europeans also has a hard time understanding who is responsible
for what in the union.

The European Commission, the EU's executive body, is the only institution that can take legislative initiatives, and yet it is weak. It comprises
twenty-eight commissioners, each appointed by his or her national government, making it a large and politically inconsistent group unable to act
forcefully. The European Parliament, counting more than seven hundred
members, is the EU's only directly elected body, but it cannot take any
legislative action not first initiated by the commission. Nor does it have a
full say on the European budget. We have turned the rallying cry of the
American Revolution on its head: representation without taxation.

And then there is the European Council, comprising the twenty-
eight heads of state and government. Technically it is the union's least
powerful institution, but in practice it has the final say on everything. Or
more correctly, it is where legislative proposals go to die. Most of the
time, the council members cannot reach a consensus. One could easily
characterize the council as the graveyard for much legislation proposed
by the commission and approved by the parliament.

The Brentano constitution structured the union much more simply,
as a normal federal state. The European political community would have
stood on a purely federalist footing and might have developed into a re-

spectable counterpart of the United States. A federal Europe would have spared us untold grief and heartache over the decades.

THE UNITED STATES DID IT, AND SO CAN WE

Anyone familiar with the Brentano constitution will understand straight away that a democratic and efficient union on the US model—with clearly defined powers and transparent institutions—is no pipedream. We simply need less bloated, more effective institutions; a small, efficient European government whose members stand up for all European citizens, not just for those who belong to their own national support base; a government accountable, as in any democracy, to a directly elected, fully empowered parliament able to initiate proposals and initiatives itself.

Anyone who claims to see in this the creation of a superstate is either acting in bad faith or willfully blind. A federation would also put an end to the "à la carte Europe," whereby each member state picks and chooses its own form of European Union via opt-ins, opt-outs, earmarks, and enhanced cooperation. This kind of cherry-picking would become a thing of the past because the practice not only weakens the union as a whole but also renders it unworkable. The expectation of enjoying a thriving internal market while refusing to participate in basic tasks necessary to its operation is no longer acceptable.

This leads to the idea—also found in the Brentano constitution—of introducing a two-tier membership: full and associated. This would immediately answer the question of how Great Britain will leave the union: as an associated member, as member of the internal market, or merely as a country with which the EU has concluded a trade agreement. Britain's departure and the need to redefine its relationship with the union is the ideal occasion to put two-tier membership back on the table. But we must also define exactly what these two types of membership entail. In other words, Brexit could provide the groundwork for a complete overhaul of the European project.

Having a two-tier form of membership gives all member states the same option. Full membership entails participation in both the internal market and the political governance of the united continent. Any state choosing associated status—which guarantees only participation in the internal market—would no longer be involved in all the union's decisions.

A GOLDEN AGE OF UNION

A good historical illustration of the power of a federation—demonstrating that political unity and economic and cultural openness are not opposites but rather reinforce each other—is the Netherlands in the seventeenth century, an era, known as its golden age, of tolerance and migration, of openness to the rest of the world. At that time, the Netherlands was a safe haven for political and religious refugees from the southern Netherlands as well as from France and Portugal. Those refugees brought with them tremendous intellectual gifts. The period was also one of unprecedented economic growth and produced many cultural and intellectual luminaries—painters like Rembrandt and Vermeer and thinkers like Spinoza.

It was also the era of the Dutch East India Company, whose story illustrates perfectly how in a world where both competitors and foes impose themselves on a global scale, only integration and consolidation can save you. In the 1600s, the Netherlands were called the Republic of the Seven United Netherlands. Its constituent provinces had their own merchant fleets, each separately under heavy pressure from Spain and England.

In 1602, the decision was taken by the States-General of the Dutch Republic—on grounds of both economic and political logic—to amalgamate these fleets. The economic logic, clearly, was to increase profitability. The shareholders of the individual fleets saw only too well that a merger was the only way for their shipping business to survive. By pooling their capital, they were able to transport more goods on more ships. The political logic behind the merger was not just to collect more taxes but also to create a maritime military power that could successfully compete with the Spanish fleet. All these small companies, after all, were no match for the Spanish. A united company, on the other hand, could and would serve as a powerful economic and political weapon.

No doubt every province of the Netherlands believed that it had to protect its identity. Holland is not Frisia, after all, and Frisia is not Zeeland. No doubt everyone also thought it absolutely necessary for each province to have its own merchant fleet. Yet no one thought for a moment that a merger could not take place for those reasons. The Dutch golden age thus dawned thanks to the construction of a federation: a federation of provinces and a federation of merchant fleets. In its heyday, the Dutch East India Company had over one hundred ships in its Indies fleet. It had 3,000 employees in the Netherlands and no fewer than 25,000 in Asia. The company was the world's very first multinational enterprise. The economic boost that this brought about also initiated a period of cultural flowering, including a dazzling array of art: in this period, the Netherlands produced an estimated 3 million paintings by no fewer than 5,000 artists.

In short, a union—for expediency, for survival, for profit—birthed one of the most magnificent and enviable periods in European history.

TWO PATHS FOR EUROPE

The United Netherlands nicely illustrates why we badly need to build a European federation. Yet the idea also has a scientific basis. In *Why Nations Fail: The Origins of Power, Prosperity and Poverty*, Daron Acemoglu and James Robinson clearly show that strong institutions are necessary to generate wealth. The day-to-day governance of a country and its short-term politics matter less than the durable establishment of democratic institutions and bodies.

Why Nations Fail begins with the story of Nogales, a city on the border of Mexico and the United States. A fence divides the city into a northern, US part and a southern, Mexican part. People of the same ethnic backgrounds occupy the two sections of the city; the same sun shines over them, and soils and sicknesses pay little heed to the fence separating them. Yet the US side is prosperous and healthy, while the Mexican side is much less so. In every area, the southern sections fare worse, even though the same people populate both parts. Only the absence of strong economic and democratic institutions in the south and their presence in the north explains the developmental differences between the districts.

That is the choice we face in Europe. Do we want to work toward strong European institutions that work efficiently, that enjoy the confidence of citizens and entrepreneurs, so that wealth is created, so that we have not just top schools and universities but also excellent health care, innovative businesses, and so forth? Nothing more, and nothing less, is at stake. Do we want our children and grandchildren to live in northern or southern Nogales?

* * *

A FEDERAL EUROPE means more than a radical change in how we make decisions. Above all, it represents the only way we can rid ourselves of the tormentor within us, the nationalist delusion that still haunts Europe. Pretty much every member state is under the spell of its national identity. Pretty much every member state excludes population groups, especially if they are small or weak or too different from the national norm. We see this in the restriction of linguistic diversity, in discrimination against minorities, and in the imposition of the same cultural or religious prescriptions across whole societies.

A federal Europe is the antidote to such practices. In Europe, we can count the countries where multilingualism is the norm on one hand. Even then, these languages are merely tolerated as a curiosity, a kind of cultural heritage; they are rarely officially recognized. This shriveling of linguistic diversity stems from two hundred years of dominant nationalist thinking in Europe. A federal Europe, on the other hand, rests on the opposite foundation: on the preservation of pluralism, multiculturalism, multilingualism, and diversity in all its forms and guises.

A federal Europe does not sweep away those differences; instead, it goes looking for that which connects us, which gives us common ground, the values, ideals, and principles we share: democracy, a free market, social responsibility, freedom of expression, tolerance, freedom to pursue any religion or hold any worldview, and equality of the genders. Every European society operates on this range of fundamental beliefs. The European Union must not only write these values into its constitution but defend them in practice.

What all kinds of populists and nationalists maintain—that Europe is suffused with social bases and values so different as to be incompatible—is nonsense. The Greeks are not born with an irresistible urge to corruption. The Italians are not fraudsters by nature. The Portuguese are not inveterate idlers. The strongest-growing regions, declared the "Four Motors for Europe," are, along with Baden-Württemberg in Germany, Lombardy in Italy, Catalonia in Spain, and the Rhône-Alpes region in France—three regions in southern Europe. The entrepreneurial spirit is not northern European, it is *European*, as are solidarity with the vulnerable, the pursuit of justice, and a commitment to democratic rights and obligations and to civil liberties. All of these principles are universal across Europe. These were the ideals of both the French Revolution of 1789 and England's Glorious Revolution a hundred years before. They are the principles that guide not just Germans or Spaniards or Italians but all their fellow citizens in each member state of the European Union.

I do not believe there exists an exact, one-to-one correspondence between economics and art or that a mathematical model can express the relationship between the two. I do believe, however, that both art and economics need free space to thrive and that it is impossible to separate the realm of one from that of the other. Europe provides such a free, creative space, both economically and culturally. Yet we do not make optimal use of it, which is an enormous waste of talent. If we do not build a European federation above it, European society will remain fragmented, incomplete, and overregulated. Europe lacks a common digital marketplace, as well as a common labor market and a common capital market. Yet we know that we can only tackle the challenges we face at the European level.

The claim that a European federation is impossible due to vast differences among the constituent states is nonsense. Many EU countries have unsustainable debts and deficits. There is no material difference between The Hague's bureaucratic centralism and Paris's Jacobinism. There is no unbridgeable chasm between the welfare states of Italy and Sweden. The social fundamentals are the same. Every European government is based on the rule of law. Every member state offers a welfare safety net, paid for by direct and indirect taxation of employers and employees. The ratios of citizens' contributions may vary from state to state, but that is a mere detail. Former British prime minister Gordon Brown underlined this crucial point during a "remain" rally when he pointed out that the European Union had put in place social policies like a minimum maternity leave and maximum working hours that he wished to see safeguarded for all Europeans, including British workers. The underlying principle of insurance and solidarity is indeed identical, no matter where you are in Europe. In the Brexit hangover, the so-called differences between Great Britain and Europe suddenly seem dwarfed.

Let us also look at things from the opposite perspective. Do we really lose our national identity if we tackle climate change together via a federation? Or if we draw up rules together to prevent the spread of toxic financial products? Or if we demand from the banks a contribution linked to their risk profiles or the size of their financial transactions—money that should serve to recapitalize the European banking sector, which still has not fully recovered from the financial crisis and needs to be made healthy again? Belgium, Finland, Sweden, France, and the United Kingdom already have such a contribution in place at the national level. Is it so illogical to impose this at the European level rather than—as at present in countries like Italy and Spain—forcing national taxpayers to pick up the tab when another bank topples?

Logically, our common currency reflects a common economic policy and to some extent also a common social and fiscal policy. We must also back up this currency with a common authority, a European federation. There are states without a currency, but there are no currencies without a state. We therefore need to move past the existential fear that by making policy at the European level, we become less effective or lose our identity. The very opposite is true: only together can we remain effective, independent, and prosperous.

PART II

DELUSION

CHAPTER THREE

AMNESIA

S O WHAT IS AT THE ROOT OF EUROPE'S PROBLEMS? GIVEN ALL WE
now know about the antiquated nationalisms, as well as the petty
squabbling and small-mindedness (to be addressed in the chapters to
come), if a deeper and more democratic federal union is the solution to
our problems, why are we unable to create it? Why do Europeans keep
wallowing in the past?

The diagnosis is that Europe is so sick it can't realize how far gone
it is.

FORGETTING THE "FOUNDERS"

In 1889 Sergei Korsakoff, a neuropsychiatrist at a university clinic in
Moscow, found that some of his patients had lost the ability not only
to form new memories but even to retrieve old ones. If left untreated,
the disease destroyed their ability to interpret reality correctly. In the
final stages, patients became trapped in a dream world in which they
systematically overestimated their capacity to face challenges. Reflexes

continued to exist, so at first sight, they appeared to function relatively normally, but they couldn't cope with change or hold a coherent conversation. Having lost the ability to store contextual information, they typically resorted to fantasies and confabulations. Conversely, they could be fooled into "remembering" events that had never taken place.

The malaise from which the European Union suffers today bears remarkable similarities to Korsakoff's syndrome, an acute form of amnesia. Europe has an ever-expanding blind spot regarding the entire political reconstruction of the European continent after World War II. The European Union, as we know it, exists on a foundation of fantasy and forgetfulness.

We believe the European Union—as we know it at the beginning of the twenty-first century—embodies the project as envisaged by our founding fathers. But today's Europe does not even remotely resemble the structure Winston Churchill, Robert Schuman, Alcide De Gasperi, and Paul-Henri Spaak—in short, the whole postwar political generation—had in mind. They had big ambitions and far-reaching political aspirations, in stark contrast to the political leaders of today. One could almost say they had *revolutionary* plans for Europe: plans that would have put the European Union miles ahead of where it is today. Today's union is a mere confederation of nation-states, whereas the founders hoped to forge a truly "united Europe," a bloc with no room for the ancient rivalries and inherited hatreds among nation-states.

Immediately after World War II, French prime minister Robert Schuman expressed it this way: "We are working to implement a grand experiment, the fulfillment of the same recurring dream that has concerned us Europeans for ten centuries: the guarantee of perpetual peace." Schuman set out a vision of biblical proportions: the European community had to succeed where the "Roman Church failed." He described the European project as the new "Utopia" and referred to "Dante, Erasmus, Rousseau and Kant"; according to Schuman, a united Europe would be the implementation of "the frameworks of these audacious minds." But Winston Churchill expressed better than anyone else the dream of a united Europe when he advocated the establishment of a "United States of Europa" at the University of Zurich in 1946.

As mentioned, in March 1953 these federalist calls culminated in a first version of a European constitution, drafted by a twenty-six-man constitutional committee headed by the German Christian Democrat politician Heinrich von Brentano. The text, which has now lapsed into obscurity, reads like the US Constitution as signed on September 17, 1787.

However, failure by the French parliament, on August 30, 1954, to ratify the proposal to create a defense community put an end to this first European constitution, as well as to European political federation. The dream of the so-called founding fathers was consigned to history. With what remained from the draft constitution, the "European Community," a mere customs union and the first step toward what later became the common market, was established at the Messina Conference in Italy in 1955. Almost sixty years later, the single European market remains incomplete.

I deliberately write "so-called founding fathers" because we don't do them justice by qualifying them as the founders of the current European Union, which in no way resembles their ideal. According to what we learn in school or from the brochures of the European establishment, a straight line runs from the end of World War II, through the creation of the European Coal and Steel Community, to the 1957 Treaty of Rome. We hear not a single word about the failed attempt to ratify a European constitution or to build a European federal union.

THE REASONS WE UNIFIED

Rather than purging the project of Europe's founders from memory, we would do better to put it back on the agenda. We should also remind ourselves that since World War II, every bit of progress in our economic prosperity and social welfare has been linked to a leap forward in European integration. That was the case in the years after World War II, in the 1950s and 1960s, when the customs union was launched and the six founding members developed a common policy in the domains of coal and steel and agriculture. During these decades, the "initial Six" realized growth figures of more than 3 percent of gross domestic product.

But the relationship between economic growth and European integration became even clearer in the late 1980s and early 1990s. The energy crises of the 1970s and 1980s bogged the European economy down in a huge depression. High inflation and unprecedented unemployment levels presented themselves simultaneously. German economist Herbert Giersch dubbed Europe's manifest inability to turn the tide "euro-sclerosis." Every single day, news reports compared the European economy with that of the United States and especially the Japanese miracle, which created seemingly effortless growth. The solution devised by the European Union, particularly then European Commission president Jacques Delors, was as ingenious as it was simple: to use the benefits of a fully integrated internal market as a remedy for the downturn. Delors assured the business community that such a unified internal market—the free market without obstacles that Europe has today—would be in place on January 1, 1992.

Immediately companies, not just multinationals but also small and medium-size enterprises, anticipated an enlarged internal market and new sales opportunities. They began to invest as never before. The launch of the single market heralded the rebirth of the European economy. The inflationary, shrinking economy with high unemployment of the 1980s transformed into a growth engine that pushed unemployment back more than 25 percent. A contraction in economic growth turned into an average growth of 3 and even 4 percent—figures we can only dream of today.

In short, today we are not witnessing the first time the European project has attracted huge criticism, but our response to the euro-sclerosis differed completely from our response today. Then, we took a giant leap in the integration of our markets. This historic fact pinpoints our problem today: the completely wrongheaded attitude of our current political class, whose members are afraid to make the jump previous generations have. The general public in Europe is deeply dissatisfied with the lack of results. But instead of removing the causes of this dissatisfaction by implementing pan-European policies, our politicians talk endlessly about it—as if they believe they can absorb the discontent by regurgitating it in their own political discourse.

ARROGANT FANTASIES

Europe is suffering from more than memory loss alone. The next phase of Korsakoff's syndrome has manifested: we place ourselves outside reality by creating our own fantasy world. The examples are legion.

Europe continues to think it still dominates economically because it constitutes the world's largest market. The tough-sounding statements repeated in all official documents of the European Commission and in the conclusions of the European Council have a pathetic quality. Again and again, we repeat our desire to become the most advanced knowledge economy, while in fact all indicators point to our heading in the opposite direction. As it happens, no other continent in the world is "growing" as slowly as Europe.

Rather than opening their eyes and making the correct diagnosis, the member states—particularly France and Germany—continue to think they can meet the challenges on their own without making use of the full European scale.

❋ ❋ ❋

THE WAY EUROPE tackled its banking problem after the outbreak of the financial crisis speaks volumes. Every economist knows that healthy banks are the precondition for economic recovery. Virtually every financial crisis of the past (in Japan, Sweden, and Argentina) has shown that it is impossible to turn the tide without first restoring confidence in the banking system. Time and again, first stabilizing financial institutions by forcing them to clean up and recapitalize proved crucial. No matter how unpopular banks may be today, they are and will remain the transmission mechanism that pumps money into the real economy—especially in Europe, where bond issuances barely finance companies and banking credit funds the bulk of investment.

That banks and financial transactions know no borders does not seem to penetrate the brains of our political leaders. You would think they had learned their lesson after the collapse of Lehman Brothers set fire to the global economy. Not so. Although the Lehman debacle shook the European economy and the euro to their very foundations, our policymakers continued to swear by a fragmented national approach.

It took them five years to understand that the banks are so intertwined that only a European banking union—one that transcended national borders—could provide the required assistance. After much back-and-forth, the European Central Bank took on the task, albeit not wholeheartedly. For five years, the German government insisted that the European Central Bank would not receive a mandate to supervise banks. When Berlin finally caved, only the banks representing a "systemic" risk—a mere 130 of them—were placed under continental supervision, leaving the door wide open for more unforeseen disasters. Moreover, the rules and procedures for rescuing a failing bank are so complex that it is impossible to implement them over the weekend, let alone overnight.

This long-awaited "solution" is being implemented at a snail's pace. The quality of the so-called stress tests that should provide an X-ray of the shape of our banks is lamentable. We have conducted several rounds, as if they were merely academic exercises. A few years ago, a number of financial institutions underwent such testing, but that did not prevent banks in Ireland, Cyprus, Greece, Italy, and Spain from getting into trouble or even collapsing. The greatest danger is that this will reoccur because, once again, Europe's politicians grossly underestimate the scale of the problem. More fantasies.

Philippe Legrain of the London School of Economics, a former advisor to the European Commission president, and with him a whole host of other financial experts, said the tests were simply "not stressful enough" and that they rested on "the notoriously over-optimistic forecasts of the European Commission." If this diagnosis is correct, Europe will find itself forced to pump hundreds of billions in fresh money into its banks. That's ten times more than the European Central Bank is officially taking into account.

The way we dealt with the banking crisis—or rather, avoided dealing with it—is just one example of the syndrome afflicting Europe. We have stumbled off the path mapped out for us sixty years ago by the union's founders. We ignore the tremendous speed with which the globalization permeates the world, a world we refuse to recognize, as we are trapped in our own fantasy version of it.

✳ ✳ ✳

BASICALLY THE WHOLE world is calling on Europe to get its house in order and establish an economic and political union as soon as possible in order to complement the currency union. The International Monetary Fund, the Organisation for Economic Co-operation and Development, and the US Treasury have echoed the same sentiment: Europe can only escape the crisis by taking a new step toward integrating the continent. But Europe only seems able to deliver more national rivalries and more national egotism.

If Europe does not take its medicine, its leaders will continue to make empty decisions at EU summit after EU summit. They will continue to draw meaningless conclusions devoid of content. And they will continue to formulate objectives that everyone knows will never be achieved. Meanwhile, the necessary interventions and reforms will be postponed, spread out over time, and retarded. The longer we leave our condition untreated, the more difficult it will be to cure.

CHAPTER FOUR

THE EUROPEAN DWARF I

The Middle East

Two events, thirty years apart, show the fundamental decline in Europe's military power—and consequently its ability to project real influence in the world—over the decades following World War II. And Europeans' inability to project power has devastating consequences for the good we can inject into troubled corners of the world as well as for the very security of our citizens.

EMPTY-HANDED

On the night of November 5, 1956, British and French paratroopers landed in Port Said, at the entrance to the Suez Canal. They were embarking on the last major military operation carried out by two European nations without the assistance or blessing of the United States. The crisis ended two months later with a humiliating retreat of British and French troops under pressure from the United Nations, which—

spurred on by the Soviet Union and the United States—strongly con-
demned the action.

The immediate motive for the controversial operation was the 1956
nationalization of the Suez Canal by Egyptian president Gamal Ab-
del Nasser. Because France and Great Britain owned practically all the
shares in the Universal Company of the Suez Maritime Canal, Nasser's
maneuverer had created a deep financial liability. In addition, the Suez
Canal was of great strategic importance for France and Great Britain—
not just because it was the gateway to the Indian Ocean but also because
of the oil resources in the surrounding areas. At that time, the United
Kingdom had no fewer than 80,000 troops stationed in the region, at
one of the largest military bases in the world.

Nasser's decision to nationalize had been contentious, but the international community eventually accepted it because Egypt compensated
private shareholders fairly. But the British and French were determined
to reverse this outcome. The Suez Canal's geopolitical significance not-
withstanding, they also needed to bring a former colony back in line.
But Nasser was unstoppable. At the beginning of October 1956, he
managed to get the UN Security Council to accept a resolution recognizing Egypt's ownership as long as free passage of international freight
was guaranteed. Nasser believed that this would stave off a British military intervention. He was wrong.

In the meantime, France and Great Britain had entered into a secret
agreement with Israel with the aim of forcing the situation militarily.
After Israel had sent its troops into the Sinai on the flimsiest of pretexts,
France and Great Britain both went in two days later to secure free passage of the Suez Canal. The French and British troops disembarked in
Port Said, and the British flew bombing raids over Egypt. Nasser immediately withdrew his troops from the Sinai and took up positions around
the Suez Canal, which he also blocked. More than 2,000 Egyptian soldiers lost their lives. That did not prevent the Arab world from praising
the Egyptian resistance as an act of true heroism.

Surprisingly enough, the United States also supported Nasser.
President Dwight D. Eisenhower regarded the conflict as a violation

of international law by France and England. Together with UN media-
tor Lester Pearson—the future Canadian prime minister portrayed by
the British media as a "traitor to the British crown"—he imposed an
international peacekeeping force on the warring parties, which ended
hostilities two months after the invasion. The last French and British
troops withdrew in March 1957. France and England, which had completely misjudged the situation, were left empty-handed, their images
tarnished.

The Suez Canal reopened a month later under Egyptian control. As a
result Nasser's leadership was stronger than ever. He used this situation
to tighten citizenship by military order and by amending the Egyptian
nationality law of 1950, forcing many French and British inhabitants,
and also Egyptian Jews, to leave the country. The Franco-British blunder
had rendered Egypt less international and less supportive of the West.
In addition, the country lost its Jewish community, which, together with
the Coptic Christians and Muslims, had always guaranteed its strongly
multicultural character.

For the European great powers, the Suez crisis ended in disaster. Afterward, America's hegemony was a fact. The year 1957 marked the end
of the European nation-states as world powers.

"NEVER AGAIN"?

Thirty years after the Suez crisis, Europe's backyard burst into flames
once again. In the aftermath of the fall of the Iron Curtain, the Balkans
erupted as they have so many times in the past.

After the Yugoslav federation crumbled into individual states—and
following the ethnic cleansing in Srebrenica and Bosnia-Herzegovina—
the violence spread to the Serbian province of Kosovo. Serbia, which
had never accepted loss of its dominant position in the former Yugoslavia, began a real witch hunt against the Kosovo Albanians (many of
whom were Muslim, with ethnic Serbians mainly Orthodox Christian).
Albanian newspapers were closed, and radio and television broadcasts
were censored. Exclusion of all Kosovo Muslims from work in banks,

hospitals, post offices, and schools followed quickly on the heels of mass dismissals of public administration officials. In June 1991, the faculty boards and university board of governors of the University of Pristina were dissolved, and all Kosovo Albanians were replaced by Orthodox Serbs. Teachers of Kosovo-Albanian descent were denied access to schools, and pupils with the same ethnic background were sent home.

Only a few decades after the horrors of World War II, the European continent had descended once again into genocide and violence. Despite pledges of "Never Again," some of the blackest pages of our history threatened to repeat themselves. The international community negotiated one peace agreement after another, to no avail. The fighting and ethnic cleansing continued unabated. When, in January 1999, forty-five Kosovars were murdered during the "Racak massacre," the North Atlantic Treaty Organization (NATO), led by the United States, decided enough was enough.

The international community proposed a peace operation, which the Serbs refused. When a final mediation attempt by US Special Envoy to the Balkans Richard Holbrooke also failed, President Bill Clinton went on American television to announce air raids on Belgrade: "We have acted with resolve, for several reasons. To protect thousands of innocent people in Kosovo from a mounting military offensive. We act to prevent a wider war. To defuse a powder keg at the heart of Europe that has exploded twice before in this century with catastrophic results. . . . By acting now we are upholding our values." "Kosovo," Clinton continued, "is a province of Serbia, in the middle of southeastern Europe, about 160 miles east of Italy. That's less than the distance between Washington and New York and only about 70 miles north of Greece." The American president went on to explain that Slobodan Milošević, the Serbian leader, had used violence not only against the Kosovo Albanians but also against Croatia and Slovenia, two countries that would soon become members of the European Union.

As a European—one who believes in the ultimate power and promise of the EU—I find Clinton's television address uncomfortable, even alarming: an American president describes European geography and the European political situation and then invokes *American* values to justify intervening in the heart of the European continent. Clinton went on television to sell to millions of American viewers an intervention by the American army on the other side of the Atlantic, on a continent thousands of kilometers away from the United States. The inhabitants, known as "Europeans," were apparently unable to put their own house in order. If you didn't know better, you might think that Europe was some developing country without sufficient armed forces to intervene itself.

However, Europe did not lack military capacity. After the United States, the states of the European Union together form the second-strongest military power in the world, albeit spread over twenty-eight member states. The union did, however, lack political will, courage, and, above all, unity.

Each of the major European Union member states had—and still has—its own interests in the Balkans, its preferential links to one or another former Yugoslav republic. Germany remains close with Slovenia and Croatia, a legacy of World War II. France maintains a strong relationship with Serbia, a relic of their "common struggle" against the Ottoman foe in the late nineteenth and early twentieth centuries and the close cultural and economic links that arose as a result. And Britain maintains excellent relations with Montenegro. Nobody wants anything to do with Bosnia-Herzegovina and the Kosovars.

Europe behaved disgracefully during the Kosovo tragedy, which raises a question: What right do we have to judge the rest of the world if we ourselves are not willing to defend our values within our own borders? Once the Americans had done the dirty work, we rushed to send tons of good advice and an army of 4 × 4 vehicles to Pristina.

We call this "soft power." "Cowardice" seems more apt.

HEADS IN THE SAND

Since then, "cowardice" and "lack of unity" have become Europe's trademarks in every foreign crisis.

Our lack of unity has never been so clear as at the time of the American invasion of Iraq. The operation was based on a lie: the supposed presence of weapons of mass destruction (WMDs) in and around Baghdad. Hans Blix, the Swedish envoy of the United Nations, never found any evidence of their existence and concluded that Saddam Hussein simply did not possess them. Today we know that the American and British intelligence services manufactured this "WMD" intelligence, based on which the United States, supported by a number of allies, invaded Iraq.

The real reason for the invasion was that George W. Bush had never gotten over the events of September 11, 2001, which he regarded as an attack on his family and himself rather than on the United States. "They tried to kill my family," were his shockingly thoughtless words when I met him at the White House, ten days after the attacks. Bush embarked on a crusade against the evil that—he believed—had targeted him and his family.

He found inspiration and vindication in a book written by Russian immigrant and former Israeli minister Nathan Sharansky. In *A Case for Democracy*, Sharansky sets out his views on how to resolve the problems in the Middle East. In his view, both the Israeli-Palestinian conflict and the Islamist terrorism it feeds can only be eliminated with creation of stable democracies in the entire region, because only democracies can make stable agreements and achieve peace. *A Case for Democracy* became the new bible for Bush and all American diplomacy. Every audience with the American president began and ended with a reference to that book.

The invasion of Iraq fit seamlessly into that story. It was the first step in Bush's master plan to make the Middle East a haven of freedom and democracy, after which terrorism would disappear of its own accord. Tragically, he achieved precisely the opposite. The invasion of Iraq engendered the Islamic State (IS), which today threatens the world with its murderous, terrifying fanaticism.

In the 2002 meeting of the European Council, discussion of the impending American invasion of Iraq lasted less than sixty seconds. French president Jacques Chirac said there was no sense in talking about it, since there was no agreement. Tony Blair endorsed Chirac's statement.

Discussion closed. Five EU member states—the Netherlands, Great Britain, Poland, Italy, and Spain—fought alongside the United States. France, Belgium, Germany, and Luxembourg remained opposed until the end. The rest abstained. Our disunity helped create the tragic mess in the Middle East today.

❉ ❉ ❉

GENERAL COWARDICE, FAR more than lack of unity, characterizes Europe's inaction in the long-standing Syrian conflict.

We have forgotten that the revolution in Syria was, in essence, no different from those in Libya, Egypt, and Tunisia. The coffin of twenty-six-year-old Tunisian street vendor Mohammed Bouazizi, who set himself on fire because of the hopeless economic and social situation he found himself in, was draped in the red flag of his country, not the green flag of Islam. At the outset, the Arab Spring was about freedom, democracy, social opportunities, and human rights, not religion. The millions of young people in the Muslim world who had no income and no future were no longer willing to accept the hopeless situation in which their rulers had trapped them. That was also the case during the March 2011 uprising in Daraa against Bashar al-Assad. Ordinary citizens—lawyers, doctors, students, and tradesmen—took up arms against Damascus. Jihadists, or Muslim fighters, only entered Syria later, from all over Europe and especially from Iraq, when it became clear that the West refused to come to the aid of the Syrian people.

Time after time, we kept looking the other way while the Syrian leader systematically massacred his people. After the slaughter in Homs in 2012 and 2013, we did nothing. After the bloodbath in Aleppo in July 2013, we did nothing. Even after the chemical weapons attacks in Damascus less than a month later, we did nothing. Under the watchful eye of the United Nations, we brought the weapons out of the country and allowed Bashar al-Assad to go on his way. The message from the international community was catastrophic: you can safely bomb and massacre your own people, just as long as you don't use chemical weapons.

The terrible truth about Syria is that we simply abandoned the Sunnis to their fate. We made no attempt to declare a no-fly zone or set up humanitarian corridors. We supplied no weapons to the moderate, democratic opposition, the Free Syrian Army (FSA), weapons that could have broken the impasse and forced Bashar al-Assad to his knees. On several occasions FSA commanders pleaded for the necessary equipment with my Cairo-based special advisor for the Middle East. Time after time, they warned that if the resistance fighters did not succeed, extremists of all kinds would take their place. To no avail.

We have left 4.7 million refugees—men, women, and children—to their fates, to be herded into camps on the borders with Turkey, Lebanon, and Jordan. When it comes to taking in Syrians fleeing the violence of war, Europe has shown its worst side. Only Sweden and Germany have accepted their responsibilities.

Meanwhile, in Syria, we have created a dangerous vacuum that, as predicted, has sucked in the most extreme elements of Sunni jihad: al-Qaeda, Jabhat al-Nussra, and the Islamic State. But is that any surprise? Some substance always eventually fills any vacuum. If we had given the Free Syrian Army proper assistance from the beginning, there would have been no jihadi cruelty and aggression. Thousands of Islamic fighters would not be traveling to Syria from our own Western towns and cities.

The "Coalition of the Willing" made the capital error of invading Iraq under a false pretext. Ever since, the country has been in chaos, an orgy of sectarian and religious violence. In Syria, we made an equally great mistake by not intervening at all. So that country, a birthplace of our civilization, has retained a dictator fallen and into the hands of an army of jihadists who are little more than criminal psychopaths.

* * *

THE STORY IS similar for Libya. There too we abandoned our responsibilities after we had bombed Muammar Gaddafi to a standstill at the gates of Benghazi and could thus have prevented a bloodbath. The Libyans could not create order out of the chaos that Gaddafi left behind. The country no longer had any public institutions or security services and barely had any legal framework. The Libyans realized that they could not do the job alone and asked the international community for help and advice. But little was forthcoming. A peacekeeping force that, after the necessary NATO intervention in Benghazi, could have prevented the deadly rivalry between the militias was not even considered. The little assistance granted came late.

In May 2013, some two years after the fall of Gaddafi, I sat in the plane that brought the first EU Border Assistance Mission (EUBAM) delegation to Tripoli. EUBAM aimed to help the Libyans secure their 4,348-kilometer border—an urgent need in view of the massive arms trafficking from Libya to insurgent groups like Boko Haram. The Libyan authorities welcomed the EUBAM delegation with open arms at the airport. Almost four years later, EUBAM had still not seen any borders at close quarters. The delegation mainly spends its allocated budget of €30 million per year on its own security.

Libya lies barely 140 kilometers from the Italian island of Lampedusa, the southernmost border of Europe. Syria borders Turkey, a country with which the EU has been conducting accession negotiations for some time. In other words, Libya and Syria are both in Europe's backyard. Both have become hubs of terrorist networks that not only carry out attacks in Europe but, above all, disrupt whole societies in the rest of the world.

✳ ✳ ✳

IN RECENT YEARS Africa has tried to tackle the terrorist movement Boko Haram, which translates literally as "Western education forbidden." What, in 2002, seemed a marginal phenomenon restricted to the northeast of Nigeria has grown into an internationally organized band of jihadists in Chad, Niger, and Cameroon.

Boko Haram has thousands of fighters. From a subsidiary of al-Qaeda, it has grown to become that organization's backbone. It spreads death and destruction throughout the west of the African continent, razing villages, beheading unbelievers, and abducting schoolgirls; anyone who crosses its path risks having his throat slit. It has already taken at least 5,000 lives and left no fewer than 1.5 million refugees.

In 2012, two weeks before the presidential elections, mutinying officers and soldiers staged a coup d'état in Mali, organized under the cynical name "National Committee for the Restoration of Democracy and the State." The coup degenerated into a civil war, during which the national committee came to an agreement with Islamic terror groups, including Boko Haram.

City after city fell, and when the strategically important town of Konna was taken and 1,200 Islamic fighters threatened to attack the nearby garrison town of Mopti, France decided to intervene. At the end of the day, Mali is a former French colony, and by the good old logic that applied in the interwar years, France had to clean up the mess. Similarly, it is Belgium's responsibility—and not all of Europe's—when problems arise in Congo, Rwanda, or Burundi. Europe still parcels out its strategy for dealing with African problems in colonial areas. At no time did it view the need for military intervention in Mali or the development of a strategy to combat the atrocities of Boko Haram or other jihadists as a global European problem requiring a global European approach. It simply left Mali and Boko Haram to the French.

In the end, Denmark, Great Britain, and Belgium sent a few transport aircraft and a medical detachment—purely a token gesture to convince the public that the EU member states supported France. But that's as far as it went. However, Boko Haram is not just a "French problem"; it threatens the whole of Europe. It is a fundamentalist terrorist group that opposes Western culture and values. Boko Haram swears by a fundamentalist interpretation of the Koran. It recently replaced its flag, which used to figure two Kalashnikovs, with the symbol of the Islamic State.

Whether we like it or not, Europe stands in the middle of a clash of civilizations. But we are reacting as though we still live in the world of 1940, when each European country ruled its own colonial empire.

MISSED OPPORTUNITIES

Things could have been very different. On December 6, 2012, the democratic opposition to Assad finally united in Antalya, Turkey, giving a backbone to the poorly organized Free Syrian Army. All the secular and prodemocracy guerrillas came under a unified command. Most of them were highly educated middle-class people—doctors and lawyers who had never used a firearm, let alone an antiaircraft gun. But all of them were absolutely convinced of their common ideal: "freedom and democracy for all Syrians, irrespective of their religion or ethnicity."

There in Antalya the different factions that constituted the secular, democratic opposition to the Assad regime made a serious attempt to give the newly created FSA the necessary capacities. Subcommands were established, Salim Iddriss was selected as supreme commander, and a "code of conduct" was drawn up. Only arms and equipment to fight with were lacking. Europe sat on its hands and repeatedly questioned "who those people really were," not in the hope of obtaining a clear answer but rather as a pretext for doing nothing.

The FSA soon found itself in a precarious situation that still holds today: on the one hand, Europe does not want to supply any arms because it regards the secular FSA as insufficiently competent or even unreliable; on the other hand the FSA cannot show what it is capable of because of a serious shortage of weapons. Time and time again, and more and more loudly, the FSA made its predicament known, announcing, "We are not Islamists; we are fighting the Islamists just as intensively as we are fighting Assad." But absolutely no support came. Europe did not even supply night-vision goggles or training.

Meanwhile, small brigades in Syria, such as Jabhat al-Nussra, received more and more money and arms from the successor to al-Qaeda in Iraq. After the death of its leader, Abu Musab al-Zarqawi, the latter group reformed as the Islamic State with grandiose and bloodthirsty ambitions. It had become reinvigorated after the disintegration of the Iraqi army, from which it eagerly recruited. Moreover it had found a new "inspiring" leader in Abu Bakr al-Baghdadi, who has a doctorate in

Islamic studies and comes from a tribe said to be descended from the Prophet. The beginning of the protests against Bashar al-Assad in Syria in the spring of 2011 provided a perfect opportunity for IS to show that its program of establishing a cross-border Islamic caliphate was more than just the boasting of a band of madmen.

Be that as it may, from 2012 massive quantities of aid goods and, above all, arms began to flow from IS in Iraq to supply the small group around al-Nussra, previously of virtually no significance in the patchwork of the Syrian rebellion. Suddenly, al-Nussra could pay its soldiers up to $200 per month. From then on, unsurprisingly, it gained more and more ground, not only at the expense of the regime in Damascus but equally to the detriment of the other rebel movements, including the Free Syrian Army. Ultimately, al-Nussra controlled so much territory that, no longer dependent on generous gifts, its members could live by looting. Before everyone even realized what was happening, it had been wholly absorbed into IS, giving rise to a genuine state with an administration that imposed and collected taxes. Thus the Islamic State came into existence because, thanks to the decline of the Free Syrian Army, it became the only viable opposition to Assad.

The longer Europe remained inactive, the worse the FSA fared and the stronger IS became. Even after several warnings, Europe continued to look the other way: the dramatic situation in Syria was not "our" problem. On one occasion, exceptionally, we did promise to send arms, but the supplies never arrived. Today, therefore, it should come as no surprise that the whole Syrian question exploded in our faces, first with mass migration to Europe and not much later with fresh attacks by radicalized young people who were born and bred here but received their military training in Syria or Iraq. We in Europe were stunned when Abu Bakr al-Baghdadi proclaimed the caliphate in Syria and Iraq on June 29, 2014. But we should reserve our shock for how we watched from the sidelines and did nothing to prevent it.

Immediately after the November attacks in Paris, at a very late stage indeed, we declared war on the Islamic State under the leadership of France, which invoked the solidarity clause in Article 42 of the Treaty on European Union, and alongside Russia, which had found itself compelled even before the attacks to rush to the aid of the imploding Assad regime.

Ironically, not IS but the last remaining strongholds of the already seriously weakened democratic opposition and of the Free Syrian Army were the first targets of the Russian bombing. The Russian aim is clear: to keep Assad in power at all costs. In order to achieve that end, first Moscow must eliminate the regime's legitimate democratic opponents. Only then will it be time to tackle the monstrous illegitimate caliphate.

✱ ✱ ✱

IT WOULD BE a capital error for Europe to join in Russia's strategy and thus be guilty of a second misjudgment over Syria. There will be no peace in the Middle East and Islamic terrorism will persist so long as Assad remains in power, just as Iraq will never regain stability if it is autocratically governed by a Shiite minority.

The caliphate of Syria and Iraq, mind you, is merely a pawn in a far wider power struggle between Sunnis and Shiites, one that concerns the geopolitical interests of two regional powers, Iran and Saudi Arabia, more than religion. Falling oil prices and the end of the sanctions against the regime in Tehran merely exacerbate that rivalry. Europe would be wrong to allow one or the other to use it as an instrument, a role that the Americans have already accepted for themselves for decades in relation to Saudi Arabia.

Both regimes are reprehensible. Both are autocratic. Both directly and indirectly support terrorist organizations. Iran supports Hezbollah. Saudi Arabia supports the Taliban in Afghanistan, al-Qaeda, Lashkar-e-Taiba, and al-Nussra.

We should not aim for a pact with either devil. We should put our hopes in the millions of younger people belonging to the educated and free-thinking middle class who took to the streets and made their voices heard for the first time during the Arab Spring. We should support those thriving secular forces by all democratic means and help them to gain power, as happened in Tunisia, the very country, indeed, where the Arab Spring originated.

We must also take sides and stick our necks out with regard to the regimes in Riyadh and Tehran themselves. We must no longer accept a situation in which they use the money we pay them for fossil fuels to perpetuate a medieval model of society based on the darkest sides of Islam and the Koran, insofar as such inhuman commandments actually figure there. And the chance of rejecting that status quo has never been so good as it is now.

Fundamental geopolitical changes have occurred in recent years: the exploitation of shale gas by the United States; the oversupply of energy; steeply falling oil prices; Iran's impending entry into the international oil and, above all, gas market; and the worldwide climate agreement reached in Paris, which will ultimately put an end to the use of fossil fuels. Because of all these factors, oil will no longer be a weapon. The threat it presented for decades will cease to exist. There will be no more blackmail by the Organisation of Petroleum Exporting Countries. We shall see no more artificial price rises due to Saudi production restrictions. The oil- and gas-consuming nations will gain the upper hand.

That will make it possible for us to attach conditions to our energy purchases. If we do this in relation to countries and companies that still use child labor, we must also do it in relation to Saudi Arabia, where women have no rights, where adulterers can be stoned and executed. We must also do so with regard to Iran, which after the lifting of the sanctions now wishes to conclude lucrative contracts with a whole range of multinational gas and oil companies. As with the Saudis, those new contracts should apply pressure to compel Iran to take steps toward democratization and the opening up of its society.

To repeat, we shall not defeat terrorism if, both here in Europe and there in the Middle East, we fail to shoulder our full responsibility. And that means, among other things, fully and unitedly supporting the moderate democratic opposition, both in Syria on the battlefields and in Geneva at the political negotiating table. International action against IS does seem to be getting more streamlined, and the organization is suffering its first reverses in Syria and Iraq. But that struggle will certainly continue for a long time in a region increasingly being sucked into a spiral of violence and conflict by Iran, Saudi Arabia, and their respective regional allies.

❦ ❦ ❦

IN ORDER TO shoulder its full responsibility, Europe will have to adopt a different approach to that which has served it for the past sixty years, which basically involved contracting out our role on the international stage to the Americans. At that point it will be high time to dust off the European defense community and place it on the agenda. Shortly after the November attacks, France invoked Article 42 of the Treaty on European Union—a significant precedent, because normally a NATO country that came under attack would invoke Article 5 of the NATO Treaty, concerning "collective defense." By invoking Article 42 of the Treaty on European Union, the clause concerning "mandatory solidarity," France obliged the other twenty-seven member states to support it militarily.

This could be a step toward what we really need: a European defense community that can intervene when the security of all Europeans is at stake. Article 42, after all, has nothing whatsoever to say about the form assistance to the country in need should take militarily. The leaders of our European member states ought to understand that we cannot tackle the international challenges we face in as noncommittal a way as the treaty currently implies, a way that will only cost human lives.

For far too long, we have felt secure under the American umbrella. But what if American military policy increasingly shifts its focus to the Pacific Ocean? What if the oil fields in the Middle East become increasingly irrelevant to the United States? Then we shall stand alone, without a unified command, rudderless.

CHAPTER FIVE

THE EUROPEAN DWARF II

Russia

EUROPEAN STATES HAVE BEEN COMPLETELY OUTCLASSED BY THEIR rivals. Our relationship with our largest neighbor, Russia—or, to be more precise, with its autocratic leader, Vladimir Putin—demonstrates this state of affairs.

I distinguish the country from its leader on purpose because I love Russia and the Russian people. I do not, however, like Putin, although, I must confess, this has not always been the case. He impressed me when I first visited him in the Kremlin in December 2000, not long after he succeeded Boris Yeltsin as president. After the usual formalities, he invited me to a private dinner, even though this was not on the official program. He was the leader of mighty Russia; I, the prime minister of comparatively tiny Belgium. Before the meal, he showed me around his private apartments. In the fitness room, by the tatami mat, he spoke enthusiastically about his passion for judo; at the table, the conversation turned to his European dream for the Russian Federation. He envisioned a democratic Russia, with its limitless resources of raw materials and fuel, as an ideal partner for Europe.

Sitting before a Russian leader who was neither a Communist nor an alcoholic and who understood that Russia's future lay with Europe—that Russia had always been a European country and belonged to the same civilization, sharing its culture, literature, and architecture—I was hooked.

Many more meetings would follow, in Brussels and in Moscow. I remember well our last, in March 2007 at Putin's dacha near Moscow. Suddenly, he had had enough of the official meeting between our two delegations, the obligatory speeches being fired from both sides of the table. He beckoned to me and suggested that we leave the meeting to the two foreign affairs ministers and the diplomats. Later, we walked all around his estate, talking together. He proudly pointed out the Orthodox church, its gold decoration shining in the midday sun. Next came the ranch with all its horses, and a little pony, obviously Putin's favorite, came galloping up at his call to have its head stroked.

Later, we sat in his apartment, lounging on a huge, dark brown leather sofa, drinking coffee and picking up the thread of the political discussion that we had left to our foreign ministers in the meeting room. I asked about the murder of Russian journalist Anna Politkovskaya, allegedly by an organization close to the Kremlin because she had been too critical of Putin's regime. The man who answered me was not the man I had first met in Moscow. He remained friendly and courteous, but you could feel behind every word his irritation with a Westerner who had the gall to explain to him, the leader of mighty Russia, the importance of democracy and freedom of expression. He swore that the Kremlin had had nothing whatsoever to do with the whole business and that he had done everything in his power to track down the assassins. But he did not convince me. Sitting before me was the sole ruler of Russia, a man trained by the KGB and the East German Stasi but unable to find Politkovskaya's killers. I did not believe him.

When, a year later, Putin reaffirmed his autocratic rule—by becoming prime minister "under" puppet president Dmitry Medvedev—our love affair was definitely over. I saw him clearly as a leader who would do anything to stay in power, even amend the constitution.

Since his accession to the prime ministership, not one democratic election has taken place. The Kremlin keeps a few opposition parties alive as marionettes, helping to convey the impression of democracy to the outside world, and constantly manipulates the media—both public and private. Meanwhile, the state and society are stripped of their riches. Putin stands, as anticorruption activist Alexei Navalny puts it, at the head of a criminal gang in Russia: an organized band of oligarchs and bureaucrats out to enrich themselves who spend most of their time abroad and have no qualms about making those who stand in their way "disappear."

This is what happened to the journalist Anna Politkovskaya and her colleagues Paul Klebnikov and Anastasia Babourova. Political opponents are not safe either, as the murders of opposition politicians Sergei Yushenkov and Boris Nemtsov demonstrate. Lawyers who stand up for the rule of law, like Sergei Magnitsky and, before him, his colleagues Stanislav Markelov and Natalia Estemirova, are killed in cold blood. Even former KGB agent Alexander Litvinenko, on the run and living in London, ultimately lost his life.

❋ ❋ ❋

SINCE THE WOOL was lifted from my eyes, I have tried to support Russian opponents wherever possible: Mikhail Kasyanov's republican party Parnas, the liberal Yabloko, and anticorruption activists such as Alexei Navalny and Gary Kasparov. I stood on a podium before 100,000 protesters, in temperatures of minus twelve degrees, when Russian riot police cleared Pushkin Square. But I have most to do with Arseny Roginsky, Sergei Kovalev, and Lyudmila Alexeyeva, the historic leaders of Memorial, the nongovernmental organization (NGO) that has for decades fought totalitarianism and defended human rights and the rule of law in Russia. Just six years ago, the NGO won the Sakharov Prize. Today, I see in their eyes only sadness and disappointment in having fought so hard against the Communist Soviet dictatorship only to live under a regime that is scarcely any better.

Above all, I look with disbelief at the self-delusion that has taken control of Europe. We keep pretending that Putin will not go too far, that he will show restraint of his own accord. We cherish the idle hope that a few tough declarations and shabby sanctions will stop him. That is a mistake, as these have little effect on him. Putin pursues the agenda of a dictator seeking to hold on to power for as long as possible, including by further enslaving Russia and its neighbors. Because never forget: for Putin, Russia is still the Soviet Union. He is a product of the Soviet Union, not of resistance to it.

Whenever a former Soviet republic so much as tries to steer its own course, chaos results. The invasion of Georgia took place in 2008. Nicolas Sarkozy flew to Moscow, where the Russians promised to withdraw their troops from the occupied areas of Abkhazia and South Ossetia. European public opinion was euphoric: the French president had shown leadership on behalf of the European Union. "Sarkozy's deal bears fruit," wrote European correspondents. Sarkozy patted himself on the back for achieving the "breakthrough." In the corridors of the European Council building, people even believed for a moment that Europe had not completely played out its role on the world stage. The German minister for foreign affairs described Europe as the only "honest broker" capable of defusing this conflict.

The Americans were less enthusiastic. US Secretary of State Condoleezza Rice said coolly, "I have just had the French on the line. Let us hope that the Russians keep their word." Soon enough, it turned out that Sarkozy was acting on his own initiative, unable to convince the rest of the European Council. He struck the deal as president of France, not the representative of a cohesive European bloc. While he spoke for those who believed Russia should back down, a number of member states felt that Georgia had provoked the aggression. The European discord was sufficient reason for the Russians to dismiss Sarkozy's journey as "back-page news." Moscow consigned his six-point plan to the wastepaper basket on the same day; the Russian troops stayed put and continue to occupy one-fifth of Georgia's territory. Nobody still believes that Sarkozy brokered peace there, except perhaps himself.

❊ ❊ ❊

GEORGIA MERELY PROVIDED a foretaste of what was to come. In 2014, soldiers with no recognizable insignia moved into the Crimea. It soon became clear that these were Russian troops. The peninsula, given to the Ukrainian Soviet Socialist Republic by Nikita Khrushchev in 1954, was absorbed into independent Ukraine in 1991, with a special "lease" to Russia of a military base in Sebastopol for its Black Sea fleet. Vladimir Putin decided, after a pro-European majority came to power in Kiev, to put an end to this "insolent" independence.

Under the pretext of protecting the Russian-speaking majority, Putin's troops took over the whole of the Crimea. A few weeks later, a pseudo-referendum allowed the Crimean populace to choose, under the watchful eye of heavily armed Russian soldiers, between joining Russia or becoming a small independent nation. Everybody knew that the second option was neither politically nor economically viable. The choice simply to remain with Ukraine did not appear on the ballot.

Russia proclaimed victory with a turnout of 87 percent of inhabitants of the Crimea, 97 percent of whom had voted to return to Mother Russia. No international observers were permitted at the elections. When the Russian president's own Human Rights Council accidentally released the real estimated turnout online, the truth was revealed: barely 30 percent of Crimeans had gone to the polls, and less than 30 percent of those who did had voted to join Russia.

Meanwhile, Europe cried that the annexation was a scandal and that Russia had breached the 1994 Budapest Memorandum stating that it would respect the territorial integrity of Ukraine. But protest remained verbal. Putin was well aware that Europe would take no action.

The Russian military presence in the Crimea was not decreased; on the contrary, a new Russian invasion followed in August 2014 in eastern Ukraine, the industrial heart of the country. Just as in the Serbia-Kosovo conflict, the United States—not Europe—finally decided to intervene. The Americans tightened sanctions against Russia and gave the poorly equipped Ukrainian army materiel and logistical support.

Meanwhile, Europe was again quibbling about the best approach to take toward Putin. Most argued that tougher economic sanctions would affect only the European economy. All agreed that military options were completely out of the question. So Angela Merkel and François Hollande went to Moscow. However, they were in the same position as Sarkozy in 2008: they represented only themselves, not a united European Union. European Council president Donald Tusk took a hard line against Russia, while foreign affairs representative Federica Mogherini pleaded for "appeasement" and sought to ease sanctions against Russia. As a result, two weeks later in Minsk, a beaming Putin solemnly promised another cease-fire but made not the slightest effort to call the so-called Russian rebels in eastern Ukraine to order. On the contrary, American satellite images showed fresh Russian troops and tons of weapons crossing the border every day.

Europe's faintness of heart came as no surprise to the Ukrainian population. Even before the Russian invasion of the Crimea, the EU had already lost a huge amount of credit, especially with the demonstrators on Maidan, the square in Kiev where for months protesters had called for an independent Ukraine and for an end to corruption, nepotism, and cronyism. The German, French, and Polish ministers for foreign affairs had negotiated an agreement between pro-Russian president Viktor Yanukovych and the opposition—stipulating that the utterly corrupt Yanukovych would stay in power for another full year.

I was standing on Maidan on February 21, 2014, when the compromise was announced. The response was scathing. Not even one demonstrator would leave the square if Yanukovych were to stay in power—especially as that very morning snipers, most likely Russian elite troops, had shot a number of protesters dead. Only when the police finally sided with the demonstrators and members of parliament from Yanukovych's party defected to the opposition did the president flee for Moscow.

Just as in 2008 during the Georgia crisis, the ink had barely dried before the agreement negotiated by Europe was already defunct. Once again, the Americans picked up the pieces. US Vice President Joe Biden and Secretary of State John Kerry flew in to assure the Baltic states of military cover if Russia got any more crazy ideas. And the United States also took the lead in imposing sanctions against the Putin regime. The European Council followed reluctantly one or two weeks later, as though it *wanted* to give Putin's supporters enough time to pull their assets out of Western banks.

In the short time between the flight of Yanukovych and the appointment of a new prime minister who could count on a majority in the Rada, the Ukrainian parliament, a telephone conversation between US Assistant Secretary of State Victoria Nuland and the US ambassador to Ukraine was leaked. When the ambassador asked whether Europe needed to be involved in forming the Ukrainian government, Nuland answered with a heartfelt "Fuck the EU." For the Americans, Europe is now a troublemaker, a dwarf, more likely to get in the way when things get serious than to make meaningful contributions.

Putin's intent is crystal clear: he plans to bring all former Soviet republics to heel and rule them with an iron rod, directly or indirectly, either by keeping in the saddle a dictator who thinks and behaves as autocratically as Putin does himself, as in Belarus, or in the event of a country's pursuing an independent course, by inciting conflict, provoking disputes, or letting latent tensions escalate as a pretext for sending in troops. Russia can then justify stationing troops in the rebelling republic with the logic that such conflicts will never be settled in the field or resolved at the negotiating table.

Diplomats have a name for this strategy: "frozen conflict." Rather than completely occupying a country, as the former Soviet Union did, Russia can tighten its stranglehold on several countries at once with a minimum of military resources. Frozen conflicts have emerged in almost all the republics that became independent after the breakup of the Soviet Union: in Transnistria, part of Moldavia; in South Ossetia and Abkhazia, significant parts of Georgia; in Nagorno-Karabakh, part of Azerbaijan; and lastly (for now), in the Crimea and eastern Ukraine. You could call this a post-Soviet tactic. The Kremlin always offers the same justification for intervening: the protection of Russophones, the Russian-speaking minorities. That is a pretext, because most Russian speakers have no desire to live under Moscow's rule. Those Russians or other ethnic groups who do were mostly transported by the Russian authorities not so long ago from other parts of Russia, often Siberia, to the borders of the "empire."

In this way, Putin is simply building on the system of so-called voluntary, repressive, and preventative settlement set up during the Soviet era, which aimed to create Russian-language dominance in those parts of the Soviet Union where other languages were spoken. The Crimea serves as a particular example. In May 1944, the Defense Committee of the Soviet Union ordered that the Crimean Tatars, an estimated 250,000 people, be loaded into railway cars and transported to Central Asia, primarily to Uzbekistan. Such actions continued a long tradition of Russification stretching back to tsarist Russia, which spared no tactic, from cultural assimilation, such as forcing local language communities to use the Cyrillic alphabet or to practice the Orthodox religion, up to and including widespread population displacement.

We have forgotten, however, that until the 1917 October Revolution, Russia was always a European nation. The Russian tsar led the coalition of European states against Napoleon in 1814. And Russia, together with France, the United Kingdom, Prussia, and Austria, formed part of the "Concert of Europe," the five powers that after the Congress of Vienna, in various coalitions, determined affairs in Europe throughout the nineteenth century. Russia not only has political and diplomatic links with Europe but also forms part of the European civilization. Travelers from Paris and Brussels to deep inside Russia, past Moscow, on toward the Volga, will find themselves immersed in the same cultural milieu as in Western Europe. Although they will hear a different language, they will see the same architectural splendor in every city: classicism, art nouveau, modernism. On the journey eastward, bookshops will display similar titles and authors, including works by the great Russian writers: Pushkin, Tolstoy, Gogol, Bulgakov. Every national radio station will play familiar music.

Russia is part of Europe. A European continent, and certainly a European civilization, is unimaginable without Russia. What is more, the European Union and the Russian Federation should have a vested interest in exploring the possibility of a single integrated economic area more quickly. It is a mistake to view the European Union and the "Eurasian Customs Union" as competitors between which neighboring countries must make an existential choice—as has happened to Ukraine. The merging of both markets to form one large economic area would create enormous opportunities. Instead of unleashing geopolitical conflict, it could unlock new prosperity in both the European Union and the Russian Federation. This could also create a new starting point for approaching the lack of the rule of law and the fundamental lack of democracy in Russia more constructively and resolutely.

PUTIN'S TRICKS

In 2013, anticorruption campaigner and former opposition candidate for mayor of Moscow Alexei Navalny was put on trial. The accusation was corruption. What better way of sowing doubt among the population about Navalny's good intentions than to drag him through the courts on such a charge.

Even I have experienced this unrivaled manipulation by the Putin regime. Several years ago, I appeared on Russian state television, which broadcast one of my meetings with Alexei Navalny, recorded by a hidden camera in a hotel room. I had been unaware that we were being filmed but was not surprised to learn as much. This happens in Russia. In the images, you saw me meet with Navalny and a few colleagues. The broadcast stated that Navalny was a traitor, and now everybody could see for themselves how he sat plotting with a "foreign agent" (me). In reality, we were discussing a number of cases of corruption that Navalny had uncovered in Russia and agreeing that I would investigate which companies, accounts, or establishments in Europe the money had been diverted to.

Meanwhile, Vladimir Putin has placed me, together with eighty other Europeans, on a "blacklist," and we can no longer enter Russia. I can't say that I'm heartbroken about this. But I am sad that I can no longer visit my many "comrades" in the kaleidoscope of organizations and movements that make up the Russian opposition.

✳ ✳ ✳

PUTIN IS A master manipulator; compared to him the leaders of our twenty-eight member states are dwarves. He is once again rushing to arm the Russian Federation and takes every opportunity to deploy this military force. In addition, knowing better than anybody that Europe is not only militarily but also politically weak, he never misses a chance to exploit the divisions in Europe. While he dismissed the Ukrainian protesters on Maidan as a "band of fascists" and compared the West to Hitler, he himself has intensive contact with the leaders of the extreme right. Anyone with an antimigration and anti-Europe agenda he welcomes with open arms. The English *Guardian* summed up his close connections with France's far right leader Marine Le Pen as follows: "It sounds like a chapter from a cheesy spy novel: a far-right European party, in financial trouble, borrows a big sum of cash from a hawkish Russian president. His goal? To undermine the European Union."

The *Guardian* described not fiction but the bitter truth. The Front National received a loan of no less than €9.4 million from a bank in Moscow and another €2 million from a mysterious company in Cyprus, the European Union member state holding more ruble deposits than any Russian city. These sums are rumored to be part of a larger package of €40 million. In short, Marine Le Pen is entirely dependent upon Putin's goodwill for the financial survival of her party and her intended 2017 run for the French presidency. Incidentally, it is no coincidence that the Russian loan took place after François Hollande postponed delivery of two Mistral warships to Russia, a deal worth €1.2 billion.

Le Pen is certainly grateful to Putin. She makes no secret of her admiration for him. Thus she supports the annexation of the Crimea and calls it a completely legitimate action. She also maintains close contacts with Russian deputy prime minister Dmitry Rogozin, who in 2005 started an antimigration campaign under the unequivocal slogan "Let's Clean Up Moscow's Trash." Together with Vlaams Belang, the party of Geert Wilders, and other racist, often outright fascist parties, Front National forms a pro-Putin faction of thirty-six members in the European Parliament. Individuals from this faction obediently showed up as "independent observers" at the rigged "referendum" that Putin hastily organized after the occupation of the Crimea.

It was a disgraceful display: self-proclaimed patriots serving themselves up for use by a totalitarian. Other leaders of right and extreme right groups in Europe have allowed the Kremlin to press them into its service. Nigel Farage of the United Kingdom Independence Party named Putin as the world leader he "most admired," perhaps because Putin unconditionally chose the side of Bashar al-Assad, the Syrian dictator waging a brutal civil war against his own people. Farage is full of praise for the "brilliant" way Putin has "handled the whole Syrian affair." Nick Griffin of the British National Party described the Duma elections as "more honest than the British [elections]" and praised the propaganda broadcaster *Russia Today* as "truthful."

Political Capital, a research institute in Budapest, characterizes the Russian influence on extreme right parties as "a phenomenon that is seen all over Europe." This is a well-known Kremlin strategy, whereby it forges close links with fascist parties such as Jobbik in Hungary, the Slovakian People's Party, and the Bulgarian nationalist and anti-EU Attack movement. As a result, even the political elites in these countries have become increasingly pro-Russian in the past few years.

It's not difficult to understand why Putin is fueling the anti-European and xenophobic voices in the EU: he wants to weaken the union. His KGB logic dictates that it is better to have Europe as a weak neighbor than as a prosperous trading partner. He deliberately encourages discord over sensitive issues such as migration and economics—a perverse attitude that we can do little about. We must understand that in the process Putin is also undermining the foundations of our free and open society and finding it all too easy to make use of our political weakness. The Kremlin has discovered that the European political system is, as Luke Harding puts it in the *Guardian*, "weak, permeable and susceptible to foreign cash. Putin believes that European politics can be bought."

STANDING TOGETHER

The Putin situation perhaps best illustrates how countries like France and Great Britain, which imagine themselves to be great, have become toothless. And thanks to WikiLeaks, we now know that the Kremlin paid Italy, under Silvio Berlusconi, in the form of extensive, cheap gas deals. Despite their pompous behavior, France, Italy, and the United Kingdom have all become playthings in the hands of the great powers.

The European Union's founders foresaw this. He who wants to win a place in the modern world must begin by creating unity. We are no longer competing with nineteenth-century nation-states; rather we must face up to continental great powers. Unity, as the founders knew, assumes a single political community and a single defense. Only by devising these can the dwarf Europe once again play a meaningful role on the world stage.

CHAPTER SIX

THE CHRONIC CONDITION OF NATIONALISM

W HY DO THE EUROPEAN NATIONS—SO PROUD OF THEIR HISTO-
ries and their achievements—allow themselves to be so outclassed? Simply put: because the delusional spirit of nationalism still
haunts the continent.

On May 4, 1945, when British field marshal Bernard Montgomery accepted the unconditional surrender of all German forces from General-
admiral Hans-Georg von Friedeburg, it marked the provisional end of
two centuries of nationalistic delusion.

Not three decades before, an effort had already been made to cure
Europe definitively of nationalism. After the conclusion of World War I,
President Woodrow Wilson set up the League of Nations. This was the
first attempt to found an international community aimed at the peace-
ful settlement of conflicts and the promotion of democracy worldwide.
Wilson also enforced referenda throughout Europe with the aim of setting borders once and for all, democratically, without weapons.

The whole undertaking fizzled out. As though the patient Europe had failed to complete its course of antibiotics, the disease of nationalism reoccurred, this time in a much more extreme form. Nationalistic madness led to the death camps, the Shoah, and the extermination of European Jews. Contrary to what most nationalists—another word for "Euroskeptics"—would have us believe, the Shoah did not occur out of the blue. It grew out of a long tradition of walled ghettos in various European cities built to isolate Jews from "clean" citizens, who were white and Christian and scrupulously spoke the official national language at home. The gates to the Jewish ghettos were regularly closed: from the inside, as when the Jews needed to protect themselves from an impending pogrom, or from the outside, for example, at Christmas and Easter to prevent the Jewish population mixing with the "legitimate" (i.e., Christian) inhabitants of the nation.

THE RETURN OF NATIONALISM

The primary goal of the European project was to cure Europe once and for all of the plague of nationalism. The results of the past sixty years might seem to indicate that the cure worked. But it has become apparent that this is an illusion. Virulent nationalism is once again on the rise.

It is as though we are being catapulted back in time, to the turbulent, terrifying years before World War II. In Hungary, the paramilitary troops of the ultranationalist party Jobbik patrol the streets, wearing black with a matching cap embroidered with the party logo. You would have to be blind to miss the similarity to the Nazi SS. Jobbik won three consecutive elections and represents 20 percent of the Hungarian electorate. It describes itself as "a radical Christian party" whose "fundamental mission" is to "protect Hungarian values and interests." It rejects "global capitalism and Zionism." This rhetoric sounds familiar.

In Greece, Golden Dawn troops scour the streets, beating up immigrants. And anybody who thinks that these are marginal phenomena in "crazy" Hungary or crisis-ridden Greece is hopelessly naive. In the Netherlands, Denmark, Sweden, Finland—in all these so-called tolerant northern and Scandinavian countries—nationalist and racist parties are on the rise. Some have names that leave no doubt about their true nature, such as Finland's True Finns; others, such as the Freedom Party of Geert Wilders in the Netherlands and its namesake in Austria, the Swedish Democrats, and the Danish People's Party, shamelessly usurp terms like "freedom" and "democracy," when they stand for the complete opposite, in the hope of winning the votes of unsuspecting citizens.

But developments in Germany are just as worrying, if not more so. In a number of towns there, Pegida (Patriotic Europeans Against the Islamization of the West) frequently organizes large anti-Islam marches. The party's rhetoric uncoincidentally bears similarities to the writings of Norwegian terrorist Anders Breivik, who in 2011 carried out a massacre in Oslo and on the island of Utoya, killing seventy-seven young people. The politicians of the traditional German parties are outraged by Pegida's scandalous rhetoric and unscrupulous political aims but conveniently forget that they themselves have jointly set the tone.

Alternative for Germany, the right-wing party that backs Pegida, as well as prominent figures such as Christian Democrat and Bavarian party leader Horst Seehofer have declared that *multikulti*, German slang for multiculturalism, is dead. Until recently, we heard such language only from the extreme right. Even Chancellor Angela Merkel said not so long ago that "multikulti had utterly failed." With a finger raised, like an old-fashioned schoolmistress speaking to a class of children, she added, "Immigrants had better do their best to learn German." Even the German socialists are saying much the same. Central banker, Social Democratic Party of Germany member, and, above all, frightened white man Thilo Sarrazin wrote a book with the panic-stricken title *Germany Abolishes Itself*. The message is always the same: Christian culture and German values are under pressure because Muslims are taking over. In short, Pegida's rhetoric does not arise out of nowhere; it has its counterparts among almost all mainstream political parties in Germany.

But this rejection of "multiculturalism," of course, reflects much more than just complaints about immigrants with inadequate knowledge of the German language or appreciation of German culture. It is about drawing clear distinctions regarding who does and does not belong to a community. In the interwar years, eastern European countries required Jews to abandon Yiddish in favor of German, Czech, or Polish, promising them full participation in political and economic life in exchange for assimilation. Today we are well on the way to making the same dangerous mistake and the same hypocritical promises with regard to a generation of nonwhite, non-Christian fellow citizens.

FRENCH "VALUES," FRENCH "IDENTITY"

France, a pillar of the union, has witnessed the same developments. It has long served as the textbook example of a "good" open society, free of narrow and closed nationalism based on ethnicity and characterized by a broad-minded and open patriotism based on the shared values of the republic: liberty, equality, fraternity—the legacy of the French Revolution. These values have never been fully achieved; instead every generation must fight for them again and again.

A mistaken attempt to appropriate this identity occurred in recent memory. On February 9, 2010, then president Nicolas Sarkozy announced a national debate intended to define, once and for all, what it means to be French, what features and characteristics "Frenchness" entails. This shortsighted attempt to win back votes from the far right Front National backfired; instead of bringing in votes, the discussion strengthened the Front National by placing its bigoted theme at the center of public debate. The official website dedicated to this national discussion quickly degenerated into a repository for sordid and racist utterances that would shame even the Nazi-allied Vichy regime.

A political stunt intended to boost French pride—and disempower the extreme right—ended up revealing the ugliest side of France and French nationalism. Entire ethnic groups were written off as garbage. One of the politer comments on the website suggested that young people looking for work should start by renouncing Islam. The core values of the French Republic were nowhere to be seen. France didn't seem to be the textbook example of "open" nationalism at all.

Fifty years after the death of French Algerian novelist Albert Camus, a Nobel Prize winner and one of the world's most important twentieth-century authors, France seems further removed than ever from the ideal "open society" it claims to be. The national debate makes clear that many French people still hold monarchist, rightist, and downright anti-Semitic opinions, reflexes prominent in certain circles until the late nineteenth and early twentieth centuries that are now resurfacing. This is worrying in the country of the heirs of the Enlightenment and the 1789 French Revolution.

⁕ ⁕ ⁕

WE EUROPEANS THOUGHT that, in and through France, we had definitively settled the ideological conflict that flared up in the eighteenth century between the nation-state and enlightened humanism, between Immanuel Kant and his dissenting pupil Johann Gottfried von Herder. We imagined that, throughout Europe, the general, everlasting, universal human values of the Enlightenment had triumphed over the *Volksgeist*: the glorification of the nation and the exaltation of national individuality and associated ingrained customs and traditions.

Sarkozy's debate on the national identity of France was an embarrassing spectacle, an affront to the French spirit, and an insult to French intelligence. The use of national identity as a starting point in politics is nothing more than a further disguise for nationalism itself. It has absolutely nothing to do with the legacy of the French Republic.

As Alain Fienkelkraut argues in *The Defeat of the Mind*, the eighteenth-century German philosopher Herder is the true father of this vicious identity-based thinking, known today in Europe as "identitarianism." It reveals itself in the banning of loan words, in the rediscovery of folk songs, in the return to the past and "authenticity." All this is necessary, Herder and his followers argued, because the Enlightenment has cut us off from our roots and landed us in a vacuum, without guidance or security. The nation is not a social contract concluded between independent and equal people; it is a superior form of organization that transcends humankind and has a life of its own. Therefore, humankind must adapt to society, not the other way around. The nation thus becomes the breath of human existence. Without the nation, humankind dies.

In the delusional identitarian worldview, "mankind" itself is a misconception. There are only Frenchmen and Germans and Belgians, compatriots connected to each other subconsciously. Precisely this collective subconscious acts as the driving force of society. Thus every society and its members must seek to learn precisely what this collective subconscious contains and to express it in the form of an individual national perception, one that acts as a cloak under which a secure, recognizable, and homogenous social life takes place. Tradition and conformism keep the nation flourishing, strong, and healthy; therefore they are far more important than democracy or rational thought, which merely serve to undermine and weaken a society. These are harrowing ideas, especially after the horrors of the past century.

The debate between Herder and Kant would have remained purely philosophical if the French Revolution had not erupted in 1789. The ideas of the Enlightenment triumphed. Revolutionary France spread the republican values of freedom, equality, and fraternity by force throughout Europe, engendering a revolution without borders for a republic encompassing all citizens, until a coalition of European states ultimately defeated Napoleon at Waterloo.

But force of arms could not defeat the ideology of the French Revolution and the Enlightenment. For many decades, two virtually irreconcilable Europes faced each other: an enlightened, revolutionary, and republican Europe on one side and a conservative, traditional, monarchical Europe on the other. An essentially French, rational, universal view of society stood opposed to the German, emotional, identitarian approach. You *are* a German. You *become* a Frenchman. And, in this way, everyone should be able to *become* European.

This contrast reached a new, violent highpoint with the 1870–1871 Franco-Prussian War. The German poet Heinrich Heine, in exile in France since 1831, warned of a "German answer" to the French Revolution. This answer came in 1933 with Adolf Hitler's seizure of power, described by Nazi propaganda minister Joseph Goebbels as "the end of the French Revolution."

The 1870 Prussian conquest of Alsace-Lorraine perhaps still provides the best insight into the irreconcilability of republican values and the concept of "national identity." For the Germans, this annexation was an obvious step, a matter of incontestable historic destiny—in short, a legitimate deed based on race, language, and tradition.

Not so, argued French philosopher Ernest Renan. While the inhabitants of the old German province might belong to the German race, this did not negate their claim to be French. Renan—rightly—considered their desire more important than their ancestry. The delegates from Alsace-Lorraine reiterated this desire in the French Assembly on the day the contract sealing the transfer of the territory from France to Germany was approved. With their protest, the Alsatians demonstrated better than anyone that national consciousness rests not on one form or another of determination—as the followers of identitarian thinking claim—but on an independent decision, a sovereign will.

PEOPLE, NOT PLACES, ARE SOVEREIGN

The nation is not a matter of language, race, religion, interests, geography, or even military necessity. Nor is it any longer a matter of social history, historical coincidence, or some vague feeling of unity. The nation is an ongoing reflection of conscious solidarity, the manifestation of a deliberate decision to live together according to shared laws and principles. "A nation presupposes a past, but exists today as a result of a tangible fact: consent, a clearly expressed wish to live together. A daily referendum which—like the existence of the individual himself—is a continual confirmation of life," as Renan put it. Thus it is a contract, a "referendum that has to be renewed every day." People are not captive to identity or nationality; they are its justification.

Does this mean that "identity" is now an empty word? No. Quite the contrary. But it is an illusion to think that an identity can protect us from the risks present in the world. We must not repeat the mistake made at the end of the eighteenth century, when the word was misused. What the eighteenth century called the Enlightenment we now know as globalization. If the Enlightenment was criticized for divorcing people from their natural pasts, globalization is now blamed for upsetting the balance of our planet, for turning the world into a madly spinning top that leaves humankind to its fate. Identity is thus a sure point of reference, a magic word that offers stability in uncertain times on this unstable planet.

I am the last person to deny people such an anchor. And yet I question whether identity can provide a sure foothold. The idea presumes that identity is a clear and established fact that applies to everybody within a society. And this is not the case.

There are always as many identities as there are individuals. Every person is unique. To lump them together under one label is to do them an injustice. It reduces individuals to reluctant cogs in the machine called "society." Amartya Sen makes crystal clear in his book *Identity and Violence: The Illusion of Destiny* the vital difference between a "monolithic identity," a term that we politicians use all too often, and the complex identity of all people who populate the real world. A one-dimensional collective identity does not exist. It is a dangerous illusion that results from an almost irresistible compulsion to classify the world in terms of religion, culture, language, or race.

A person is not just a Christian, a Jew, or a Muslim, just black or white. A person is a unique personality who, in addition to his or her skin color or religion, lives in a neighborhood, in a village or a town, in one region or another of a country, with family and friends, personal preferences, and individual feelings and desires. He or she may be gay or straight, married or single, raising a family or childless; may like rock, classical, or jazz music, the Beatles or the Rolling Stones; may have a penchant for Mark Rothko or for the precision of realistic landscapes; may live in a trendy neighborhood or an abandoned factory somewhere in a run-down part of town; may be a sports fiend or a smoker, a cyclist or a jogger, a homebody or a partygoer.

In short, there is no such thing as a clear identity—at least not in the real world. The construct is a figment of sociologists' and political scientists' imagination, a denial of our human capacity to wrest control of our own destinies. In the identitarian world, identity is etched in stone, pinned to the group. A person can only discover it during his or her life.

The identitarian approach, according to Sen, reflects a reductionist view of reality: a narrow-mindedness that ignores that each person has a whole range of identities and characteristics. The identity approach reduces people to mere observers, to passive beings. In a certain sense, identity humanity is barely distinguishable from the animal kingdom, whose members must also accept their environment as it is and have just as little free will. Everything is predetermined. Everything is a reflex or an instinct.

❋ ❋ ❋

STANDING DIAMETRICALLY OPPOSED to this reductionist worldview is belief in the freedom of choice of every person in the real world. This freedom is not unlimited or the same for everyone; there are limits, often—regrettably—determined by birth. But according to this perspective people not only inherit their peculiarities and personalities but also create and build them up themselves. In the modern world, mankind is increasingly its own creator. Contrary to what nationalists would have us believe, the boundaries of freedom lie not in the history of a nation, the character of its institutions, or its language but in the capacities and characteristics of all individuals themselves, in their intelligence, characters, and emotions—in short, in their personalities.

The one-dimensional, collective identity that forms the basis of nationalistic thinking is of a completely different order. It leads to the construction of inescapable ethnic, national, cultural, or religious "bunkers" in society. Each bunker braces to face the enemy, inevitably generating hatred: riots in the neighborhood and wars in the wider world. Author Amin Maalouf calls this "deadly identity."

The murderous twentieth century is a tragic illustration of this. It taught us that the gas chambers of Auschwitz are the ultimate outcome of this type of identity thinking. It is not difficult to see why this is so.

We use identity to assign to a group of people characteristics that often differ radically from those ascribed to our own group. Individual differences get swept aside; only the group differences matter. At a stroke, a whole group of people becomes "different." Anything different arouses suspicion and creates fear. The step from "different" to "enemy" is very small.

Just as significant is the fact that identity can also lead to extreme conformist behavior and the disappearance of critical thinking. People blindly obey traditions, which get passed on from one generation to another without discussion, even if this demands outright discrimination against somebody with a different ethnic background or of the opposite gender. The consequence is often violence against the "other." Because humanity is reduced to one's own group, noble principles such as justice, tolerance, or nonviolence apply only *within* the group.

After the terrible wars in Yugoslavia, identity prevented Serbia from handing over war criminals for more than a decade. Identity caused German courts in the aftermath of World War II to mete out to Nazis ridiculously light punishments. Identity prevented the global Islamic community from excommunicating Osama bin Laden. Identity also explains why, after the attack on *Charlie Hebdo,* so many within the Muslim community expressed sympathy with the perpetrators.

In short, it is impossible to build a peace-loving society on the foundation of identity. A society of identity is a society of exclusion and conflict. A society clinging to identity has usually passed its peak and seeks desperately to restore its (questionably) glorious past. More generally, identity is a symptom of our inability to accept the world *as it is.* In this sense, to speak of an "identity crisis" is misleading, because, in truth, we only turn to such words when we in fact have a *societal crisis*, when society feels unsure and unsafe.

The future of Europe cannot rest on national identity—certainly not on twenty-eight different ones. The Europe of today, *l'Europe des Nations*, is a relic of the past; it is as good as dead if only because it cannot face the challenges of the living. Above all, it barely plays a meaningful role in the multipolar world of the twenty-first century. Like it or not, we have a clear choice before us: we can once again submit to the rise of identity thinking in Europe, or we can openly combat it.

Many political leaders have already made their choice. They have opted to abdicate. The CSU, the Christian Democratic Party, in the south of Germany; the center-right in France, which under the new-old leadership of former president Sarkozy uses the kind of language that makes it sound as though Sarkozy himself, not Marine Le Pen, were the leader of the Front National; the British Conservatives, who are moving heaven and earth to take the wind out of the sails of the United Kingdom Independence Party, the party of the "little Englander": it is as though none of them has learned anything from the past, as though none of them remembers the catastrophes to which identitarian thinking led in the nineteenth and early twentieth centuries.

Luckily, we have the young generations. Regardless of the member states in which they live, they believe in Europe and will not be imprisoned by their so-called national identity or stopped by national borders. They know that the future of Europe lies *beyond* nationalism—if it is to have any future at all.

CHAPTER SEVEN

"QUICK FIX" POLITICS

O N SUNDAY, MAY 3, 2009, FOR THE FIRST TIME SINCE STEPPING down as Belgium's prime minister, I was participating in the European elections. I stood before a jam-packed auditorium at the University of Leuven, discussing my new book. Although in retrospect it was completely crazy, this book bore the hopeful subtitle *How Europe Can Save the World*.

At the end of my presentation, I showed three world maps, colored to show the growth outlook of each continent as projected by the International Monetary Fund (IMF) "if policy remains unchanged," as they say in the economic community. These included one for 2009 and estimates for 2011 and 2013. The entire 2009 world map was colored red, with every country and region in a severe crisis. The whole world was in financial turmoil, and world trade had all but ground to a halt. The map for 2011 showed a little more variation. The crisis was over in Asia and Africa, and the United States was gradually getting back on its feet. Those continents turned orange. Only the European continent remained red. On the 2013 map, the entire world was colored green (indicating high growth) save for one red spot: the European Union and, in particular, the countries of the eurozone. The IMF did not make these projections on a whim. Its first premise was that newly elected US President Barack Obama would effectively implement his planned banking and investment strategy. The second was that Europe would remain paralyzed by the lethargy that had crippled it since the financial crisis crossed the Atlantic Ocean the year before. Economists are often reproached for doing a better job of explaining away incorrect past analyses than correctly predicting the future. On this occasion, however, they proved right.

In stark contrast to the American authorities, who took swift and clear action following the failure of Lehman Brothers, European politicians appeared to have no strategy. They shuffled glumly from the edge of one abyss to another—the mortgage market crisis, the banking crisis, the sovereign debt crisis and the resulting economic crisis, first in Greece, then in Ireland, then Portugal, then Spain, and then in Greece again—all without a coherent response or serious reaction.

Not that Europe did not cause a commotion. On the contrary, extra summits, crisis meetings, and special meetings of the European Council were called every other day. These, however, did little to help matters. At the end of each, Mario Draghi, president of the European Central Bank (ECB), was left to improvise and hastily avert a crisis. Draghi, however, was an unelected technocrat with no mandate to design a new architecture for the eurozone. He could do no more than apply quick fixes—than plug leaks with duct tape, so to speak.

While Draghi endeavored to save what could be saved, the United States tackled the crisis with great rigor and efficiency. The Americans established an impressively coordinated series of programs—a three-stage rocket, if you will—to tackle the financial crisis and its ramifications. Our own insufficient response was but a far cry from this effort.

BLASTOFF

The first stage in the American program was the Troubled Asset Relief Program (TARP), introduced in October 2008 to clean up any unsound

American banks. The American government purchased more than $400 billion in toxic assets, tidying up individual banks while restoring confidence across the entire banking system. The funds remaining from the program were used to bail out vital businesses such as General Motors and General Electric.

This first stage of the rocket was extremely successful because of the speed and thoroughness of its implementation: less than two years later most businesses no longer needed their state guarantee or were able to repay the amount injected by the government. The American government sold the last of its financial holdings in late 2014, essentially ending the program.

America has a sound financial sector once again. The banks trust each other and lend to businesses as if the crisis never occurred. The car industry in Detroit, which everyone had doomed to failure, was not only saved but reinvented itself. US industry is back on its feet and—perhaps—even stronger than ever.

This crucial first step for recovery simply never took place in Europe, leaving us still, in effect, at square one compared to America. The European Central Bank did provide the financial institutions with additional liquidity, but this financial stopgap did not bring the credit crunch to a halt in Europe. Above all, Europe has failed to grasp clearly the true extent of the problem. Seven years after the outbreak of the financial crisis, the stress tests intended to identify the toxic assets on bank balance sheets—and inform us of how resilient our banks would be to all manner of financial risks and events—have still not been carried out fully.

At the outset of the crisis, each country shored up its own banks using its own methods. State guarantees, full and half bailouts, a range of liquidity lines provided by one national bank or another: there was no discernible pattern. Such an approach is lethal to a cross-border, multinational sector in which a guaranteed, unequivocal approach alone can restore the confidence of financial institutions. Seven years after the outbreak of the crisis, we still lack a unified policy that might reorder the continent's finances.

* * *

A BANKING UNION that encompassed the whole of Europe could have prevented this fragmented response. Such an option was on the table in 2008 and might have saved the union its current existential crisis. It could still save us further despair down the line.

Such a European banking union should have authority for the entire financial sector, not just the 130 banks deemed "significant." Even a local mortgage bank in a remote corner of Europe can have a destabilizing effect on an entire country and thus pose a risk to the euro, as we are seeing once again in Austria, where the Hypo Alpe-Adria-Bank, which collapsed in January 2009, is still causing trouble in 2016. If the crisis demonstrated just one thing, it was the member states' spectacular lack of competence in the field of banking supervision. Not one of the twenty-eight national regulatory authorities warned that the credit bubble was on the verge of bursting.

On October 15, 2008, at the height of the financial crisis and ten days after the United States launched the TARP, German federal chancellor Angela Merkel opposed the creation of a European banking union at a summit held at the Elysée Palace. In her opinion, banking supervision should remain a purely national matter. At most she would tolerate cooperation between the national supervisors of the member states.

In typical misguided fashion, no less than three institutions were established for that purpose. One of those, the European Banking Authority (EBA), carried out the first stress tests together with the European Commission. The reassuring results were published in September 2009, after the Anglo Irish Bank had collapsed only eight months earlier.

The failure of one of the largest banks in Ireland not only threatened to drag the country into an unprecedented crisis but proved that the stress tests—and indeed the entire European Union economic program—were completely ineffective. Instead of restoring confidence among the banks in Europe, the stress tests caused even greater turmoil.

When the European institutions tried to make up for their initial failure, they only revealed their own shortcomings once again. The new stress tests were reported to be more comprehensive and thorough than those in the previous round, incorporating the balance sheets of the 130 largest banks across the twenty-eight member states. The conclusions were, again, suspiciously reassuring. This new review claimed that the European banks had a capital shortfall of no more than several billion euros, which flew in the face of previous studies claiming that, in truth, several hundred billion euros were missing. Using an alternative model, the renowned Stern Business School of New York University concluded that there was a capital shortfall of €450 billion for the banks in ten European countries. Europe estimated the shortfall for the same banks in the same countries at barely €20 billion—less than one-twentieth of the amount reported in the Stern study. After a shameful first round, it would seem that the European Union decided to offer the *appearance* of health rather than doing the deep work of actually fixing its banking system.

Nevertheless, recapitalizing the banks is still the very first step in successfully tackling a crisis. The longer it takes to complete this cleanup, the more stubbornly the crisis will persist. This proved to be the case in Japan, which spent more than thirteen years recapitalizing its banks after the outbreak of the mortgage crisis in 1990. The crisis endured for so long that it was dubbed the "Japanese winter," a drawn-out period of economic stagnation that would persist for twenty years.

By contrast, following the outbreak of a mortgage crisis in 1992, Sweden cleaned up its banking sector immediately: two banks were nationalized, and a "bad bank" was established for the purpose of removing all bad loans from the balance sheet. This cleanup, combined with a sizeable depreciation of the Swedish currency, generated a spectacular economic recovery. The United States followed the Swedish formula to great success. Europe, on the other hand, landed in the same situation as Japan in the 1990s and risks slipping into a persistent downward spiral of stagnation and deflation. This is a direct consequence of failure to implement the right strategy in time.

* * *

THE SECOND STAGE of the American anticrisis rocket consisted of quantitative easing (QE) by the Federal Reserve Board, which is the US central bank in all but name. While some find it controversial, QE involves no more and no less than expansionary monetary policy that aims to stimulate the economy when standard monetary policy (e.g., interest rate hikes) has become ineffective. In concrete terms, the central bank purchases financial products—from private or public institutions—and thereby injects money into the economy.

Although the United States already had its banking system in order, it decided to employ QE as an additional remedy to further shore up the economy. The American government and the Fed wanted to be absolutely certain that credit reached the real economy—in other words, that the banks would once again lend money to individuals and companies seeking to invest in new houses, businesses, or product lines.

Despite the sensible nature of the American policy, in Europe we have been discussing it fruitlessly for years. Our indecisiveness stems from the national governments and central banks of various countries' applying the brakes or vetoing discussion, Germany in particular. The result has been a complete deadlock both within and outside the governing bodies of the European Central Bank, with opponents of QE prevailing for many years.

In the latter months of 2014 and early 2015, as a result of our ongoing economic difficulties, prices began to fall dramatically across Europe, sparking fears of deflation. There was a real risk that individuals and businesses would freeze even more money rather than reinvesting or spending. So soon after the 2008 financial crisis, this could have signified a final knockout for the European economy.

While the politicians continued to argue the benefits of QE, Mario Draghi again came to the rescue and averted a crisis with his quick fixes. Contrary to the wishes of the German Bundesbank, Draghi announced that the ECB would roll out a QE program worth more than €100 billion over two years to prevent the European economy from falling into the abyss. But where the American provision employed goods and QE intelligently to accelerate and secure a swift economic recovery, Europe used QE as a measure of last resort, taken only at the last minute, to avert deflation, the most ruinous scenario possible in a crisis.

Again, Europe was caught running to catch up with the crisis instead of containing it ahead of time—when we'd had a chance of bringing it to a halt.

❋ ❋ ❋

THE THIRD AND final stage of the American anticrisis rocket best illustrates the differences between the American and European approaches. Less than one year after the outbreak of the financial crisis and immediately after the presidential elections, Congress passed the American Recovery and Reinvestment Act, better known as the "Stimulus Package."

Although Republicans voted against the investment package, many did not miss the photo opportunities that were only possible thanks to their share of the federal check of no less than $831 billion offered to their home states. This enormous amount will have been directly injected into the American economy from 2009 to 2019. Broken bridges and sewer systems were repaired. New roads were laid. Additional subsidies were granted for innovative research. Taxes were reduced for families and businesses. States encountering difficulties, such as Florida and California, received federal bailouts.

Here in Europe, we have sat twiddling our thumbs for seven years. The European political elite, conservatives and socialists alike, became bogged down in an unproductive discussion as to whether to follow austerity or stimulus policies. The former Barosso Commission got no further than the brilliant idea of "project bonds" amounting to €200 million, just one-four-thousandth of the commitment of the Americans. Only now—more than seven years after the crisis—is an investment fund of any size being launched. This fund, for roughly €300 billion, relies primarily on private investors. No spade has yet broken ground, however.

FLORIDA

Another example of our lack of competence and power is our handling of derailed public finances in the member states. Rather than actively dealing with the enormous Greek public debt of 180 percent of gross domestic product at the very outset, as the United States did with Florida, we allowed the Greek crisis to develop into political theater, a battle between Germans who refused to yield and Greeks who opposed reform.

Ultimately, there was but one solution: the creation of eurobonds or a European debt redemption fund through which eurozone countries could refinance and manage the problematic part of their public debt together. This would allow us to clean up the mess with a single swipe, not only for Greece but also for other eurozone countries stuck in a negative spiral of austerity, a shrinking economy, and growing debt. The German Council of Economic Experts, which advises Angela Merkel, strongly advocated such a European debt redemption fund because it would protect the weaker eurozone members against aggressive speculation, providing them with the breathing space needed to make reforms that would take some time: cleaning up tax systems and social security and ridding them of corruption. Merkel outright disregarded the opinion of her high-level advisors.

The introduction of such a European debt redemption fund could resolve the problems for Greece, European creditors, and European taxpayers. For Greece, because the country would be able to finance its debts and restructuring at an acceptable interest rate. For the creditors, because access to the debt redemption fund would be subject to the implementation of real reforms: deregulation of the labor market, privatization and streamlining of state enterprises, and, in particular, extirpation of corruption and ever-present patronage. Lastly, for the European taxpayers—the Germans first and foremost—because their tax revenues would no longer disappear into the coffers of banks and financial markets within and outside Europe. Such a fund would have maintained the solvency of the euro and the European Union.

＊ ＊ ＊

THE DIFFERENCE BETWEEN the approaches adopted in Europe and the United States is nowhere more evident than in the results: 3 percent growth in the United States compared to just over 1 percent in Europe. This is precisely what the International Monetary Fund predicted back in 2009, when it warned that drastic measures were needed in the European Union in order to put the economy back on the road to recovery. And although the European economy might seem to be doing a little better lately, all experts agree this is a temporary and artificial rebound, fueled by low energy prices, low interest rates, and an expansive monetary policy resulting in a weak euro. The structural problems of the European economy are far from over. With clocklike regularity, recommendations and analyses published in all quarters of the world called on the Europeans to set their house in order. A *new* Washington consensus has even developed around the subject in America.

Neither the Democratic left wing nor the Republican right wing understands why Europe is not taking the final plunge toward a full-fledged federation. Alan Greenspan, former chairman of the Federal Reserve and figurehead of right-wing America, stated, "The euro can only be saved via a real political union." Nobel Prize winner Paul Krugman, the rock star of left-wing America, said something similar: "Because monetary union wasn't accompanied by political union, the continent as a whole is pursuing what amount to insanely restrictive policies.'"

Krugman also drew a comparison between the approaches taken in Spain and Florida. Both fell victim to the same type of phenomenon: as popular destinations for pensioners, they confronted a real estate bubble that signaled a whole host of later economic difficulties. How did their respective governments react? Washington's transfers to Tallahassee amounted to no less than 4 percent of Florida's gross domestic product. As a result, the Sunshine State made a quick recovery, and Florida now ranks among the American states with the highest growth rates. The picture in Spain is a little less rosy. Spain had to handle a real estate bubble and a banking crisis while at the same time swallowing reduced tax revenues and coughing up higher unemployment benefits. Whereas part of the solution in Florida was for unemployed residents to relocate to another US state, such an exodus from Spain would mean a further erosion of the tax base. After all, every Spaniard leaving the country further reduces tax revenues for the treasury in Madrid. "Granting federal aid to Spain," explains Krugman, "as we did with Florida, is not possible in Europe as it currently stands. That is a major issue."

And it is not only Capitol Hill that has reached a consensus on how Europe should tackle the crisis. The International Monetary Fund is likewise crystal clear: "The crisis has exposed critical gaps in the euro area's architecture." The solution to these structural flaws lies in the creation of a "fiscal union for the euro area." The IMF states that the European countries will need to adopt a common approach to tax revenue management. This alone can avoid excess risks. Anyone wishing to get the European economy back up and running must first complete the EU *political* union project.

The United States has every interest in a strong European economy. The trade that flows between the European and American blocs is the largest in the world and can increase only when the new Transatlantic Trade and Investment Partnership enters into effect. It is therefore unsurprising that the Americans are watching Europe's poor growth with increasing unease.

Yet their tough analysis is motivated not only by self-interest or economic calculations but also by their own experience. The United States has not forgotten how the loose confederation of thirteen colonies that formed the United States in 1776 was unable to deal with the challenges it faced. The rule of unanimity blocked most decisions. The confederation was thus expanded into a federation eleven years later out of pure necessity. Shortly after that, just prior to the end of the eighteenth century, the dollar was introduced as the national currency. In Europe we have done things the opposite way around.

It takes little effort when comparing the two historic experiments—the dollar and the euro—to arrive at a correct diagnosis. A currency is viable only if supported by a political entity. It is possible for states to exist without their own currency; for instance, some states use another nation's currency. The reverse, however, is impossible. A currency cannot exist without a state. All currencies require a stable base.

Europe is continuing to deceive itself. Rather than thoroughly addressing the problems at hand, we keep fiddling about. Any attentive observer can see that European politics often entails little more than ploys, wrapped in nice sentences, to give the outside world the impression that problems are indeed being addressed, when in fact these gimmicks have very little meaning and are of no help whatsoever. Such stratagems have one thing in common: they prevent us from having to make hard choices. They keep us from addressing difficult issues and allow us to continue taking half measures, when desperate times call for desperate measures.

TRICKS OF THE TRADE

The arsenal of ploys employed by the European political elite shows a seemingly inexhaustible ingenuity. The most frequently used of these ploys is the "politics of announcements," whereby we repeatedly launch major objectives and projects without first ensuring the necessary resources are available for their completion. The decision to introduce a common migration policy was announced in the Finnish city of Tampere in 1999. More than fifteen years later, no action had been taken with regard to this policy. One year later, under the Portuguese presidency, we announced the Lisbon Strategy, an ambitious project to make the European economy "the most advanced knowledge-based economy in the world." Since then, the European economy has experienced a constant downward trend. In 2006, under the British presidency of Tony Blair, at the stately Hampton Court Palace in London, we announced that we would establish an energy union with the aim of reducing our reliance on the Russians. Almost ten years later, action is also still forthcoming in this regard. Now, following Vladimir Putin's invasion of the Crimea and the eastern provinces of Ukraine, the project is being dusted off post-haste.

A second ploy closely associated with Europe's "quick fix" politics is the preference for a so-called soft but intelligent approach. "Soft law and soft power" is our motto. Instead of making hard decisions—and requiring member states to uphold them—we apply "soft law," a contradiction in terms. "Best practices," "benchmarks," "peer review," "blame and shame": these are all simply nice English terms for tactics to put pressure on the member states and encourage them to do what is right of their own free will. Fifteen years' worth of evidence shows that this method does not work. It is simply paperwork. Documents. Deception. It is like receiving a report card, but without consequences, like being allowed to progress to the next grade or class regardless of whether or not you have passed.

The eurozone has demonstrated the failure of this approach more than anywhere else. A monetary union requires more than mere coordination of strategies and policy measures or spreadsheets, slides, and comparative tables. An area of shared currency requires a high degree of convergence and, in some cases, even complete harmonization. Where not achieved voluntarily, this level of convergence must be imposed. It is one way or the other: either you have a single, shared currency and therefore shared obligations, or you do not, and each country can proceed as it pleases.

This choice betrays another ploy used in Europe today: where strict rules apply—and serve the powerful states' interest—they are treated as holy writ. The stability pact, introduced as a type of constitution for the monetary union, is a fine example. The two largest member states underwriting the agreement, Germany and France, had already violated it within a few years. Nobody felt bound by the pact after that. Only when the financial crisis struck and the rating agencies took a closer look—which they had neglected to do for several years—did everyone suddenly remember that the pact existed—as Greece was the first to experience. Greece was not entirely without blame; however, the fact is that when the smaller member states (Ireland, Portugal, and Greece) are at issue, the rules are strict; when the larger member states (France, Germany, and Italy) are at issue, the rules are considerably more accommodating.

The rules are tightened each time in the case of the former and stretched or revised each time in the case of the latter. In 2003, we relaxed the rules in favor of Germany and France. In 2010, we tightened them again, when Greece, Portugal, and Ireland ran into difficulties. Under the rubric of "flexibility," we relaxed the rules once again in 2014, after the new European Commission took office—to the benefit, not surprisingly, of France and Italy. The controversy surrounding the application of the stability pact has thus become a true phantom haunting the Union. Not only is the pact applied inconsistently but the proceedings leading to sanctions depend largely on the member states themselves. Why would you make things complicated when evaluating the budget figures of a colleague if that same colleague will then be evaluating your results afterward?

We pay scarcely any attention now to the actual cause of our difficulties: the fact that a monetary union cannot endure without a full-fledged economic and political union. The member states prefer to focus on debating the application of the stability pact rather than taking a serious step toward the economic and political integration of the eurozone.

Lastly—and this is likely the main cause of "quick fix" politics—the union can make no progress without the unanimous agreement of all member states, a state of affairs in effect since the Luxembourg Compromise of 1966, when Charles de Gaulle won the right of member states to opt out of any collective policy against their national interest. Officially, the veto has been abolished; in essence, however, it still exists, particularly for the large member states. This means that every rule is a carefully molded compromise. Perfect solutions and simple choices are not possible within the European Union. Today's European politics are always a case of drawing a complex comparison between twenty-eight member states, each of which wants to have its cake and eat it too.

Conversely, in those areas in which unanimity is an official requirement, we employ all manner of subterfuge to avoid having to achieve it. We use legal trickery—so-called passerelle clauses, alterations that don't require *formal* amendments to the treaties—to circumvent unanimity and adopt decisions with a qualified majority. And when that does not work—because passerelle clauses also require unanimity—we set up "enhanced cooperation," actions and policy measures that do not include the participation of all twenty-eight member states. If that too proves impossible, we create some form of other instrument or vehicle outside the European Treaties, independent of the European institutions, using, for instance, the "intergovernmental method." In short, where a rule does not exist, we apply one; where the application of a rule is officially required, we do our utmost to avoid it.

✱ ✱ ✱

THUS THE EUROPEAN political community employs an inexhaustible array of deceptions. In some cases, we politicians use simple magic tricks, deceiving ourselves and others that the mirage of European unity is real. In other cases, we employ practices that are completely fraudulent, resolving problems by simply denying that they exist (as was the case during the bank stress tests). In almost all cases, we use these illusions to fool ourselves into thinking that, with just a few minor interventions, we can achieve the same results as we could through extensive reforms or by taking a major step forward—for example, with regard to the economic policy of the eurozone, where we continue to believe that loosely coordinating the economic policy of the member states is sufficient.

This denial of reality—this craze for never looking at the merits of the case and getting to the crux of the problem and instead focusing on details or secondary symptoms and thereby creating the impression that we are doing things right—has gradually become second nature to us.

We must ultimately ask ourselves why we are no longer capable of seeing the truth in front of us. What explains this blind spot? Europeans have a reputation for rationality, for thoroughly analyzing problems using their powers of judgment before seeking appropriate solutions based on well-reasoned arguments. That is what the founding member states of the European Union did, at any rate. They survived the horrors of World War II and concluded that we could only put an end to the nightmare through European cooperation and integration.

It has now also become clear that in a globalized world dominated by empires such as China, India, and the United States, only "an ever closer Union" can play a significant role. How have we lost this capacity and insight?

I believe that the answer to this question is implicit in the beliefs of the current generation of political leaders and, more specifically, in the unwillingness and powerlessness of today's national elites. We have lost our way due to the unwillingness of some, who refuse to transfer sovereign power to the supranational level based on their convictions, and the powerlessness of others, who are no longer able to sell the European dream due to public opinion. In a certain sense, all of our political leaders—some due to their convictions, others out of pure opportunism—have become clones of Margaret Thatcher and Charles de Gaulle, both of whom shortsightedly imperiled the European project by championing so-called national purity.

Many of today's political leaders are followers rather than front-runners, politicians who stick their fingers in the air to determine which way the wind is blowing rather than mavericks who fly in the face of public opinion where necessary.

CHAPTER EIGHT

THE HUNGARIAN DISGRACE

Anyone seeking to understand the dangerous shift in Europe—from democracy to autocracy, from the triumph of human rights to the new ascendancy of the state—need look no further than Hungary's prime minister, Viktor Orbán. I first met Orbán in December 1989, back when he was a dyed-in-the-wool liberal. Today, he aims to make his country into an "illiberal state." No one would have imagined this transformation twenty-five years ago.

I still vividly remember our first meeting in a Budapest hotel. At the time I was leading the Belgian opposition with the liberal Party for Freedom and Progress (PVV). I had never been to the Eastern Bloc. Honoring the Communist satellite countries of Eastern Europe, let alone the Soviet Union, with a visit was not the done thing among liberal politicians of my generation. Western socialists often made the trip, seeing those countries as comrades. But for those of us who believed in the basic democratic consent of the governed, the implicit freedom and security of a market economy, and the paramount importance of human rights—we liberal politicians of Western Europe—they were the enemy, both politically and ideologically. Yet the Berlin Wall had recently fallen, and the Iron Curtain had just been torn down, and we were now seeing liberal protests and liberal ideals springing up among our eastern neighbors.

Night after night, we watched on the news how history was altering course in a way that we would never, ever have thought possible, even in our wildest dreams: the collapse of the almighty Soviet Union and the implosion of its most fanatical ally, East Germany. I was born in 1953 and had always thought that the wall would remain standing forever. Who or what on earth was powerful enough to undo this disgrace and bring the wall tumbling down? Was change really in the air, or was this just another revolt in the Eastern Bloc that the Soviets would again suppress, as they had in Budapest in 1956 and Prague in 1968?

For months already, we had been closely watching the revolution in Poland, the events in Gdansk, and the activism of Lech Wałęsa. No response seemed forthcoming from the Russians. In Hungary, the Communist rulers themselves seemed to be cutting holes in the Iron Curtain. Who exactly was this Soviet leader Mikhail Gorbachev—a hypocrite attempting to maintain a corrupt system or a reformer acting in good faith?

I was overcome by a kind of euphoria that I have never since experienced in my political career. We liberals suddenly felt compelled to travel to Eastern Europe as soon as possible, and did so, because history was being written there. The atmosphere was comparable to that of the American Revolution or the French Revolution. We had to be there, side by side with kindred spirits, instead of at home, in front of our television sets.

GOING EAST

So the Flemish liberal party hastily organized a mission to the Eastern Bloc countries to size up the situation and, more importantly, to make contact with our brothers, the numerous liberal parties sprouting everywhere. These included political movements returning from exile as well as entirely new parties springing up of their own accord.

We mapped out an entire route. We would begin at the farthest point, in Romania, where the liberals needed the most help. They had to fight against the remains of an old regime that had rid itself of Nicolae Ceauşescu but was determined to hold on to power and keep the country as far away from democracy as possible. We would then call in at Budapest, followed by Prague, and finish in East Berlin. The journey to Bucharest was something of a shock: we spent over three hours on a flight with Tarom, the Romanian state airline in its heyday, with twenty centimeters' legroom. It was my first painful introduction to the material world of the Communist single-party state.

The visit to Bucharest itself was even more awful. The city was like a dilapidated theater, with wide avenues and high-rise, ostentatious facades that concealed not houses but slums. In the center of the city lay a megalomaniac's presidential palace that deserved to be knocked down. In the city itself, we saw beggars in the streets and prostitutes in the bar of our hotel. With increasing astonishment, I wondered how anyone could ever have had an ounce of credence in the blessings of the Communist utopia.

We received a warm welcome from Radu-Anton Câmpeanu, the historic leader of the National Liberal Party, Romania's oldest liberal party, who had remained in exile in Paris since the Communists took power and returned to Bucharest shortly before we arrived. His party headquarters looked just as cheerless as the streets of Bucharest, consisting of one rickety table, a few wobbly chairs, and a worn-out typewriter. Due to the sheer poverty of his surroundings, we later sent him a truck containing state-of-the-art office equipment, stencil duplicator machines, and computers. The cargo was completely destroyed shortly after it arrived by the storm troopers of interim president Ion Iliescu, during a demonstration by the Front de Salut National. We sent a second truck to Bucharest, which even included broadcast radio equipment to set up a pirate radio station. Known as Radio Contact, it would remain on air for over ten years.

After Bucharest, Budapest was a breath of fresh air, like a return to civilization, European culture, and modern society. The city even displayed the great European architectural styles of the nineteenth and early twentieth centuries: art nouveau, art deco, and modernism. This was how I ended up as head of a delegation of Belgian liberals in the lobby of a hotel in Budapest. After enjoying some breakfast, we were mobbed by a series of large and small political movements, think tanks, political parties, action groups, and nongovernmental organizations (NGOs) with a common interest in preaching liberalism. Ten of them had assembled in the arrival hall to extol their own virtues. Each one hoped that we, the Western liberals, would recognize it as the definitive voice of liberalism in Hungary.

We were curious. In our Western society, liberalism had always found itself on the defensive, but in Hungary and other former Eastern Bloc countries, a dozen liberal movements waited in the wings, seemingly unconcerned about this whatsoever. They were not afraid to make their liberal views known—quite remarkable in countries where only a short time before there had allegedly been universal acceptance of the illiberal state.

Excitedly, we told them our views and gauged their expectations. The first free elections would soon take place. We first met Péter Esterházy, Imre Kertész, and Geörgy Konrád, representatives of the Hungarian liberal Alliance of Free Democrats (Szabad Demokraták Szövetsége, SZDSZ), which enjoyed the support of the majority of Hungarian intellectuals. Immediately afterward we met with Fidesz, a party led by a flamboyant young man who introduced himself as Viktor Orbán. He and a few of his companions explained that they were actually the student branch of the SZDSZ. Surprised, I asked him directly why, if he was in the student section of the SZDSZ, he was not a member of that party's delegation. Orbán glanced left and the right at his companions, as if seeking their agreement on what he was about to say, and then explained that they had had a serious dispute with the parent party. They were hardly ever given favorable positions on candidate lists and had therefore decided to participate in the elections independently. But there was no need to worry, as the election took place over two rounds. If SZDSZ became more popular than Fidesz in any electoral district, they would sacrifice their candidate in the second round. Yet they hoped for the reverse. I thought back then that Orbán had guts: he was representing a student organization rebelling against its parent party. I had a habit of treading on the toes of my own party leaders, but I had never submitted my own candidate lists. As to whether Fidesz candidates would be elected, I had serious doubts.

But I was mistaken: Fidesz debuted in the first freely elected, post-1989 Hungarian parliament with twenty-one members. During the 1998 elections, it outperformed even SZDSZ. Left with barely 24 seats, the parent party had practically been gobbled up by its offspring, which became the largest political group with 148 seats. At the age of thirty-five, Viktor Orbán became Hungary's youngest-ever prime minister, and his government pursued a strictly liberal policy. He reformed the country's rotten administration, brought spiraling inflation under control, and jump-started the economy with substantial tax cuts. During his first term in office, Orbán also introduced maternity leave, completed the pension reform started by his predecessor, and reformed both health-care and agricultural policy.

In that period, I met him regularly at the meetings of European liberal politicians, which he attended from 1990 onward. He was a bold leader who made great strides in bringing the people in the former Eastern Bloc country onto the path toward a free and democratic society. He was a role model; we all looked up to him.

Then the electoral tide turned. He lost the 2002 elections, and the socialists regained power. That was not unusual in the former Eastern Bloc in those days. In fact, the opposite would have been a miracle. The changeover of power at every election was practically the rule. The Czechs, Poles, Slovakians, and Hungarians were all disappointed in the political parties that they had elected to power. You could bet your life that they would choose to help the opposition into power at the next opportunity. In short, no single party ever held on to power for more than one term. But Orbán could not accept his defeat. He joined the opposition, seemingly humbly, but on reflection concluded that liberal policies would never help him win back power. And power, it seems, proved dearer to him than his values. Orbán embraced Hungarian nationalism as his new creed, joined the conservative European People's Party, and left the liberal movement.

A CHANGED MAN

Since then, Orbán has been an out-and-out nationalist. It must be said, he backed the right horse. He returned to power, as the head of the Hungarian government, but he is no longer the same man I met in that Budapest hotel lobby in 1989. He has become a liberal-hater, a populist, and a traditionalist. He spat out the writer friends with whom he had stood on the barricades in 1989.

The man I met for the first time as a result of the fall of the Berlin Wall and the Iron Curtain is now building a fence of concrete and barbed wire, one measuring 150 kilometers in length, right along Hungary's border with Serbia. It is intended to keep Serbs and all other non-Hungarians out of Hungary. Just like the wall between Israel and Palestine, it is nothing less than an act of nationalist aggression.

Orbán is firmly convinced that the Western model has run its course and that the future lies in copying regimes such as that in China. Autocratic leaders such as Vladimir Putin and Recep Erdoğan are the role models, and on that basis Orbán is increasingly turning into a mouthpiece for the Kremlin. He has become the parrot of Russian propaganda within the European Union. He called the invasion of Ukraine a "legitimate" means of protecting the Russian minorities there. And he uses more than words to demonstrate his support.

In the middle of the Ukrainian crisis, while the West had to tighten its sanctions against Putin for the third time in a row—and at exactly the moment when the European Commission announced its plan for an energy union (intended to make Europe less dependent on Russian gas)— Orbán stood before the assembled world press shaking hands with none other than Vladimir Putin. Smiling broadly, he announced a gas deal between the two countries, adding, "The details are yet to be hammered out." Clearly Orbán was making a statement; he wanted to show the rest of the world that the European Union was not absolutely unanimous in its rejection of the Russian invasion.

Orbán employs a tactic characteristic of every autocratic leader: keep the people in their place and systematically place the blame for personal failures on others. The corrupt energy giants are "tyrannizing the Hungarian people," he cried out recently. In truth, the price of energy in Hungary is below the average in Europe, but it takes up a larger chunk of the average Hungarian's household budget simply because wages there are so low.

In the meantime, Orbán is doing everything he can to maintain Europe's energy dependency on Russia and the high prices associated with it. For example, his ministers have helped to sabotage the European Nabucco pipeline project and ensured that the Russian retort in the form of the South Stream would succeed. He also throws himself into the arms of Russia where nuclear energy is concerned: he concluded a major deal with the Russian energy giant Rosatom for the construction of two nuclear reactors. The total cost of the project was no less than €12.5 billion, with a €10 billion loan agreement attached to it, granting the Russians no less than 10 percent of Hungary's gross domestic product. Independent energy experts don't consider Orbán's energy strategy the slightest bit sensible.

Orbán and his party are also following a dubious path economically. Over the past few years, Hungary's economic growth has invariably been lower than that of the other former Eastern Bloc countries. Moreover, the country is on a collision course with European institutions due to its excessive debt levels. An excessive deficit procedure was initiated in 2004 and dragged on for nine years, becoming the longest in EU history without any result worth mentioning.

✱✱✱

OF GREATER CONCERN than his economic or energy policy is Orbán's treatment of Hungarian civil rights and freedoms, which he deems of lesser importance than "the national interest." He, of course, determines exactly what that is. With the support of a two-thirds majority of seats in parliament—even though he won well below half the votes in the last election—he is pursuing one constitutional amendment after another at a brisk pace.

One such amendment altered the electoral system in his favor (again); another curbed freedom of religion; another gave him greater control of the magistracy. He dismisses questions about these actions, raised openly by the Supreme Court or renowned academics, as "political maneuvers" instigated by the opposition. And he brands anyone who dares obstruct him as an "enemy of Hungary." This quasi-totalitarian method of banning your legitimate opponents from the public sphere is well known: the West and international capitalism are trying to finish off Hungary.

As a result of this classic portrayal of "others" as the enemy in order to obscure failing policies, Hungary has lagged behind its neighbors for years. In one sense, Orbán resembles Benito Mussolini, with his blend of anticapitalism and antisocialism: opponent of both big business and trade unions and initiator of a new national order that purports to speak for the people, who, by the way, want to reintroduce the death penalty.

Orbán has appointed himself defender of the free market against the trade unions in order to keep wages as low as possible. Yet he does not shy away from nationalizing private pension funds, thereby squandering the savings of the middle classes. On the other hand, he is all too pleased to present himself as the voice of the common man and the enemy of major corporations, which, in his words, are "sucking Hungarians dry," while he himself has fixed the prices of just about all the country's utilities by decree.

In order to spread this utterly incoherent tale—and disguise the overall poor results—Orbán manipulates the media, which he monitors closely to determine who reports on his policies and how. Depending on the outcome of this screening, Orbán personally determines, using every means necessary, who will be tomorrow's winners and losers among

Hungary's media. Employees of the state broadcaster who do not toe the Fidesz party line are dismissed. Those who bring Orbán's political opponents into disrepute—by doctoring images if need be—are promoted.

✽ ✽ ✽

UNDOUBTEDLY THE MOST effective weapon Orbán employs to keep everyone in line is taxes. He determines, almost personally, which profits of both Hungarian and foreign companies (especially if they operate in the media sector) are considered normal or "luxury" profits. In other words, profits amassed unfairly, in his view, must be taken in taxes.

To this end, Orbán rushed a new media act through parliament in mid-2014, as a result of which advertising revenue was taxed at up to 40 percent, an unprecedentedly high rate both within and outside Europe. That measure made it possible to control the media (a sector already experiencing difficulty at the time) more effectively and particularly targeted the largest player, German-owned broadcaster RTL Klub, which Orbán was determined to bring to heel. He uses taxes to determine which broadcaster survives and which goes bankrupt.

Despite warnings that this act would severely undermine an independent and pluralistic media sector in Hungary, it still entered into force—but not with the same effect for everyone. While RTL Klub had to pay the full amount, TV2, a broadcaster loyal to Orbán and his party, received a special exemption. For those who still doubt the intentions of the new media act, Fidesz cabinet chief János Lázár made them crystal clear: "RTL is threatening the country. It would be good if they would practice this at home in Germany, and not in Hungary." By "this" he meant independent news coverage and reporting. To cap it all, a financial solution has been worked out for the fiercely loyal but unprofitable TV2, whereby CEO Zsolt Simon, who has close links with Fidesz, became the broadcaster's new owner and received a credit line on the basis of "future profits."

Radio showcases an even harsher situation: Fidesz, as a political party, appropriated the most popular commercial radio frequency without a word spoken in opposition. The head of the Hungarian media authority, unable to stop it, ultimately took the honorable way out and resigned. Meanwhile, the European Union watched idly as the pro-Fidesz broadcaster Class FM became the most listened to in the country as a result.

And that case is not unique. All commercial broadcasters that use reports preapproved by Orbán get privileged radio frequencies or popular cable network positions. Klubradio, one of the few remaining broadcasters that support the opposition, has already submitted fifteen requests to extend its frequency, and it has been refused fifteen times.

The situation is not much better with online media. Last year, the news website Origo exposed a scandal regarding Orbán's confidant János Lázár, who had spent a fortune on trips abroad at the taxpayer's expense. Lázár refused to reveal all but the minimum of information about the purpose of these trips under the pretext of "national security." Once again, the EU remained silent. Knowing that he cannot fully control the Internet and that more and more people, particularly the young, are using it as their source of information, Orbán toyed with introducing an Internet tax. That was a bridge too far. He withdrew the measure after Hungarians took to the streets in protest.

Under the leadership of Viktor Orbán, the scale of measures to restrain media has included everything from financial assistance for sympathetic outlets to political threats and shifted advertising budgets for those whose reporting deviates slightly from Fidesz's wishes and expectations. NGOs that denounce these media laws or practices and the increasing level of associated corruption are next in line to face trouble. Fidesz rhetoric consistently describes them as "foreign agents" and as "false" and "spurious" because they work with "a hidden agenda."

In June 2014, a letter arrived at a number of NGOs, including the leading human rights organization, the Hungarian Civil Liberties Union, the women's organization NANE, Transparency International, and the anticorruption organizations K-Monitor and Atlatszo. It urged them all to present their accounts to the Hungarian Government Control Office, responsible for financial inspections. The office had "serious questions and objections" concerning the subsidies that these entities had received as part of a Norwegian government program. During raids of the Hungarian branches of these organizations, the control office seized computers and other equipment. Orbán triumphantly announced that he wholeheartedly supported the crackdown on these "left-leaning" and "problematic" NGOs. The Norwegians were shocked and enraged. The Norwegian minister of European Economic Area and EU affairs, Vidar Helgesen, wrote in a letter that he was disappointed by the absence of any EU response. The Norwegians could not understand how shameless practices worthy of a banana republic or Putin's Russia could take place in the heart of Europe. In the following month, Orbán boldly declared, "I don't think that our European Union membership precludes us from building an illiberal new state based on national foundations."

THE THREAT FROM WITHIN

The whole of the free world looks on open-mouthed as Hungary treads this path. The *New York Times* wrote, "A once-promising democracy is rapidly sliding toward xenophobia and authoritarianism . . . as the population sees its freedoms curtailed. What makes this extraordinary is that Hungary is a member of both NATO and the European Union and blatantly defies the core values of both."

Countries that wish to accede to the European Union must meet the highest standards with regard to democracy and human rights. The so-called Copenhagen criteria require "stability of institutions guaranteeing democracy, the rule of law, human rights and respect for and protection of minorities." Any country that wishes to accede to the union undergoes careful screening and receives checklists of required adjustments and how to go about them. Every EU directive, every regulation, and every European court ruling must be observed and applied. Elections must take place securely, by secret ballot, and prisons must be livable; citizens must be able to participate in decision making at every level and must have a "visible influence" at a political level. Courts must be politically independent, the press and trade unions free and independent of political influence.

The list is endless, as are the reports and the associated paperwork—
it still is the European Union after all. So what is going wrong? The
Copenhagen criteria are applied extremely stringently in relation to accession to the EU but vanish from the radar afterward. Once a member
of the EU, a country is no longer tested in any way to ensure that it is
upholding the union's most fundamental principles. At the very most it
receives some finger wagging or criticism written in incomprehensible
official language.

When Orbán breached EU regulations with his new Elections Act—
which restricted political campaigns to such a degree that his own party
enjoyed a significant advantage—then EU justice commissioner Viviane
Reding offered a sleepy response: "While limitations may be acceptable
in some cases, they would only be lawful if they are duly justified and
proportionate." Such a statement only leaves us guessing whether the
European Commission believed the act in question constituted a problem and a breach of EU law.

Orbán understands the weakness of the system. He even used the
possibility of Hungary's being fined for his actions as a tool; he merely
promised to pass such a financial burden on to Hungarian taxpayers,
handing the EU a public relations nightmare.

Rather than stridently rejecting a member state leader's holding his
own citizens hostage, Reding responded, "The implementation of this
provision would mean that Hungary would introduce an ad-hoc tax
on Hungarian citizens. . . . This could undermine the authority of the
Court of Justice and could constitute a violation of the duty of sincere
cooperation in Article 4 (3) of the Treaty on the European Union on
the part of Hungary." No one could understand such bureaucratic language, let alone understand the issue here. This type of legalese nonsense completely fails to respond to the severity of what is happening
in Hungary.

The United States, again, has shown us the proper way to discuss
such blatant posturing. Victoria Nuland, US assistant secretary of state
for European and Eurasian affairs, was far less inclined to mince her
words: "How can you [Orbán] sleep under your NATO Article 5 blanket

at night while pushing 'illiberal democracy' by day, whipping up nationalism, restricting free press, or demonizing civil society?" But the EU is simply too cowardly to kick out a member for violating the very letter and spirit of the union's founding treaty.

In the meantime the Hungarians can only tremble while they wait to find out whether they will be punished twice: first by Orbán's unfair Elections Act and then by the EU fine that he intends to recover from them.

Who would be surprised to hear that the European Union is losing Hungarians' esteem? Who could champion a spineless EU that capitulates at the slightest hint of resistance and goes back on its promises? That responds only with words and never with actions?

The European Union's culpable failure to act in the case of Hungary stems, of course, from the fact that Orbán belongs to the union's largest political family, the European People's Party, which for years has done nothing but minimize the scandal surrounding Hungary. The European People's Party, embodying the political center of Europe, has become completely spineless, when it should be radically defending its values: namely, democracy, tolerance, and openness. In Europe, it is doing the opposite and surrendering to an off-the-rails figure such as Orbán simply because he can win votes, seats, and power.

Is it any surprise that Orbán gains followers? In Poland, the new government of the deeply conservative Law and Justice Party (PiS) raided the independence of the judiciary. It crippled the Polish Constitutional Court by decreeing that thirteen of the fifteen judges must be present before a verdict can be given, and all decisions must be reached by a two-thirds majority. A number of newly appointed PiS judges will thus be able to prevent the court from exercising its constitutional control duty in one of the largest countries of the union. Questioned on that point, the new foreign minister, Witold Waszczykowski, said, using pure Orbán-style rhetoric, "The land will be healed" from "diseases" after "25 years of liberal indoctrination." Putting his words into action, a new media law was hastily adopted putting the public broadcaster under full political tutelage. The minister of finance will appoint every manager in public TV and radio directly. The same will hold for the appointment of other senior officials. The exams to hire and internally advance civil servants introduced by the previous government were annulled so that PiS could place its pawns directly at the helm of the administration. Again, the European Union will likely be watching, toothless.

What moral authority do we have as a defender of democracy and human rights in the world if we are incapable of upholding these values within our own borders? With the Hungarian and Polish scandals, we have relinquished our right to rap the knuckles of Russia, China, Turkey, or anyone else, because we don't bother to defend the most basic principles of the rule of law in our own territories.

Margaret Thatcher was right when she said, "They're a weak lot, some of them in Europe."

CHAPTER NINE

THE MASS GRAVE OF
THE MEDITERRANEAN

Migration and Security

STORIES ACROSS THE WORLD TELL OF THE UNSPEAKABLE HORRORS
that come with refugees seeking a better life in Europe. As a result it
is easy to lose focus, to forget that behind the statistics are fully realized
human beings with likes and dislikes, hardships and friendships. For me,
one remarkable woman made this clear.

Her name is Shpresa. She works as my family's cleaner. She is
thirty-eight years old and a real ray of sunshine in our home. Shpresa
is Kosovan—Kosovan Albanian to be precise. She is married to Genti,
who is forty-eight and also from Kosovo, more specifically, from Gjilan.
They have three children: a daughter, Yllka, and two sons, Lirim and
Arta.

One day in September 2013, Shpresa was celebrating. We drank
champagne, while she drank fruit juice: she, her children, and her hus-
band had been granted Belgian nationality after almost fifteen years
spent traveling around Europe. Her experience is not unique, although

it exemplifies the scandalous way we treat the less fortunate of the world, those who see Europe as a promised land and want to play an active part in our society but are not allowed in.

FOR A BETTER LIFE

Shpresa's story begins on February 10, 1997, when her fiancé, Genti, is hurt in a serious motorcycle accident near their house in Kosovo. With severe injuries to his right arm and shoulder, he is taken to the hospital, where doctors make the mistake of giving him physiotherapy rather than operating straight away.

When, six months later, he has no option but to undergo the knife, the damage has already been done. The surgeons try to save what they can and transplant two nerves from his leg into his shoulder and forearm, but Genti will live the rest of his life with a paralyzed arm and wrist drop. However, he cannot and will not resign himself to this future. He decides that, whatever the cost, he will go to the West for treatment. On top of all this, war is raging, threatening his family, his country, and his future.

In March 1999, together with a pregnant Shpresa, he makes a first attempt. His father pays the local mafia boss the equivalent of €6,000 for a fake visa, which they use to fly to Frankfurt. The German authorities stop them and, three days later, put them on a plane back to the Balkans.

Two months later, in May 1999, they try again. Once again, the family hands the equivalent of €6,000 over to the mafia. This time, they risk the crossing to Italy aboard a small boat. Together with forty-five others, they squeeze onto the wooden benches of a shabby barge barely equipped to carry fifteen people. The boat suffers engine trouble and has to turn back. The next morning, they set out again. By this point, Shpresa is nearly seven months pregnant. She is terrified during the crossing, which takes almost seven hours. Eventually, however, they reach the Italian port of Bari, where the police pick them up off the coast. This is what paradise looks like: uniformed officers and a refugee camp where they receive a place to sleep and a small allowance to live on.

After a month, they have saved enough to buy a train ticket to Milan and, from there, to travel on to Brussels, where they arrive in June 1999. A friend of Genti's father picks them up and takes them to an address in Ghent, where Shpresa gives birth to her first child in August.

❊ ❊ ❊

AT THIS POINT the second phase of the saga begins: battle with a rogue landlord and bureaucrats.

Shpresa and Genti have just one goal: to avoid deportation and build a future in Belgium for their children. With this in mind, they apply to the Office of the Commissioner General for Refugees for asylum. They receive a white card, a temporary, one-year residence permit. Two years later, they are issued an orange card: a sign that they will be asked to leave the country in the foreseeable future. At the end of 2002, after a third hearing, the verdict is delivered: they are ordered to leave Belgium.

In the meantime, they have gotten tangled up with a rogue landlord who is charging them exorbitant rent for a little "corner house." As I was able to see for myself when I took over a few items of furniture, "tenement dwelling" would be much more apt: the living space included three tiny rooms with hardly any light and mold on the walls.

Shpresa and Genti cannot find a way out. Their lives are heading in the wrong direction. They are now residing illegally in the country, the Public Center for Social Welfare (OCMW) has stopped providing any form of assistance, and their debts are piling up at a frightening rate. Only with the help of the church and what my wife manages to slip them are they able to keep their heads above water. Medically, things are hardly going to plan either. New operations in Bruges and Paris fail to deliver the hoped-for result. Genti's right arm remains paralyzed. It has lost all muscle strength and turned blue and is causing him excruciating pain.

However, this paralyzed arm might actually prove their salvation by preventing their deportation. In line with the international refugee convention, Belgian law applies a special procedure for people suffering with health problems. In such cases, it is possible to apply for a permanent residence permit. Having no other option, they decide to take the chance.

In 2005, six years after their arrival in Belgium, they receive a permanent right of residence. Finally, they are no longer living in the country illegally. The OCMW starts assisting them again and helps Genti into sheltered employment. Together with the service vouchers that Shpresa is earning as a cleaner, they are able to make ends meet. They eventually decide to apply to become Belgian nationals.

But their troubles are not yet over. In 2011, the rogue landlord seizes their property. Their rental arrears and the interest owed now exceed €13,000. They are evicted from their home. In the end, my wife gives Shpresa most of the small inheritance she received from her late mother to get this evil landlord and his bailiff off their backs for good. In 2013, fourteen years after their arrival, Shpresa and her family receive Belgian nationality.

Yllka, Lirim, and Arta are now part of the new generation of Belgians who, I am sure, will be the pride of our country and our continent in the future. Arta and Lirim are outstanding students. Yllka plays the piano and attends a music school. She dreams of continuing her studies at the college of music in a few years' time. Who knows, she might one day take part in the Queen Elisabeth Competition for young musicians and be crowned a laureate.

A BITTER WELCOME

Shpresa and her family finally got their happy ending, but for millions of other asylum seekers and migrants, life in the promised land is hell. They find themselves without a roof over their heads or, worse still, lose their lives while risking the journey by boat, inside the hatch of an airplane, or locked inside a container. This is a tragedy on a colossal scale. According to the United Nations High Commissioner for Refugees, between January 2014 and June 2016, more than 10,000 people died while crossing the Mediterranean. This sad and shocking number means that we can now regard this crossing as the world's most deadly route.

The European Union has responded to this appalling tragedy shamefully. When European Commission president José-Manuel Barroso visited the island of Lampedusa, he announced, "That image of hundreds of coffins will never get out of my mind. Coffins with babies, coffins with the mother and the child that was born just at that moment." And yet his words proved empty: not a single substantial commission initiative to prevent people from drowning followed.

We shift budgets this way and that. We send out a few boats and helicopters under the banner of the European agency Frontex, not to carry out targeted search and rescue operations, as that is not part of Frontex's mandate, but to combat illegal migration. After all, rescuing people who get into trouble at sea remains a merely *national* matter. Frontex's budget is now a paltry €114 million a year, on a par with the transfer fee paid by Real Madrid for footballer Gareth Bale. Less than 30 percent of this amount is allocated to joint sea-border operations. What is more, during the latest round of budget talks, Frontex's budget was actually cut again by around €30 million, or 25 percent. Rescuing migrants is a matter of secondary importance.

During the last major refugee crisis, which took place between 2010 and 2013, the European Union stuck its head in the sand. Frontex received some modest extra funding, and member states rejected a distribution program drawn up by the European Commission with a view to taking in several tens of thousands of refugees, a figure that paled in comparison to the total number. "Mandatory" acceptance of refugees became "voluntary" acceptance. In other words, this approach simply does not work.

On the day Barroso visited Lampedusa's refugee center with Italian prime minister Enrico Letta in order to assess the situation with their own eyes, local resident Salvatore Ragonetti voiced his indignation: "I don't care if he comes here or not." Reading between the lines, he was saying, "It makes no difference." Another resident said on *Euronews*, "What are they [the representatives of the European Commission and the Italian government] coming here for? To see that everyone is dead?" Ultimately, the European Commission's delegation practically had to flee Lampedusa. Boos resounded from the other side of the fences, a protest against an inhuman policy that deliberately skirts any solution. The European Union has failed here bitterly.

The member states themselves bear a heavy responsibility for the human dramas playing out every day on the Mediterranean. The Italian government, for example, suddenly suspended its own sea-patrol operation, "Mare Nostrum," which included maritime search and rescue activities, simply because of the high costs. "Mare Nostrum" was hurriedly succeeded by "Triton," a Frontex operation restricted to border patrols only; rescue operations fall outside its remit.

Ultimately, this means that no one is taking responsibility for the boatloads of refugees arriving on our shores. Certain countries are considering criminalizing individual rescue operations, for example, by fishermen who happen to be in the area. In other words, they want to bring the people who rescue these poor souls before the courts for assisting illegal immigration and the criminal organizations behind it. "Culpable negligence" is the most generous term you could apply to this attitude, but the only truly accurate word is "murder."

❋ ❋ ❋

THE EUROPEAN UNION and its member states are really to blame for the tragedy we are witnessing on a daily basis at the southern fringes of our continent. More than fifteen years after the summit in Tampere, Finland, we still do not have a common asylum and migration policy. Although the Schengen Agreement creates a single common area, within it we still have twenty-six individual sets of legislation with far-reaching differences among them.

These differences play into the hands of unscrupulous human traffickers with no qualms about forcing penniless refugees to pay for their transport with their organs. We are actually driving asylum seekers and migrants into the arms of these criminal organizations because we allow them to apply for asylum only on European soil. When it comes to reaching that little corner of Europe, whatever the cost, asylum seekers are entirely at the mercy of ruthless rogues and smugglers, who exploit them financially and sometimes even abuse them physically.

What on earth is stopping us from setting up a more humane system? Why do we not allow refugees to apply for asylum via our countless embassies and consulates or the foreign representatives of the European Union? Why do we not make it standard practice to set up humanitarian zones close to conflict areas so that refugees can live in dignified conditions?

The Balkans have become a scene of mass migration, the Mediterranean has become a mass grave, and the European Union is the gravedigger. Every year in early spring, when seas are calmer, the flow begins of men, women, and children—entire families trying to escape war, violence, or persecution and find a better and, above all, safer life.

Every time there is an accident, every time a vessel capsizes, the European political classes trot out solemn statements, each starting with the same obligatory phrases: "We would like to express our condolences to the families of the victims. This tragedy must mark a turning point in European policy." Turning point? What turning point? We remain stuck in a quagmire of false indignation, good intentions, and recommendations, and these stand in stark contrast to our complete lack of action.

CAUSE AND EFFECT

This migration pressure is obviously a direct consequence of the many conflicts playing out on our doorstep, in North Africa and the Middle East. For many years, we believed these conflicts did not affect us and hoped they would resolve themselves, just as we did initially in the case of Kosovo and Bosnia-Herzegovina. We were just playing ostrich.

To turn a blind eye to these problem areas, as we are doing once again in Libya and many other failed African states, is the worst decision we could make. In a few years' time, we will see that conditions have become intolerable in these countries and that the local population has no choice but to leave. We have watched this happen in recent years in Syria, where we simply left Bashar al-Assad to his own devices instead of supporting the Free Syrian Army from the outset, even if only by creating a number of safe zones or humanitarian corridors. As a result, alongside the emergence of Sunni jihadist organizations, the country and the region as a whole now face an unprecedented humanitarian crisis.

Tens of thousands of Syrians are currently starving in Turkey, Jordan, and Lebanon. At least half of Syria's children have received no education for over two years and, together with the rest of society, are slipping irretrievably behind or, worse still, falling victim to child labor, recruitment by armed militia groups, or forced marriage. In mid-2015, there were 11 million refugees in Syria and neighboring countries, almost 4 million of them staying in border camps. In 2016 this number rose further to 5 million: 2.7 million in Turkey, 1 million in Lebanon, 655,000 in Jordan, 247,000 in Iraq, and 117,000 in Egypt. Civil war has already claimed more than 200,000 Syrian lives; 1 million Syrians have been injured, and four out of five are living in poverty and destitution.

Between April 2011 and January 2016, Syrians lodged more than a million asylum applications in Europe, of which the twenty-eight member states approved not even a third. This paltry figure of 307,000 admissions led to uproar in Europe about which member states were doing too much and which were not doing enough. In 2011, in the wake of the Arab Spring, France and Italy engaged in a similar struggle regarding the acceptance of 25,000 Tunisian migrants—a shameful spectacle during which the foreign ministers concerned made no attempt to hide their desire to see those refugees' backs.

The Libyan story is exactly the same. After turning the tide in favor of the rebels by implementing a no-fly zone, we washed our hands of the country. Instead of sending in UN peacekeeping forces, we left everything to rival militia groups. Chaos now reigns.

What is more, alongside Egypt, Libya is the departure point for tens of thousands of Syrian, Palestinian, and Sudanese refugees hoping to take the leap and build better lives in Europe. Around 140,000 Syrians are living in houses along the Libyan coast close to Zuwara and Benghazi, as well as around the Egyptian ports of Damietta and Baltim, near Alexandria, where they are waiting for a spot on one of the many rickety fishing boats that will carry them to Italy or Malta. Hundreds of them cram into vessels barely large enough to hold half their number, running considerable risk of perishing if the boat capsizes or sinks. Countless people succumb to the heat on deck, and pregnant women give birth in dirty cabins.

The list of vessels lost in the Mediterranean goes on and on. Reports that several hundred migrants have drowned off Lampedusa barely come to our attention, eclipsed by reports that another vessel has sunk, with even greater casualties, off Rhodes or Malta. There is simply no end in sight.

***

IN THE ABSENCE of a common approach to the problem—other than sending out a few rescue ships—Europe is trying to hold back the flood by transferring its responsibility to the countries of transit themselves. The worst case is undoubtedly the deal the twenty-eight member states struck with Turkey. They outsourced the migration crisis to a regime that, even before the failed military coup of July 15, 2016, and the massive purges that ensued, had become a deeply authoritarian state under the rule of an autocratic leader, Recep Tayyip Erdoğan. We asked this new Ottoman despot to prevent refugees from entering Europe. In exchange the Turks received €3 billion and visa-free travel. Weeks after the deal was communicated, Human Rights Watch and Amnesty International reported that Turkish border guards were shooting refugees at the Syrian border. Not a single European leader deemed it necessary to react to this barbaric act. Have we abdicated all moral principles?

The European Union has entered into "collaborative arrangements" with many other "partner countries," such as Egypt, Tunisia, and Niger. In many cases, we are asking unstable states with limited resources to deal on our behalf with migrant flows from sub-Saharan Africa and the Middle East, even though these countries themselves face poverty or mass influxes of refugees themselves. More than 130,000 Syrian refugees are living in Egypt. As much as a third of Libya's population is now living in Tunisia. Niger is one of the ten poorest countries in the world and, since the mid-1990s, has dealt with a flood of asylum applications from pretty much all of its neighbors.

Our attempt to shift the burden of taking in and supporting asylum seekers to a handful of impoverished countries is a disgrace. We should be assuming responsibility ourselves and making sure that these refugees are received in a safe and dignified manner in the immediate vicinity of the conflict itself.

A MISSED OPPORTUNITY

We are perfectly aware of the causes of this unbridled migration and how we should tackle them. However, not every form of migration is a problem. On the contrary, in many cases, it presents an opportunity that Europeans are failing to grasp, as we have neglected to put in place not just a common asylum policy but also a common policy for legal migration.

In Europe, we have failed to develop a coherent and common policy that transforms migration into an opportunity to achieve economic benefits. Doing so would dramatically relieve the pressure of illegal migration. It would rid us for good of the criminal organizations responsible for human trafficking and eliminate the large-scale abuse of asylum and refugee status that we currently face. Above all, it would mark the first step toward a solution to deal with the huge demographic and economic challenge confronting western Europe, with its rapidly aging population.

As the continent with the oldest population in the world—a consequence of declining fertility and mortality rates and increasing life expectancy—Europe is sitting on a demographic time bomb. The average age in Europe has already reached thirty-eight. By the middle of the century, this will have risen to fifty-two, compared with an unchanged figure of thirty-four in the United States. In many parts of the world, however, the population is getting noticeably younger. The Middle East is even experiencing an actual "youth boom."

It will therefore be impossible for Europe to survive without migration. Today, there are four young people for every pensioner, a ratio that will fall to just two to one by mid-century. Germany in particular faces a colossal challenge. Only one other country in the world's population is aging more quickly. Without migration, the number of workers in Germany will fall from 41 million to 36 million over the next five years. By 2030, the over-sixty group will account for 37 percent of the population. And by 2050, the population will collapse completely from 81 million to 65 million, meaning that the most populous member state today will have only the third- or fourth-largest population, certainly below those of France and Italy.

In the globalized world, knowledge is power. You cannot survive in the digital world simply by copying others: you have to create things yourself. What could make more sense than attracting talented individuals and allowing them into your country, especially if you have a shortage of skilled workers in a particular field?

Countries like Canada and Australia understand this. Some time ago, they developed a points, or "green card," system for selecting individuals from the massive talent pool available around the globe. As part of this process, they assess a person's linguistic knowledge, technical skills, education, and work experience. At first this system may seem restrictive, but rather than putting up barriers or obstacles, it establishes qualification tiers that open the door to the country. The United States takes a different tack, but the aim is the same. Anyone who can present a contract from an American employer is allowed in. The United States believes that companies are better placed than bureaucrats to decide who has the necessary skills.

That is not how we look at the problem. Fearful Europeans still confine legal migration to the occasional guest worker who comes to pick fruit or the young graduate who spends a year on a research project at a university. That's about as far as it goes.

Incidentally, in Europe, legal migration is still largely a national matter and therefore subject to restrictive national legislation. Although a few European directives exist to streamline these twenty-eight sets of laws, the political thoroughness ends there. Certain member states, such as Austria, the Netherlands, and the United Kingdom, use a points system very similar to that of Canada or Australia. Others, like Sweden and Spain, follow the American model. Others still, like Denmark, use a combination of the two systems, while some hardly allow anyone in. The only common characteristic in Europe is that virtually all twenty-eight countries nervously keep the door closed to lower-skilled migrants (i.e., people with no academic background). Except in Sweden and a number of countries in southern Europe, this is a constant right across the continent.

It is an extremely shortsighted attitude, as Europe has a real need for these kinds of workers (in the agricultural, construction, health-care, catering, and cleaning industries). Often they are in greater demand than more highly educated individuals. It is not difficult to work out why: Europe's "own" workers are turning down these low-skilled jobs, with the inevitable consequence that, in the absence of a pool of legal workers, people from the former Eastern Bloc, particularly political refugees, asylum seekers, and illegal migrants, are increasingly filling these roles.

It is no accident that among EU countries Sweden is showing the strongest growth, despite having been hit by two crises in succession: the 1991 property crisis and the 2008 financial crisis. Since 2008, Sweden has implemented a mechanism for legal migration based on presentation of a contract from an employer; it is unrestricted and applies to both higher- and lower-skilled migrants.

Sweden's successful approach should serve as the starting point for integrating the twenty-eight sets of national legislation and the raft of directives to create one common, coherent system that applies to high-, medium-, and low-skilled workers. Once a permit has been issued, it should be valid and applicable in all member states, which should boost sluggish labor mobility within the union significantly. Unlike the current blue card, this permit should not be restricted to more highly educated individuals, and holders should not have to wait for several months before they can start working in a different member state from that in which they legally reside and the card was issued. This uniform system should replace the twenty-eight sets of national laws. At present, the European blue card is actually an additional twenty-ninth permit that is valid only if it is compatible with the restrictions imposed by the legislation in the migrant's destination country. Unsurprisingly, therefore, the blue card has met with very little success. Since 2013, several thousand have been issued, mostly in one member state: Germany. In the rest of Europe, national bureaucratic regulations remain in force, explaining why talented young people are increasingly giving Europe the cold shoulder.

Why is the continent whose population is aging most quickly and which objectively has the greatest need for migration acting with such caution? Fear is undermining the immigration debate in Europe: fear of migrants and the terrorist threat they supposedly pose. All rationality is absent from the discussion. Any citizen with a migrant background is viewed and treated with suspicion.

Since the Paris attacks in January and November 2015 in particular, Islamic terrorism has been directly linked to migrant communities in general. Few people still distinguish between, on the one hand, a small group of poorly integrated young people at risk of being radicalized and, on the other, the vast majority of people who have migrated to Europe to build a future for themselves and, with their talents and eagerness to work, have a great deal to offer our continent.

The French right is proclaiming that we must stop terrorism and migration by abolishing Schengen and closing off national borders once again. This is nonsense, of course, as the Paris terrorists were born and bred in France. The only border that could possibly have prevented the attack on *Charlie Hebdo* has never existed—namely, one between the center of Paris and the poor suburbs that were home to the perpetrators.

The hostility toward asylum seekers has grown even further since the assaults in several German cities and in Sweden on New Year's Eve 2015. These attacks on women were absolutely reprehensible, and the perpetrators must be immediately returned to their homelands. But I abhor the lack of nuance and the stigmatization of an entire group based on shared characteristics with the assailants. Any offense like the New

Year's Eve attacks remains a crime committed by an individual, not by the population group to which he or she belongs. The fact that both the Cologne and the Swedish police concealed the facts has no doubt aggravated the stigma.

But we cannot cherry-pick our outrage. What about the lukewarm or virtually nonexistent coverage of attacks on asylum seekers, migrants, and refugees themselves? In 2015, according to the federal German police, no less than 817 attacks were registered in asylum centers and refugee camps: arson, property destruction, hate graffiti. That's four times more than the year before. No matter the angle from which we view the situation, we must fight, with all means at our disposal, those who threaten our freedom and our values. That includes terrorists, immigrants who abuse our hospitality by committing criminal acts, and homegrown extremists who organize pogroms against foreigners.

PART III

DECAY

CHAPTER TEN

THE DIGITAL DESERT

Europe's problems exceed ostrich behavior in foreign affairs and a weak moral backbone. We also lack vigor and unity in shaping our economy. We failed to address the economic crisis. We have extremely low labor mobility. We keep ignoring the fact we have a common currency without fiscal and economic buttresses. Most of all, we are losing gigantically in the markets of the future: digital, energy, and capital. The single market created back in 1992 omitted these three crucial sectors, and we fail to include them today. Our refusal to use the economies of scale the European continent has to offer leaves us bogged down in a zero-growth scenario.

Like millions of other people, I use Spotify—every day. This app allows you to listen to music for free, while the musicians are paid from the advertising revenue generated. It's a brilliantly simple concept: You listen to your favorite music free of charge without downloading it illegally. The musicians, in turn, receive payment from their labels or record companies, which contract with Spotify, ensuring that they are appropriately compensated.

Spotify was developed in Stockholm. Its founders, Daniël Ek and Martin Lorentzon, soon relocated their brainchild to the United States, where it was much easier to conclude deals with the four major record labels, allowing the company to tap into the entire US market of more than 300 million consumers. The United States offered something Europe could not: a single legal framework when it comes to both copyright and the digital market.

For Spotify, "Europe" represented constraint by the borders of individual member states. From the company's base in Sweden, winning over Europe's 500 million consumers looked like a task that would require plenty of staying power. After all, there is no European digital market. Europe still consists of twenty-eight separate national compartments with twenty-eight different sets of legislation and twenty-eight regulators, as well as twenty-eight different licensing and copyright systems. A vast number of deals must be concluded with the more than one hundred national telecom operators active in Europe.

All of which is to say that Spotify started out in 2006 as an extremely successful European start-up but would eventually have gone under if it had not decided in 2011 to enter the US market. Now Spotify's main office is no longer in Stockholm; it is in New York, and the company has also transferred jobs there. Its profits are taxed in the United States too. Meanwhile, Europe is looking on from the sidelines.

DIGITAL DIVIDES

Spotify is just one example among many of a European invention that, thanks to the lack of a unified market in Europe, the Americans are now reaping the benefits of. We are witnessing an exodus from a continent where, in some regions, more than half of young people are unemployed. But not just start-ups and apps are suffering from the lack of uniformity on the European digital and telephony market. This situation is, in fact, most problematic for consumers.

Those who cross national borders—which people do all the time on our relatively small continent—know full well that they will lose their telephone and data signal. Your smartphone's software has to detect a new transmitter—from one of the national telecom operators in the country you have just entered—before you can make or receive a call and resume your conversation—a huge source of frustration for people like me who regularly travel from Brussels to Strasbourg on a route that takes you from Belgium to France via the Grand Duchy of Luxembourg. Although we pretend that the borders have opened, your mobile phone continues to remind you that you have just crossed an antiquated national boundary. The absence of an internal European telecom market, despite more than sixty years of European integration, is impossible to ignore.

Even in this remarkable digital age, we still think in terms of borders in Europe. I've said it already, but the point is worth hammering home: we have twenty-eight different markets overseen by twenty-eight national regulators, as well as twenty-eight different finance ministries using frequency auctions to bolster their national coffers. This backward situation reveals the true depths of European innovation and resourcefulness when it comes to filling the national treasuries.

This is a recent phenomenon, however. In the 1990s, Europe led the way in telecommunications by doing exactly the opposite: by allowing its companies to benefit from the economies of scale that a large, continent-wide market has to offer. Europe was able to innovate dramatically, creating the Global System for Mobile Communications (GSM) standard for mobile phones and the first standardization of the modern 2G (now 4G) networks, which remain the bar for global telecommunications. Researchers developed this with the help of European research funding; as a result the union allocated standard frequencies right across Europe.

The revolutionary GSM standard was adopted worldwide and formed the basis for the first networks in the early 1990s. Even America's largest telecom provider, Verizon Wireless, adopted the GSM standard at the end of 1991. European companies grew rapidly thanks to the economies of scale made possible by this worldwide breakthrough. Ericsson and Nokia became the dominant players on the mobile telephony market.

During the 1990s, six European telephone manufacturers accounted for more than half of global production.

Twenty years on, Europe has lost this lead entirely. The future therefore looks a good deal less rosy. Apple and Samsung are now the market leaders, and European telephone manufacturers have lost their position among the world's top companies for good.

❋ ❋ ❋

EUROPE ALSO LAGS behind in the area of high-speed Internet. Japan, South Korea, and the United States together have roughly the same population as the European Union but eight times more fixed broadband Internet connections and fifteen times more 4G connections. Even Russia has rolled out more fiber-optic connections than all EU countries combined in recent years.

To reverse this trend, the European Commission—at the urging of Neelie Kroes—launched a groundbreaking proposal. By establishing a European guarantee fund worth around €9 billion, Kroes hoped to encourage businesses to invest more than €100 billion in broadband connections.

But the plan was scuttled before it got off the ground. During a late-night meeting on the union's long-term budget, the heads of government slashed the value of the guarantee fund to a meagre €1 billion spread over a seven-year period.

We do not have seven years to wait for reform. No fewer than 82 percent of US households have a high-speed Internet connection, while in Europe we trail well behind at 54 percent. In rural areas, just one in ten Europeans has access to such a connection, compared with four out of ten Americans. Unsurprisingly, then, of the world's twenty-five largest Internet companies, fifteen are based in the United States; Asia has nine and the European Union just one. The ten biggest high-tech companies are also American or Asian: Apple, IBM, Microsoft, HP, Dell, Toshiba, Samsung, FoxConn, Sony, and Panasonic. These companies are the drivers of growth and new jobs. European technology and Internet companies, on the other hand, are constrained by national straitjackets. They can achieve growth only within their own national markets, which comprise several million consumers at best; the market of 500 million Europeans remains out of reach. Most Internet companies are government-owned public utilities that function more as old people's homes for aging workers than as young and dynamic businesses.

As a result, the European digital sector is generating little employment. In Europe companies founded before 1950 do the majority of hiring, whereas in the United States recent companies like Uber and Airbnb are creating jobs on a massive scale. Unsurprisingly, not one major digital company has been founded in Europe in the past ten years. Meanwhile, US companies like Google, Facebook, eBay, Yahoo!, and Amazon—the real Internet giants—are thriving.

Even more dramatic is the amount of work that young Europeans are missing out on. According to the European Commission, completely opening up the European digital market could create more than 900,000 new jobs. By acting nationally rather than on a European level, we have not only squandered our lead in the telecom sector and the digital economy but also deprived our young people of tremendous opportunity.

It didn't have to be this way. Fifteen years ago, however, a far-reaching liberalization process got under way in Europe. National regulators were tasked with creating a competitive market to break the monopoly enjoyed by state-owned companies. This increased competition on the national markets but regrettably did not lead to a single, integrated European area where European telecom providers could compete with one another. By creating a single European regulator, we could have realized such a European telecom market at a stroke.

However, the member states were unwilling to give up their regulatory powers and transfer them to the European Union. They saw this as an excessive encroachment on their sovereignty that would result in their losing far too much power. They therefore persisted with a system of informal coordination, including the exchange of certain best practices. In short, they made exactly the same mistake in the telecom

sector as they had previously in relation to union economic policy, the
eurozone, and bank regulation.

* * *

THE TELECOMMUNICATIONS SECTOR in Europe is now completely fragmented. We have hardly any global players. Europe currently has more
than two hundred telecom operators. By comparison, China has three
and the United States four. Furthermore, each of the member states
has developed its own unique legislative framework and its own way of
allocating frequency licenses. These national arrangements do not even
come under the oversight of the European competition authorities.

In Europe, telecom companies like Vodafone, Orange, and Deutsche
Telekom are regarded as giants and closely monitored to ensure that
they do not acquire a dominant position at the national level. Glob-
ally speaking, however, they are dwarves. Major players like Apple and
Google can easily dictate terms to them. National regulators lobby intensively to thwart any European attempt to give more direction to the
European telecom market. Such an approach benefits only the heads of
the national watchdogs and leaves European consumers completely out
in the cold.

The costs of international telephone and data traffic in Europe remain incredibly high. An average phone call in the United States, from
New York to Los Angeles or from Anchorage to Honolulu, costs exactly
the same as a phone call to a neighbor around the corner. In China, a
phone call from Beijing to Shanghai costs around two cents a minute. In
the EU, an international call over an identical distance costs around six
times as much. The tariffs that providers charge for use of each other's
networks vary enormously from one member state to another, the highest being more than ten times the lowest. In any case, these bear little
or no relation to the actual costs incurred because regulators in each
country employ different models. And as the regulators won't relinquish
their "right" to determine a fair price for network access, Europeans are
saddled with excessive roaming charges for mobile calls. Because in Eu-

rope you generally pay double if you make a call from "abroad," we have the absurd situation where a third of European travelers switch off their phones if they travel to another EU country.

The extremely poor functioning of the European telecom market can be seen most clearly when it comes to allocating the spectrum—that is, the frequencies that allow wireless Internet access via 4G or long-term evolution (LTE), for example. This technology is absolutely essential in many countries where there are few cables. However, these frequencies must be made available, a matter over which Europe has no control.

Each country has its own system. As a rule, frequencies are allocated not in response to market demand but when the government needs to top up its coffers. In other words, the interests of consumers who want a high-speed Internet connection are secondary to the extra funds generated to bolster the national treasuries. The union's finance ministers have already collected no less than €100 billion from frequency (spectrum) licenses. To meet the growing demand for 3G and 4G, telecom companies have therefore had to take on massive debt, which prevents them from investing in high-speed networks. This, in turn, gives them an excuse to continue charging their customers high roaming tariffs. Roaming generates 10 percent of their profits.

The European digital market now lags hopelessly behind in all areas: competition, licensing, spectrum, net neutrality, and so on. Europe is no longer a breeding ground for innovation. We have plenty of entrepreneurs with brilliant ideas, but the different regulations and lack of a common framework make it extremely difficult for successful European companies to launch their products. This explains why Europe has fallen so far behind the United States over the past decade in terms of productivity.

Further delay in rolling out the necessary Internet infrastructure will only widen this gap even more and inevitably hold back Europe's economic recovery once again. Former European commissioner Neelie Kroes clearly recognized this, especially after receiving the message, in no uncertain terms, from every other sector, including the automotive, chemicals, chip manufacturing, photonics, and robotics industries.

All these businesses had made clear that they would leave Europe if a healthy telecom sector failed to get off the ground.

In 2013, Kroes therefore came forward with an ambitious package that would harmonize the allocation of the spectrum across Europe, abolish roaming charges, and introduce net neutrality. Even before its unveiling, an unholy alliance of national regulators, finance ministers, and Europe's five biggest telecom operators (Orange, Deutsche Telekom, Telefonica, Vodafone, and Telecom Italia) ruthlessly torpedoed the plan.

Although these three groups represent different and often conflicting interests, they are united in their rejection of a European approach: the regulators refuse to relinquish power to Europe, the finance ministers refuse to give up their spectrum—their cash cow—and the telecom companies refuse to give up their roaming revenues. All the heads of government, from across the political spectrum, headed into their most recent elections promising to make the digital agenda a top priority. However, they are doing nothing to break up this unholy alliance of regulators, telecom companies, and finance ministries. The proposal to bring spectrum tariffs into line has been swept from the table and consigned to the wastepaper basket.

A SINGLE DIGITAL MARKET

The snail's pace at which Europe is plodding along is enough to drive one to despair, especially as we cannot afford to delay. It is sink or swim.

For more than seven years now, our continent alone has failed to grow. Rather than agreeing on half-baked compromises, we need to come up with a new, fresh, more ambitious, and much further-reaching package, one that will close at a stroke the gap stretching between us and the Americans and Asians. We need a package with which to stand up to the regulators and large telecom operators and deal with the taboo against stripping the member states of their telecom powers and transferring them to the European level.

The starting point for such a package needs to be a genuine European market in which consumers can subscribe to the telecom provider of their choice. Pan-European providers should be active in various countries, new developments should be rolled out across the whole of Europe from the outset, and every European should have access to a high-speed broadband connection. Two revolutionary reforms will be crucial here.

The first involves dismantling national silos in the areas of telecom legislation, copyright, data protection, and the spectrum. Developments in the field of monetary policy could serve as an example here. When the euro was introduced, we established a European Central Bank to monitor price stability in the eurozone in close collaboration with the national banks. We could apply the same model to the digital market: a single, independent European telecom regulator could ensure that European regulations are implemented in the same way in all countries, carry out independent studies, issue spectrum licenses on behalf of Europe, and develop a policy to make the European telecom market more competitive and consumer friendly.

In the United States, the Federal Communications Commission (FCC) ensures that the US market—with its fifty independent states—is open to competition, that sufficient spectrum is available, that innovation can take place on a large scale, and that the right environment is created for broadband investments. In short, the FCC ensures that the United States is a single area within which all telecom providers can compete on an open market.

The new European regulator will need to tackle two specific points as a matter of urgency. First, with regard to the awarding of more spectrum licenses, the new regulator will have to accelerate the rollout of the 700 MHz frequency by means of a pan-European auction, under which telecom operators can acquire this spectrum in a number of countries simultaneously. This will allow European companies to become active throughout Europe and therefore develop into genuine global players. The revenues generated from these frequency licenses could be put to a variety of different uses. They could be added to the European budget, reducing the contribution that member states currently have to make. Or—a much smarter option—they could fund the necessary investments in European broadband networks.

Second, the European regulator must ensure that the achievements of the internal market are applied to the telecom market without compromise. Our aim should be to trigger a second wave of economic integration within the union. We need to apply the Cassis de Dijon principle—the groundbreaking 1979 European Court of Justice judgment stipulating that a product approved by the authorities in one member state can automatically be sold in the other member states—to the sectors of the future. This principle, which requires national legislators to trust each other, must also be valid in the markets of the future.

❋ ❋ ❋

IN THE AREA of telecommunications and digital services too, we need to get back to the basis of the European Treaties and the jurisdiction that has developed from it. This will allow innovative companies like Spotify or Dutch firm Blendle to conquer the entire European market in one fell swoop—and from there, the rest of the world. Many domestic markets are far too small to make this possible.

We need to get back to the original idea: a single European system. Protracted bureaucratic procedures to acquire twenty-eight different licenses have no place in the digital era that is the twenty-first century. They will only hold back economic growth and job creation.

CHAPTER ELEVEN

THE DECLINE OF EUROPEAN INDUSTRY

I N RECENT YEARS, WE HAVE FOCUSED EXCLUSIVELY ON THE EFFECTS of the financial crisis, which blew over from the other side of the Atlantic Ocean and wreaked havoc, particularly in the south of Europe. We have paid too little attention, however, to another, slowly advancing crisis that poses an equal if not greater threat: the erosion of European industry.

The industrial base that has formed the backbone of our employment for more than a century and a half is languishing. The number of jobs in European industry has fallen by more than 20 percent over the past fifteen years. On the other hand, employment in Asian and South American industry grew rapidly. The number remained virtually stable in the United States.

Less than half of the top exporting countries in the world today are European. Whether these European countries can maintain even this position for much longer remains to be seen as each has a higher cost structure—understood as the total cost of labor, energy, and transport—

than the competition, including the United States. Even in Poland, production costs in industry are a full percentage point above those in America. Our labor, gas, and electricity are invariably more expensive.

It is no wonder that European industrial production is losing ground year after year. Over the 2004–2011 period, Europe relinquished 10 percent of its market share. Compared to our most hardened competitor, the United States, average production costs rose by 6 percent in Belgium, 7 percent in Sweden, 9 percent in France, and as much as 10 percent in Italy.

The Americans have proven that things can be done differently. They demonstrate that you do not have to be a "new economy" to do well in industry. Under Barack Obama, the production of green electricity doubled, the car industry was restored to health, both financially and in terms of its innovativeness, and energy prices fell by one-third as a result of large-scale extraction of shale gas. The United States has gone from being a net importer to a net exporter of energy.

For Europe, on the other hand, the long-term outlook is less rosy. Whereas, at the end of the last century, we were still the major industrial power of our planet, accounting for a third of global production, by the middle of this century we will be the third-largest industrial nation, after China and the United States. The twentieth century saw an industrial triangle composed of the United States, Japan, and Europe. The twenty-first century is seeing a new triangle emerge, with China as the new rising economic power, replacing Europe. Together with the United States and Japan, it will account for 45 percent of global production.

From a third of the global economy at the end of the last century, by 2015 Europe will account for just 18 percent—if we count all of the countries in the union as a single entity. Individually, Germany will account for just 3.2 percent of global production, whereas it currently accounts for 10 percent. The shares of Great Britain and France will fall to 3 percent and 2.4 percent, respectively. According to Angus Maddison, a British economist specializing in the history of the world economy, we are witnessing a dramatic shift, and "the balance in the global economy is returning to the way it was before the industrial revolution that made Europe the dominant world power."

STEEL FOR STRENGTH

This concern drove me to be the only European government leader to side with Mittal Steel in its bid to take over Arcelor in 2006.

Early on a mid-January morning of that year, I received a telephone call from Karel Van Miert, the former European commissioner for transport and later commissioner for competition, with whom I had developed close political ties since his departure for the European Commission. He asked me whether I would speak to Peter Sutherland, one of his predecessors as competition commissioner and currently adviser to Lakshmi Mittal, the Indian steel magnate. That same day I spoke first with Sutherland and then, a few hours later, with Lakshmi Mittal himself.

Mittal explained his ambitious plans for the European steel industry in great detail, first on the telephone and then a few days later in Brussels, together with his son Aditya, the company CFO.

Mittal Steel was already the largest steel company in the world, but as it claimed less than 10 percent of global production, that did not represent much. There were simply too many players in the field. Consolidation was taking place upstream in the extraction and supply of ore and coal, as it was downstream in the companies that consume steel products (e.g., the automotive industry). Moreover, Chinese steel companies were emerging at a tremendous pace: in just twenty-five years, they had increased by a factor of twelve. With an annual production of more than 800 million tons, China is now the world's largest steel producer. The European steel sector likewise had to be consolidated, and quickly, in order to survive. This meant merging the sector into a few major players and adding iron ore and coal mining to their portfolios.

Mittal was already in the process of doing the latter. The merger, which was in fact a takeover of the second-largest steel company in the world, Arcelor, would create a European group ready to compete in this turbulent global market. Furthermore, almost 40 percent of the production capacity of the new group would remain in Europe. The synergy was also ideal as Arcelor's manufacturing operations were based primarily in western Europe and South America, whereas Mittal Steel's branches were mainly located in eastern Europe, North America, and South Africa.

I was persuaded in part because I had never found Arcelor's management to have any kind of future outlook. The old Luxembourger steel barons of Arbed still held sway in the company. Having produced steel for generation after generation, they believed they could go on doing so for centuries. I must confess, however, it helped that Mittal planned to keep open blast furnaces and rolling mills, such as those in the Liège Basin, that the Arcelor management had long written off as moribund.

When, in late January 2006, Lakshmi Mittal launched his bid to take over Arcelor, the response was furious. The management of Arcelor not only brushed aside the bid with contempt but also made a number of questionable insinuations in its statement. Who exactly did this Indian think he was? If he did not take care, Arcelor would take over Mittal and not vice versa. My colleagues in Luxembourg, France, and Spain—Jean-Claude Juncker, Jacques Chirac, and José Luis Zapatero—responded accordingly, rearing up on their hind legs and braying that they would put a stop to the takeover. For them, the issue was not the future of the European steel industry but power. They feared that they would no longer have influence over what had been the backbone of their national industry for several decades.

For a while, the management of Arcelor played with the idea of getting into bed with a Russian oligarch. That, however, was also a bridge too far for my colleagues in the European Council.

Ultimately, Mittal increased his bid to twice his initial offer and promised the Luxembourg government to move the headquarters of the company from Rotterdam to Luxembourg. The final bid was approved in late June, and the company was renamed Arcelor Mittal. Arcelor Mittal is still the largest steel producer in the world by some distance. The company employs more than 220,000 workers in its mines and steel companies.

Still, the least productive rolling mills and blast furnaces that had remained open, or been reopened, had to close their doors permanently after just a few years. Mittal's ambitious project succumbed to the financial crisis of 2008. Today, Europe produces approximately 30 percent less steel than before the crisis. We are utilizing just 70 percent of our capacity.

We must ask ourselves, however, what the situation in the European steel sector would have been without Mittal's intervention. Would we have been able to respond to the tsunami of Chinese steel? I believe not. Again, we see that consolidation, while politically toxic, remains the only viable path forward for Europe.

***

ECONOMISTS HAVE LONG said that the European automotive industry is doomed. They are wrong to do so. The American automotive industry's ascent from the ashes in recent years proves the contrary. Or look at how Ferdinand Piëch forged the Volkswagen Group into the largest car manufacturer in Europe and the third-largest player in the global market. Even after the emission scandal of September 2015—a disgrace that cost the company all of the stock market value it had so carefully built up over the years—the group still remains a global player to be reckoned with and one of the few European industrial success stories. I know this from personal experience.

When Volkswagen announced the closure of its plant in Vorst, Brussels, I was distraught. Belgium is traditionally a car-producing country. We do not simply drive cars; we consume them, much as we do french fries, beef stew, and chocolate. I had told both myself and the public that no Belgian car-production plant would ever close its doors while I was in office as prime minister. Renault-Vilvoorde had shut down under my predecessor, causing a national trauma. I, personally, had managed to prevent the same thing happening to Ford Genk a few years previously.

Once the news of the closure had sunk in, I made a decision that could be called questionable, to say the least. I decreed that no Volkswagen vehicles would be purchased by the Belgian public services until VW's headquarters in Wolfsburg reversed its decision to close Vorst. Not five minutes after making this announcement, I received a telephone call from Roland d'Ieteren, importer for Volkswagen Group in Belgium and owner of many car-related companies, such as Avis, Carglass, and Touring, the renowned Italian car design company that was as successful as Pininfarina and Zagato had been in the mid-twentieth century. I stated the reasoning behind my decision but in the same breath added that I could still reverse it, if there was any way to undo the Volkswagen decision.

I discovered that Piëch was one of d'Ieteren's best childhood friends. Their fathers were colleagues: Piëch's father was the exclusive importer of Volkswagen and Porsche in Austria, while d'Ieteren's father held the same position in Belgium. Further, as a teenager, d'Ieteren had spent several years holidaying with the Piëchs in Austria to improve his German. His childhood friend later married a daughter of Ferdinand Porsche and thus became the ruler of the Volkswagen empire, a result also of his undeniable talent and stubborn perseverance.

It was thus that I came to know Piëch personally. Piëch manufactures not only Volkswagen, Seat, and Skoda but also Audi, Porsche, Lamborghini, Bentley, and Bugatti. Never in my life have I met anyone who personifies the car as much as he does. The negotiations that took place in my office were not negotiations so much as a long, drawn-out ode to the beauty of cars: Bentley, Bugatti, Lamborghini. The line. The engine. The origin. The performance. I rode the waves of the passion that I had developed at age five or six, sitting in the backseat of my father's car and listing the makes and models of all the vehicles racing by. I love *das Auto*. I am particularly fond of driving. Put me in a car, and I will drive it to the south of Italy in one stretch, no complaints, simply for the pleasure.

As the Belgian federal government I headed was prepared to slash taxes on shift work drastically, the plant in Vorst was reopened, but as an Audi, not a VW, factory that was both nicer and more modern. Thus far, it is the home base of all A1s, as it will be in the future for all fully electric cars produced by Audi.

INFRASTRUCTURE WOES

As with steel, so too with nearly every other European industry. While Volkswagen and a number of German "premium brands" are holding their own, the major motor manufacturers in Europe are constantly losing ground. Total production in Europe fell from 16 million to 12 million vehicles. This decline is visible in almost all industry sectors: the shipbuilding industry has disappeared; the textile sector is dying; the coal mines closed down long ago. No policy resolutely committed to a revitalization of European industry exists at the European level.

Anyone looking into the cause of this landslide will quickly conclude that there is no single underlying cause. A multitude of factors have together put Europe at a serious disadvantage: escalating labor costs, high energy prices, expensive transport, and an administrative and bureaucratic overload of legendary proportions.

Detailed analysis of these factors quickly reveals that, in recent years, energy costs rather than labor costs have been causing the decline in our industry. The average electricity price in Europe for industrial consumers is the second highest in the world, after Japan. This high energy bill is the reason why even new member states, such as Poland, with low labor costs are finding it difficult to keep a tight rein on production costs. Energy prices there have doubled in the past ten years, due in part to an overreliance on Russian gas, but chiefly because of the lack of a true European Energy Community. Only the energy suppliers are not aggrieved by this situation, as they can easily turn the division within Europe to their advantage.

* * *

THE LACK OF an energy community is not, however, due to a lack of good intentions. Ten years ago in Hampton Court in England, for example, a decision was adopted to develop plans for a European Energy Community. After the sudden wake-up call of the Orange Revolution—which occurred in response to the Kremlin's stranglehold over Ukraine—

pro-Western Viktor Yushchenko came to power in a fair presidential election. This was not, however, to Vladimir Putin's liking, who wanted his puppet Viktor Yanukovych on the throne.

To achieve this, he drew his energy weapon and demanded that Ukraine settle its debts regarding gas supplies. Immediately. The gas conflict between Kiev and Moscow escalated under prime minister and "gas princess" Yulia Tymoshenko, who played a questionable role and was ultimately enriched personally by the conflict. The Kremlin finally turned off the tap.

Not just the Ukrainians but also large parts of eastern and northern Europe were literally left in the cold. At that time, no less than 80 percent of the gas imported into Europe came via Ukraine. The Kremlin attempted to placate the Europeans with a vague promise to pipe the gas by other routes in the future.

Ultimately, however, it became clear to everyone that the Kremlin regarded Europe and its population as nothing more than "collateral damage." The need finally became so great that even the British, renowned for their cool love affair with the European Union, became convinced that greater cooperation between the European member states was vital. A "common energy policy" and a common "European energy grid" were needed and would be introduced in the immediate future.

Tony Blair, then holding the gavel at Hampton Court, let there be no misunderstanding: "Obviously there are already on a bilateral basis certain interconnections. There is a lot more we can do however, and it is important too that energy policy is something that we work on together as a European Union, given the fact that we import round about 90% of our oil and gas needs. That is no small amount. This is a classic example of a situation where Europe needs to do more and not less."

The fine words proved empty, however. No common purchasing and pricing policy was introduced, and the announced investments in a European grid never came to fruition. The problem remained. Gas supplies to Europe faltered once again in 2009. And a third time in 2014, ten years after the outbreak of the Orange Revolution, when a new uprising erupted in Ukraine in response to Russian interference. Yet another energy war ensued.

This time, however, it received less media coverage. All eyes were on Maidan Square, the annexation of the Crimea, and the fighting in the eastern provinces. In the meantime, the problem posed to our economy was only growing. The United Kingdom, located in the far west of the union, depends on Russia for a quarter of its gas needs; France, for half. Germany, the driving force of the European economy, depends on Russia for almost three-quarters of its gas; Spain and Italy, for even more than that. Moscow sets the prices, and we have no choice but to pay. We do not use the strength of our numbers. No collective negotiations take place—via the European Commission—with regard to the oil and gas we import. Instead, each member state holds its own negotiations with Gazprom, the Russian energy giant, which is essentially a state within a state.

✾ ✾ ✾

MEANWHILE—AND THIS IS the second reason for the snowballing costs—the union is wasting massive amounts of energy. The lack of adequate interconnections between the European countries—the so-called energy grid—means that excess wind energy produced in Ireland and excess solar energy produced in Spain do not get exported to other member states.

And that is by no means the only problem in our European energy market. Most of the member states continue to protect their national markets from foreign competitors. Even if it were physically possible, Spanish producers could not sell and distribute their energy in the French market purely because they are not French. Like the digital sector, the energy sector falls outside the scope of internal market agreements.

Continuing to take a national approach to these sectors, however, has caused us to lag so far behind our competitors that the gap has become almost unbridgeable. Moreover, we have caused our businesses great expense and made them less competitive. Our families have less disposable income available for consumption and investment.

* * *

ENERGY COSTS ALONE are not making our businesses less competitive. Logistics costs are similarly too high, due, of course, to the higher prices paid for fossil fuels and electricity in Europe. Equally important, however, is the lack of an internal market for almost any mode of transport, which causes additional expense for our businesses and citizens. It makes no difference if you are transporting by rail, road, or air: when it comes to transit across the continent, "Europe"—meaning a unified internal market—does not exist.

For road transport, we have indeed created a European driving license and introduced a number of common standards for trucks and motorways, but that is all. Neither traffic regulations nor maximum speed limits have been harmonized. Licenses for heavy goods vehicle drivers still differ.

In the air transport sector, Europe is nonexistent. No fewer than thirty-one different codes and systems exist in Europe for the effective management of air traffic, with thirty-eight air traffic controllers operating across sixty-three control towers. The United States has a single system and a single area air traffic controller operating across twenty towers, while managing a much larger airspace than Europe.

A truly unified airspace in Europe would generate tremendous profits. We would save no less than €3 billion in administrative expenses and €6 billion in operational costs. At the same time, carbon dioxide emissions would be reduced by 18 million tons, equivalent to 12 percent of total emissions.

Europe is likewise still living in the dark ages when it comes to rail transport: European trains passing through more than one country require more than one electrification system. In the Benelux region alone, we use three different types of direct and alternating current systems to power locomotives. Not even the track gauges are identical. A train traveling from Madrid to Vilnius will have to break gauge at least twice in order to reach its destination. This is because Spain and Portugal use the Iberian track gauge, the Baltic states use the Russian gauge, and the tracks between the two are European gauge. Even in western Europe, little to no harmonization has occurred with respect to rail transport. The Thalys service that operates between Paris and Amsterdam via Brussels requires no less than three different voltages and furthermore must be adapted to four different signaling systems. The Thalys service operating between Paris and Cologne requires yet another voltage and has to meet the requirements of no less than seven different signaling systems.

Not even the signaling practices are identical in Europe. A red light means something different in Germany and in France. In Germany, it means "stop in all circumstances," whereas, in France, a red light may be passed in certain circumstances. Because of these irregularities, competition within the rail sector is virtually nonexistent. National monopolies continue to hold sway, and prices remain high.

❋ ❋ ❋

LITTLE ACTION IS being taken on a European scale in terms of infrastructure either. Whereas the Americans have developed a strategy for their roads, ports, and railways that encompasses all fifty states, the prospect of doing so in Europe is inconceivable. The two largest ports in Europe, Rotterdam and Antwerp, are just a stone's throw away from one another. Everyone agrees that both would benefit greatly if they were to work more closely or even merge. This has not come to pass, however, as neither the Netherlands nor Belgium wishes to "surrender" its regional flagship.

The way we are dealing with the investment gap seven years after the outbreak of the financial crisis best demonstrates that national interests would benefit from an integrated, coherent European vision. After years of heated yet unproductive discussion with regard to what should be given priority, "savings" or "investment," the commission finally decided that the European economy would receive a boost in the form of a new European investment fund.

When asked at the time to submit proposals and projects, the member states did no more than dig up the standard lists of demands and wishes that they always come up with when the European institutions wave money around. Shamelessly, they saddled the European Union with all of the good intentions, poor plans, and electoral promises that they themselves could not realize due to a lack of public funding.

No single, coherent, and integrated investment and infrastructure strategy existed at the European level. Rather than asking the member states for input, the European Commission should have developed its own global strategy. This would have allowed it to emphasize the interconnections needed to achieve a single energy grid, to develop a fully integrated and uniform European rail network, or to set up ambitious innovation and research projects, for example in relation to energy storage and the Internet.

The United States, on the other hand, is working to develop an innovative transport economy and an intelligent energy grid in which consumers are also producers. Progressive entrepreneurs, such as Elon Musk, the CEO of Tesla, are developing pilot projects in the field of high-speed rail transport as a substitute for pollution-causing domestic flights and a new generation of lithium-ion superbattery that will store excess green energy, which previously went to waste. This is a new step in the US turnaround in energy policy. An enormous lithium battery capable of storing excess wind energy and providing no less than one hour of electricity to 10,000 families has already been constructed in California.

China is not lagging behind either. The Zhangbei project developed a battery with a similar capacity of thirty-six megawatt hours. Ultimately, all of these innovative investment and research projects will not only benefit the environment but also boost the American and Chinese economies. Here in Europe, we have made no progress on any of these fronts.

THE FRUITS OF COMPETITION

The outdated competition policy of the European Union is similarly of no help. Our bureaucrats in the European Commission appear not to have realized that we are living in a globalized world, where competition policy should be fleshed out at the continental, not the national or regional, level. Due to this national or regional approach most industry sectors have few or no "European champions" capable of competing with the other major players in the global market.

Our competition policy is European in name only. The union may well have exclusive jurisdiction in this area; however, it is failing to create European added value. This is because it either passes on dossiers created at the European level to the national competition authorities or considers competition in one or more regional or national markets to be more important than competitive conditions across the European Union as a whole.

The blocked merger of Volvo and Scania is just one of many examples. Both were, by coincidence, Scandinavian companies and, more specifically, Swedish truck manufacturers. Their merger would have created the third-largest truck manufacturer in Europe. The European competition authority rejected the bid, however, on the grounds that the merged companies would have a clearly dominant position in Sweden, while also gaining approximately half of the market in countries such as Denmark and Finland. The European Commission should have considered the merger not from a Swedish or Scandinavian point of view but from a European perspective, and then there would have been no impediment at all.

What is the sense in working to eliminate all barriers to the establishment of a single market if, when all is said and done, we continue to divide that internal market into regional and national territories? Doing so is absurd—especially since a merger of Volvo and Scania would have yielded a new, strong European player, capable of competing with other major manufacturers in the global market.

Success stories such as the European Organisation for Nuclear Research (CERN) and Airbus prove that things can be done differently. In both cases, a resolute decision was made to take a European approach. At first, however, the situation seemed hopeless. After World War II, the United States threw itself into civil aviation with great determination. Companies such as Boeing, McDonnell Douglas, and Lockheed dominated the sector entirely. They appeared to be untouchable. In 1959, the British Hawker Siddeley group attempted to get its foot in the door with a bold project with the working title "Airbus." The huge risks associated with this project compelled the Brits to go in search of partners. At the Le Bourget Air Show in Paris in 1965, they succeeded in getting German and French engineering firms on board, together with their respective governments. As usual, France feared getting its feet wet, and the project ultimately took off thanks to the increased efforts of the German federal government and private engineering firms.

The rest is history. Airbus was a major success. Today, the company has a turnover of more than €30 billion and posts annual profits in excess of €1 billion. In 2015, Airbus has grown to become an innovative and healthy publicly traded company that employs more than 60,000 people across France, Germany, Spain, and the United Kingdom. This European joint venture managed both to open up and to outclass the battened-down American market. With a 33 percent market share, the company is the world's largest aircraft manufacturer. It now produces the world's largest airliner and the first commercially viable "fly-by-wire" civil aircraft. It is a star in the European sky.

✾ ✾ ✾

CAN THE SUCCESS of Airbus be repeated? Looking to the future with the same European formula in mind, it should be possible to develop supercompanies in growth sectors such as high-speed rail connections, the digital market, or clean energy production. The number of jobs in these sectors will only grow over the coming decades. The challenge today is thus identical to that faced by the British Hawker Siddeley group more than half a century ago.

There is but one difference: competitors are emerging in the American, Brazilian, Chinese, and Indian markets. By 2050, the Americans and Chinese will hold more than 40 percent of the global economy. Our choice is as clear as day: either we fight back, as we did when Airbus was established, or the industrial decline will inevitably progress. There is no middle road.

Perhaps, when making this choice, we can reflect on the words of Barack Obama, who, during a speech in Brussels, described Russia as a "regional powerhouse." It was a subtle yet clear insult to Vladimir Putin, who has global ambitions for his country.

A regional economic powerhouse is exactly what Europe will become, however, if we do not alter our course radically and focus on furthering European integration in the years to come.

CHAPTER TWELVE

THE CREDIT CRUNCH

I N THE ABSENCE OF A FULL BANKING UNION AND A UNIFIED CAPITAL market, the credit crunch in Europe simply keeps going on. Without credit, all but the largest of companies and enterprises suffer, from businesses that employ dozens or even hundreds of workers to aspiring entrepreneurs like me.

About eight years ago, I made the bold decision to make wine in Italy. I'm crazy about wine, especially red wine. The smell. The taste. The story behind it. It's more than just a drink. I regard it as part of civilization. But purchasing the 4,000 cuttings of the two types of grape varieties that I had chosen, the construction and planting of the vineyard itself, and the purchase of a winemaking installation required finances that I didn't have.

So I took my plans to the bank to ask for a loan. The result was an ordeal of navigating a maze of dusty offices in what seemed to be the oldest functioning bank in the world, Monte dei Paschi di Siena, founded in 1472 by the Republic of Siena.

In 2011, after several visits and many months of waiting, I was offered a loan with an interest rate of more than 8 percent—truly exorbitant, especially considering that interest rates were at a historical low. In any case, it was impossible to make enough income from such an investment to be able to pay back the loan. If I had not already planted the vines, I would have given up on the venture long ago. Fortunately, a few months later, I was able to secure a ten-year loan from the Belgian branch of the same bank at a much lower interest rate.

With such interest rates, it is no wonder that investment in Italy has come to a standstill. Nowhere in Europe, except perhaps Greece, has the credit crunch hit so hard.

When I related my experience to one of the new European commissioners who had just settled in Brussels from the Far North, he told me a similar story about trying to take out a loan with a foreign bank. A capital market does not exist in Europe, except perhaps on paper, which in practice does not work well.

He had experienced this for himself a few weeks earlier when he wanted to buy a place in Brussels. Since, as a member of the European Commission, he would be staying in the city for at least five years, it seemed a sensible decision. But implementing it was not so straightforward. It was not possible to use the house he owned in the Far North as security in order to secure a mortgage in Belgium, because a European mortgage market simply does not exist.

There is no difficulty securing a loan if you can offer as collateral real estate in the country where the bank is located, but if you want to involve a house, apartment, or plot of land in another state inside or outside Europe, it's a different matter. Then your loan manager treats you like a crook.

LACK OF TRUST

The loan traffic between banks practically dried up in the months following the collapse of Lehman Brothers and the outbreak of the financial crisis. Only after some reforms did mutual trust between the banks gradually return. But the enthusiasm among European banks for doing business with each other is still far below the precrisis level.

The number of toxic loans circulating in our financial system is still ten times higher than in the United States; as a result, there is no appetite for additional lending. And as long as interbank lending does not get back to normal, people who want to buy a house or invest in a business can barely get a loan.

In the meantime, the European Central Bank has been forced to reduce its interest rates to almost zero in the hope of forcing people and companies to stop saving and start investing again. However, the experience of Japan's recession has taught us that this does not work. When customer and business confidence has been undermined, it makes no difference how low interest rates are: there is scarcely any investment. In economic jargon, this is called a "liquidity trap." In plain English, this means that people and companies see through the absurdly low interest rates and are not persuaded to invest. On the contrary, they regard them as a desperate act on the part of the central bank with no credible motive other than crisis.

✻✻✻

ALL THESE FACTORS have led to the huge credit crunch in which Europe is still hopelessly mired. After the collapse of Lehman Brothers, lending in Europe dropped by 10 percent in six years, whereas in normal economic circumstances it should have risen by 10 percent. In other words, the global credit level has collapsed by one-fifth. Only for the large companies and multinationals has there been little or no change. They can still obtain credit as easily as before. But small and medium-size enterprises often find the door slammed in their face when they approach the bank for a loan for expansion or innovation. And these small and medium-size enterprises employ three-quarters of eurozone workers.

An additional problem is that the economic culture of small to medium-size enterprises and family firms is particularly widespread in southern Europe, far more so than in the North, and consequently the

South is harder hit. Thus the economic differences between North and South are increasing as a result of the credit crunch. Small but productive enterprises in the South all too often confront the sudden loss of credit lines they were guaranteed before the crisis (and always paid off promptly). Or they suddenly have to pay exorbitant rates of interest.

José Blasco runs a successful business in Spain making beds and armchairs. He employs twenty-two people. Two years ago, his bank decided to reduce his standing loan from €500,000 to €100,000. While the Spanish government was paying 5 percent interest at that time, thanks to the assistance of the European Central Bank, José Blasco suddenly had to cough up 14 percent. His is just one of thousands of similar stories in southern Europe.

The situation forced central banker Mario Draghi to sound the alarm: "The banking sector and the financial markets of the euro area become more and more fragmented. Companies headquartered in affected countries face significantly higher lending costs than their competitors in countries that are better off." In other words, the precarious state of public finances in many southern countries is a significant burden not so much on the public sector itself as on the private economy, which is being dragged down. The conclusion drawn by Draghi, gradually despairing at the lack of action by our European leaders, is crystal clear: "If we don't solve the problem of towering interest rates in some countries, the consequences will taste bitter for the rest of the euro area as well."

For Draghi, the problem extends beyond southern Europe. The risk of contamination is great, particularly since the whole European business sector is financed almost exclusively via bank loans. Our companies are dependent to the tune of over 70 percent on credit provided by financial institutions. Only large companies can issue bonds, unlike in the United States, where almost three-quarters of companies finance themselves through bond issuances. In this way, American companies are far less dependent on the health of the banking sector.

In the first years after the crisis, the difference in interest rates paid by companies in northern and southern Europe amounted to almost 2.5

percent. In 2013, this had doubled, and today this "spread" has tripled or quadrupled.

This financial inequality also translates to the real economy. The Spanish bed maker Blasco decided he could no longer accept the high interest rates and low loan ceilings. He now works with banks in countries that offer reasonable conditions. And these are often non-European countries. The foreign percentage in the financing of his company has thus risen from 10 to 50 percent. Blasco's problem is thus—at least partly—resolved.

But the problems of the southern member states are not. These countries are sinking even further into crisis. Many companies are moving to other countries; as a result, tax revenues fall, and a balanced budget becomes increasingly difficult to achieve. Countries with a growing economy and low interest rates attract these companies and new investments. This creates an ever-widening rift within the European currency union. And that is a catastrophe in any case, especially because, unlike in the United States, in Europe there is no mechanism to reduce this rift.

Blasco's story is not unique. It is the rule rather than the exception. Economists have calculated that, since the beginning of the crisis, the European economy has lost between €700 billion and €900 billion in investments as a result of the sorts of ill-conceived stopgap measures that only brought trouble and no solutions for small business owners like Blasco.

PLUGGING THE GAPS

In addition to the investment gap in Europe, there is another bottomless pit: government finances. And like it or not, we will have to fill these two pits. We are talking about €700 billion or more that, in the past few years, has not been invested in new bridges, roads, schools, hospitals, prisons, and so on. That means that the younger generation is missing out on many jobs. Whereas the United States, after the fall of Lehman, encouraged a new wave of investments and is now back to the same level of investment as before the crisis, capital formation in the eurozone is completely paralyzed.

Between 2001 and 2007, capital in the American and European economies grew at the same pace. In that period, approximately one-third more capital came into circulation, which was used for investments. Even the blow to both economies and the drop in investments in 2008 and 2009 were the same for both continents. But in the subsequent years, the European and American economies have grown steadily further apart. Europe remains stagnant, while America has made a huge comeback.

* * *

THE ONLY EXPLANATION for this is the difference in the speed of reaction mentioned earlier. Seven years after the American stimulus plan, the European Commission has now also contributed an investment package in the region of €300 billion. This is not only extremely late but also amounts to just a third of the actual investment gap and barely a third of the amount that the Americans injected in 2009.

The launch of this European stimulus plan has not been straightforward. Its implementation risks have gotten bogged down in the institutional morass that the European Union has become. First, all member states have to be brought on board in a begging round, but they want to see specifically which works and projects they will get back before they put money on the table. The European Parliament—which must agree to the legal basis of the investment fund—is dragging its heels because people believe that creating such a fund is robbing Peter to pay Paul. The financing of such a fund always begins with taking financial resources away from the European general budget, resources intended precisely for innovation and investment. And finally, the European Investment Bank (EIB) is posturing outrageously, attacking the stimulus plan as superfluous: the EIB is *already* the investment bank for the union, even if it does no investing.

But the EIB is sitting on the sidelines while the whole edifice of European banking collapses. By its own account, between 2013 and 2015 an extra contribution of €60 billion was delivered in the form of loans, with which it hoped to mobilize an extra €120 billion from the private sector. In 2012, the EIB received an extra €10 billion from the European member states with the aim of creating additional loan capacity. However, the EIB used a large part of this sum to improve its—already very strong—capital base.

With this extra €10 billion, it would have been possible, over a three-year period, to generate a much greater amount in loans than the €60 billion that is at issue now. This extra amount could have gone to projects that the union urgently needs. Even the European leaders became irritated by the behavior of the EIB and called upon the institution to "make full use" of the latest capital increase.

The EIB treated this appeal with princely disdain. Keeping its triple-A rating was far more important than these extra loans and projects and, according to the EIB, "vital to the bank's business model." But such a business model will, of course, never solve the investment gap. The bank's rating is a means of obtaining investments, not an end in itself.

* * *

ONE THING IS certain: the credit crunch will not be resolved using the current approach. The European Commission, the member states, and the European Investment Bank see each other as competitors rather than as allies.

We must form a real European plan that enables us to tackle the investment gap, with a full banking union that is responsible for all banks, with capital and mortgage markets that are fully integrated, and with a European investment fund that is financed by European bonds. This fund must be of the same magnitude as the American Investment and Recovery Act: €800 billion. It must be covered by the issuance of European "government" bonds, whereby the whole European budget serves as the guarantee, and it must finance the projects that will enable Europe to finally make the leap into the twenty-first century.

CHAPTER THIRTEEN

THE OBESE LABOR MARKET

I GRADUATED FROM GHENT UNIVERSITY IN 1975, OVER FORTY YEARS ago. That was between two oil crises, each of which shook the very foundations of the Western economies. And yet, at no point did I think that I would end up unemployed. My parents assured me that people with a university degree were almost certain to find a well-paying job in an interesting career. For most of my peers, that was indeed the case. I worked as a trainee solicitor and, soon after, found myself involved in politics. The sky was the limit.

The outlook today is much more desperate. Unemployment among the younger generation has reached unprecedented highs. More than half of the young people in Greece and Spain are unemployed and receiving no training. Likewise, in other, mainly southern European countries, more than a third of young people have nothing to do: they're getting no training and finding no work. Youth unemployment in the European Union averages around 25 percent. This means that, at present, one in every four young adults in Europe is unemployed.

* * *

WE CAN ATTRIBUTE much of this catastrophic situation to the economic crisis. No economic growth means no jobs. That said, we can trace much of the problem back to an issue that has beset Europe for quite some time: very low levels of labor mobility. There are an estimated 1.3 million unfilled job vacancies in Europe because companies cannot find suitable candidates in their home country: people with the right language skills or level of experience. Labor mobility within the European Union is ten times lower than it is in the United States. While in 2014 almost 8 million Americans moved to another state to live and work, just 700,000 Europeans did so. In total, just 3 percent of the European labor force works in a different member state to that of their birth, despite the need for workers right over the border.

It is unclear why European politicians refuse to recognize this reality and remain blind to this problem. They fear the rise of the extreme right and populist parties like the UK Independence Party (UKIP) in Great Britain and the Front National in France, which warn of surges of Polish plumbers inundating our society. This has proved to be a complete myth.

Most alarmingly, however, moderate-minded politicians who ought to know better expound this myth. During the recent British elections, both David Cameron and his socialist opponent Ed Miliband declared that they would put an end to "mass migration from within the EU," a fiction planted in the minds of the British public by UKIP leader Nigel Farage, who claimed that the country would be overrun with 29 million Romanians and Bulgarians. In the run-up to the general elections of May 2015, a large-scale media campaign was unleashed upon the Brits to spread the fear that hordes of barbarians would be crossing not the Rhine but the Channel. In reality, exactly 32,000 Bulgarian and Romanian citizens settled in the United Kingdom—a far cry from even 1 million, let alone Farage's 29 million. The University College of London estimated that these 32,000 Bulgarians and Romanians, along with other European migrants, contributed a net total of £20 billion in taxes over the 2000–2011 period. Labor mobility within Europe, albeit limited, had colossal benefits for the British economy and the British treasury.

Extremists and populists are continuing to spin the same nonsensical yarn that, if a foreigner occupies a vacancy, that job is no longer available to "natives." First, Poles, Romanians, and Bulgarians fill positions that nobody else wants. Second, everyone knows that, irrespective of whether a person is a foreigner or native, anyone who takes on a job contributes to the economy, starts spending and investing, and thus creates new jobs. An economy is not static, with a fixed number of jobs. The more people who are working, the more the economy improves, and the more jobs are created. Migrant workers will therefore have contributed to any economic recovery experienced in the near future. In short, we must not place further constraints on our already limited labor mobility, as the populists are proposing. The more mobile Europeans are, the fewer job vacancies will remain unfilled.

In recent years, many young people from southern Europe have sought refuge in Germany or the more northerly European countries. In the difficult period immediately following the economic crisis, Latvia quickly lost 6 percent of its population to neighboring states. Such surges in migration do not pose a problem, however. European migration eases unemployment in the country of origin, and migrants contribute to the economic growth of the member states where they relocate and work. Nevertheless, the southern European and Latvian cases remain the exception. Labor mobility within Europe is still very limited. Just 14 million Europeans live and work in another member state to that from which they originally came. This is equivalent to just under 3 percent of the European population. Even the number of non-Europeans earning a living in Europe is higher (4 percent). According to Canadian economist and Nobel Prize winner Robert Mundell, this is an enormous problem for the economy of the eurozone because high labor mobility is a prerequisite for an optimum currency area.

We cannot permit ourselves the "luxury" of reclosing our borders or restricting freedom of movement, a right inextricably bound up with the internal market. Doing so would be incredibly foolish. The argument often cited as justification for such a measure—"welfare shopping," the so-called abuse by migrants of the social security benefits provided by the destination country—is utterly lacking in reason, not because abuses do not occur but because it is always possible to take action against them. Do not throw the baby out with the bathwater. Member states are free to show the door to those who abuse their social security system. The aggrieved member state does not have to turn to Brussels. Nor is any "repatriation of powers to the member states" required. In Great Britain, anyone living in British territory is entitled to unemployment benefits. There is no requirement for unemployed persons to have ever contributed a single penny. What is stopping the British government from reforming its unemployment benefits system, which some will undoubtedly label "naive"? Europe allows a member state to take extreme action if one or more population groups place an "excessive burden" on its social security system. If there truly were a problem with abuse of social security, the British could invoke this clause; yet they do not do so. The reason for this is crystal clear. The British middle class takes full advantage of the services provided by eastern Europeans, from the Romanian cleaner to the Polish laborer.

CRAFTSMANSHIP

We need to boost labor mobility drastically within Europe. This requires a number of fundamental reforms. Mutual recognition of member states' procedures and rules is needed within Europe to ensure that the transition to a new job in another country goes as smoothly as possible.

As a first course of action, we must ensure that Europeans are able to take advantage of their accrued social security entitlements when seeking a job in another country, not only with regard to pensions but also in relation to medical expenses and unemployment benefits. We should set this mutual recognition and portability of social security entitlements down in a European directive for worker mobility, equivalent to the directives we already have for people who work in their home country but deliver services to another member state or for posted workers who work abroad on a specific project for a couple of weeks or months, often in the construction business, but who return home regularly. The directive should actively remove all obstacles to finding employment in another member state, while at the same time introducing a set of minimum social standards.

Research has shown that, for the average European, the main barrier to accepting a job in another member state is that it will not recognize the individual's accrued social security entitlements.

The second major course of action is to introduce a European traineeship. Erasmus, an exchange program for university students, was a massive success. Why, then, do we not introduce the same type of scheme for people who are good with their hands? We are pumping €6 billion into a European youth guarantee scheme that provides courses and training for young Europeans who fail to find work within four months of leaving school or university. It would be even better if we were to offer every young person in Europe a "European trainee contract." I would name such a program Hephaestus, after the Greek god of craftsmen and blacksmiths. Hephaestus would enable youths to undertake a one-year traineeship working for a business in another member state, an ideal launching pad for finding work and building a career elsewhere in Europe at a later date.

Sweden and Germany may serve as sources of inspiration when setting up Hephaestus. Sweden not only has opened its labor market to highly skilled workers but also is issuing residence permits to low-skilled workers. Although youth unemployment is rising to more than 50 percent in some countries of the European Union, Sweden is increasingly looking outside Europe to find these low-skilled or technically skilled workers.

The German "dual training" experiment, which combined traditional education with on-the-job experience, may also serve as a source of inspiration. To begin with, German business managers were apprehensive about the experiment. Where would the well-oiled businesses of Germany begin with a horde of youths with no work experience? Now, German industry is unable to cope without them.

Hephaestus would give European youths with a technical or vocational education the same opportunities as those received by their

German contemporaries and by young graduates via Erasmus. In the globalized world economy of the twenty-first century, young people require a broad range of experience, including in languages, technology, and business culture. Most of all, we need to get away from the objectionable European habit of regarding technical ingenuity as inferior to academic accomplishment.

A third course of needed action is implementation of a basic European unemployment benefit, based on the American model. In Europe, we are rightly proud that we have a wide safety net in the form of a modern social security system, particularly—though not only—with regard to unemployment insurance. Nevertheless, the existence of twenty-eight different systems, each with its own checks and rules, has been a major obstacle to labor mobility.

The United States, as a rule, almost never serves as an example in matters of social security; however, the federal system it has in place guarantees workers an allowance to help them through periods of hardship, irrespective of how they have become unemployed. The federal government provides a basic allowance for three months, which can be extended in exceptional circumstances, as was the case recently in the wake of the financial crisis. We should roll out a similar system in Europe, allowing the member states to decide whether to provide any additional scheme on top of this basic allowance. This would prevent "welfare shopping" and, at the same time, minimize the risk of moving to a foreign country. This system could be funded at the European level, spreading the risk out over 500 million Europeans.

By no means would the adoption of such an approach result in harmonization of every aspect of social security. There are too many effective pension systems, such as in the Netherlands and Scandinavian countries, and too many effective health-care systems, such as in Belgium, to allow for harmonization. Our labor market policies also include various parameters that do not require harmonization at the European level at any cost.

It is in everyone's interest, however, to increase labor mobility as quickly as possible, and that requires a European approach.

CHAPTER FOURTEEN

THE DELUSION OF THE EUROPEAN BUDGET

A HAPPY BUT EXHAUSTED BRITISH PRIME MINISTER, TONY BLAIR, addressed the representatives of the European Parliament in Brussels on December 20, 2005. After months of haggling and hassling, the European Council had finally reached an agreement on the European Union's multiannual budget. In reality, this seeming triumph was a sham: a truly "European" budget is structurally impossible thanks to the squabbles among the member states.

On the face of it, Blair's victory—as president of the European Council—was real. Six months earlier, then president Jean-Claude Juncker, the prime minister of Luxembourg, had failed to negotiate a budget. Not for want of trying, however: with his wealth of experience, Juncker had expended every effort and indeed come quite close to brokering an agreement in June. And yet a mere six months before his own triumph, Blair had sabotaged Juncker's proposal.

Did Blair begrudge Jean-Claude Juncker this success? It was an open secret that they couldn't stand the sight of each other. The official version held that Blair wanted to do things differently. Rather than a multiannual budget that simply copied the previous one, he hoped to pass a new budget that would herald a break with the past. This would put an end to outdated agricultural spending, focusing instead on technology and innovation, on the future.

In practice, things didn't work out like that. Ultimately, Blair's budget differed little from the draft budget proposed by Juncker. Moreover, in order to reach an agreement, Blair had to pull out all the stops for weeks on end. He had only managed to get everyone on board by buying off one member state after another. The result was an abomination. Hardly anything remained of the initial setup.

To close the deal, Blair had to promise the member states no fewer than forty-one "gifts": compensations, rebates, and ad hoc exceptions, ranging from €100 million in aid to the Canary Islands to more than €200 million in aid for the peace process in Northern Ireland and €865 million for the decommissioning of an obsolete nuclear power plant in Lithuania. And those were the most sensible concessions. To get the Netherlands on board, Blair doubled the compensation for the member states that collect customs duties, even though these constituted union revenue to which the member states were not entitled. Value-added tax (VAT) payments were reduced to please Germany, Austria, and the other net contributors, but by a different percentage for each country. Sweden and the Netherlands also got a fixed discount on their gross national income contributions. In return for coming aboard, Poland, the Czech Republic, and Hungary, against all applicable rules, were allocated additional resources from the structural funds, as were Cyprus and the German state of Bavaria. Finland, Ireland, Italy, Luxembourg, France, and Portugal were appeased with additional rural-development allocations. Spain and the Baltic states also gained additional funds, which they could use at their own discretion, regardless of all the rules. It was horse trading with a vengeance.

Blair fervently defended the agreement but added in the same breath that this exercise was not to be repeated. Tony Blair did not admit that he had failed (he is too proud for that), but his "never again" spoke volumes.

"OUR MONEY"

Despite Blair's failure to reform the European budget, his discourse was nevertheless a breath of fresh air. It was highly unusual to hear a British prime minister offering a vision of European finances that didn't revert to the mantra "I want my money back"—five words that, better than any speech, reflect Margaret Thatcher's position, which she shared with the press after the European Council in Dublin in November 1979: "We are not asking for a penny piece of Community money for Britain. What we are asking is for a very large amount of our own money back. . . . Broadly speaking, for every £2 we contribute we get £1 back."

This statement by the Iron Lady summarizes exactly what is wrong with the European budget. It is indeed *not* a budget, and most definitely not a "European" one, at least not in the way that we normally define a budget, as a collaborative political project funded from taxes paid by residents in order to pay for common public goods and services. In Europe, the budget has little to do with the people who live there or with the companies located there. In Europe, the budget entails contributions paid by the member states to Brussels every year. Each country contributes a sum, which it then tries to recover by applying for as many grants or projects as possible.

That budget is "European" in name only, for only a tiny part of it involves truly communal and cross-border initiatives. Each member state tries to be a "net recipient" (i.e., to extract more money from the European budget than it puts in). The member states for which this is not possible (because, of course, not all twenty-eight countries can be net recipients), the "net contributors," try to keep their contributions as low as possible by demanding more money from the budget themselves, by cutting the spending of the other twenty-seven member states, or—most commonly—by negotiating rebates on their own contributions.

Margaret Thatcher initiated the practice in 1979, and now virtually all "net contributors" have followed suit. Germany, the Netherlands, Austria, Sweden, and Denmark now receive rebates.

* * *

NOBODY IS DEFENDING the European interest anymore, because doing so would involve expenditure that, despite creating benefits for everyone, would be difficult to assign to a single member state. And that does not fit the "fair return" philosophy that, since the Berlin Summit in 1999, has become the starting point of each budget exercise in the European Union. In Berlin, the German federal government made the fatal mistake of giving in to pressure by member states like the UK and officially recognizing the terms "net recipient" and "net contributor" and even attaching official numbers to them.

That was the last thing the founders of the union wanted. They did not intend the European countries to exchange the battlefield for a calculator. They had a supranational budget in mind, financed by loans and taxes and decided upon and monitored by directly elected parliamentary representatives, a budget to enable a European policy and to achieve joint objectives—collectively, side by side.

All these measures ignored the raison d'être of the European Union. It was founded not to scatter subsidies left and right but to define common objectives and, to that end, to establish a framework for common policies: objectives and policies that a member state acting alone would be too small to achieve or handle on its own, such as an internal market, international trade relations, climate change, the economic crisis, and transnational investments.

To quote Paul-Henri Spaak, a founder of the European Union, "There are only two types of states in Europe: small states, and small states that have not yet realised that they are small." The key question in the entire European story is whether or not a country has realized that it is small—but, together with other countries, strong enough to use the economies of scale associated with the European continent.

We relinquish those economies of scale if each country thinks only of recouping the money it has paid to Europe. That is as absurd as cataloguing European spending as a benefit for only one member state or another. A new motorway constructed in Poland with European money doesn't benefit Poland alone. A German or French firm may well have built it, and Belgian or Dutch logistics companies will also use the new infrastructure to the benefit of the entire European economy. In short, fair return reasoning negates and denies the existence of Europe and its internal market.

REPRESENTATION WITHOUT TAXATION

The only way to get rid of the perverse logic of "fair return" is to abolish the existing contributions and introduce a system of "own resources." Own resources are taxes that people or businesses pay directly to the European Union. Only in this way can we free the European Union from the stranglehold of the member states, in other words, from the charitable handouts they give to the union. It would also save us from the annual battle between the council (composed of member states and their representatives) and the parliament (directly elected by citizens), whereby the latter always draws the short straw. No matter how fiercely the European Parliament goes on the rampage, the outcome is a foregone conclusion: it will suffer a defeat. That is not surprising because it is ultimately not about money *for* Europe but about money *from* the member states.

Introducing "own resources" changes that logic radically. The money becomes Europe's money and does not depend on one member state's arbitrary decision. Instead, it depends on the type of tax levied: VAT, corporate or income tax, tax on financial transactions, or tax on carbon dioxide emissions. The composition and amount of revenue at the union's disposal would no longer depend on some sort of perfidious political deal, concocted in the back rooms of the council, but on the growth and success of the economic, social, and environmental policy implemented by the European Union. The greater the improvement in the economic situation of people and businesses in Europe, the greater the flow of financial resources into Europe.

* * *

WE URGENTLY NEED to abolish the current financial system for a second important reason: the total lack of democratic legitimacy. No other place in the world employs a system like Europe's, in which the parliament has control over funds and expenditures but absolutely no say about revenue. The 1776 American Revolution arose because the colonists had to pay taxes to the British Crown but received no representation in the House of Commons: "No taxation without representation," they cried.

In Europe, the exact opposite is happening. We elect a parliament, but that parliament has no control over revenue. What is the purpose of a directly elected parliament if it has no authority in performing the most essential task in a democratic society? "No representation without taxation" is as valid as "no taxation without representation."

The founders of the European Union were more aware of that than the current political elites. When the European Coal and Steel Community was formed in 1951, a levy was introduced on both coal and steel. The proceeds went directly to Europe and did not transit through the member states first. While this principle remains the same, in practice we have totally abandoned this pragmatic solution; instead we now depend on member states' "largess" in coughing up the money owed when they find it convenient. Not one elected parliament, anywhere in the world, would tolerate such a situation.

THE 1 PERCENT

Almost sixty years after the Treaty of Rome, and despite all the great leaps forward in European integration, the European budget still represents only 1 percent of the prosperity created annually in the European Union. In nominal terms, that is a huge amount: €130 billion. In reality, it is a charitable handout, namely, €250 per person per year, seventy cents per person per day. The European budget is smaller than the national budget of Greece or Belgium. No matter how loudly populists of all kinds cry out that Europe is costing a lot of money, its budget still equals less than one-fortieth of the resources that the national, regional, and local authorities together in Europe are creaming off their citizens and businesses. That 1 percent is nothing compared to government spending, which amounts to an average of around 50 percent of gross domestic product in most EU member states.

Compared to the US budget, that 1 percent is peanuts. When, in the eighteenth century, the thirteen American colonies united to form a federation, the budget was also 1 percent of their total wealth. Since then, it has steadily increased. Back in 1929 (i.e., before the outbreak of the Great Depression), the US federal budget had already risen to 7 percent of the gross domestic product, a percentage that has since continued to increase to almost 25 percent. Especially in difficult times—the two world wars, the Great Depression, the oil crisis—the budget of the American federation has been drastically increased to absorb the inevitable accompanying shocks.

We are doing exactly the opposite in Europe. Despite the crisis in the 1980s and the financial turmoil that erupted in 2008, the European budget stagnates around that paltry 1 percent, based on a legally binding capping of own resources in the multiannual budget of the European Union. And yet the union is asked to shoulder an increasingly long list of tasks. In the aftermath of the 2008 financial crisis, the real expenditure of the majority of the member states increased by 3 percent (2007–2013) and in the eurozone by 4 percent. In the same period, the union's expenditure was frozen.

The characterization of Europe as a vastly expensive machine is therefore completely untrue. Just 6 percent of the entire European budget goes to civil servant wages. In recent years, the union has not even had sufficient means to pay its invoices, even if the golden rule states that the EU should not get into debt. In 2011, its arrears amounted to €6 billion; in 2012, €16 billion; in 2013, €23.4 billion. In 2014, its arrears reached a record €24.7 billion. The European debt totals €221 billion and is, in fact, illegal.

Meanwhile, everyone is dissatisfied with the system as it now stands. The commission considers the budget too low. The member states consider the contributions too high. The European Parliament is up in arms because it has no control over revenue. The people too are dissatisfied, unsurprisingly, because their political leaders tell them daily that Europe is a bottomless pit (which is simply not the case). In short, a lot of vague rules reinforce a general dissatisfaction so that no one can see the forest for the trees.

This is why, at the end of the year, the European Union usually goes head-to-head with one or more member states that make a great fuss about the fees they have to pay. With mock indignation, they refuse to "pay extra money to Brussels," when they are fully aware that the "extra money" in question is debt they owe anyway.

Sometimes the European budget seems to work by magic, because despite increasing deficits, the union still succeeds in producing annual surpluses—by not paying its bills and putting invoices on hold. The member states encourage the union in this because everything not spent at the end of the year gets returned to the member states. After all, it is "their" money, not Europe's. The whole system has been hijacked: the "own resources" mechanism has been thrown out the window, and the European Commission has lost any kind of proper control, resulting in "demands," such as Thatcher's "I want my money back." Yet it wasn't "her" money; it was Europe's, and the union was entitled it to by law.

A COMMON BUDGET

We can draw but one conclusion: the entire horse trade known as the "European budget" is in need of urgent reform. Once again, this is not a truly European budget but rather a hodgepodge of contributions and allowances from and to the national member states that creates no added value.

We should establish a truly European budget financed by "own resources"—for example, by a VAT paid directly to the European Union. Every receipt or invoice would have to list two rates: the European rate, which would be the same everywhere, and the national rate, which would vary from country to country. In contrast to the current situation, under this regime, taxpayers would pay the European VAT owed directly to Brussels. The new financing method would not lead to an increase in taxes; all in all, citizens would pay exactly the same amount as they do now. The member states need not fear monetary losses either. On the contrary, elimination of the national contributions currently being paid would fully offset the losses incurred from a decrease in income from VAT.

This would bring to an end the current political horse trading whereby the member states have Europe in a financial stranglehold. People would, for the first time, understand exactly how much they were paying to Europe, in the same way as they currently know how much they pay in tax to their national government, city, or municipality.

CHAPTER FIFTEEN

THE QUAGMIRE OF
EUROPEAN INSTITUTIONS

T HE INABILITY TO FIND COMMON GROUND ON MANY ESSENTIAL
issues has made of the European Union a very messy patchwork.
There is not one union but many: the European Union, the euro union,
the Schengen union, the fiscal compact union, the European Arrest
Warrant union, the European patent union, the internal market union,
the judicial cooperation union, and so on. Anyone wishing to fully map
out the European Union would need at least ten different maps and to
take into account member states that obstinately refuse to cooperate in
certain policy areas on the one hand and countries outside the union that
wholeheartedly want to be part of it on the other.

STREAMLINING THE SEAT OF GOVERNMENT

In 2001, when I chaired the European Council meeting in Laeken, I conceived a bold plan to end a protracted feud raging within the European

Union: the "seat" issue surrounding the numerous European agencies that have sprouted up like mushrooms over the last twenty years.

Whenever a new agency is established, a dispute arises in the council about where to locate its headquarters. Brussels is usually the most obvious solution, given that the European Commission and the European Council are based there, as is the European Parliament, even if it does still move to Strasbourg for four days every month. Invariably, however, other member states also want a slice of the pie and welcome any European institution to their territory. Hosting an agency's headquarters brings in money from the European officials who go to live and work there. And—so it is thought—it brings the citizens directly closer to Europe.

Today, around forty agencies crisscross Europe in cities like Ljubljana in Slovenia; Riga in Latvia; Warsaw in Poland; Tallinn in Estonia; Valletta in Malta; Alicante, Bilbao, Madrid, Barcelona, and Vigo in Spain; Cologne, Munich, Berlin, and Frankfurt in Germany; Solna in Sweden; Thessaloniki and Heraklion in Greece; Helsinki in Finland; Copenhagen in Denmark; Dublin in Ireland; Prague in the Czech Republic; Vilnius in Lithuania; Lisbon in Portugal; Hampshire and London in the United Kingdom; The Hague in the Netherlands; Valenciennes, Angers, and Paris in France; Parma and Turin in Italy; Vienna in Austria; and Budapest in Hungary. And of course, there's Brussels, Strasbourg, and Luxembourg, the three official seats of the institutions of the union.

In 2001, during the Belgian presidency, four agencies had not yet been assigned a permanent seat. In order to facilitate a compromise between the member states, I extended the list to include a number of institutions that had not yet even been founded and thus only existed on paper. Soon agencies would be created for maritime safety, aviation safety, railway safety, justice, policing, visa-data exchange, asylum and migration, communication network security, external border surveillance, experimental fusion reaction, and the monitoring of drug addiction. In total, the list included no fewer than thirteen new institutions and also featured the European Food Safety Agency, established in the wake of the dioxin crisis in Belgium to closely monitor food chain safety.

This last agency in particular gave rise to an unimaginable tug-of-war. Finland set its sights on headquartering it, proffering its expertise in food chain monitoring. Silvio Berlusconi also made a bid, however. Where better to base a food agency than in a country with such rich gastronomic delights as pasta, grappa, and mozzarella? "Parma," he proposed. When the German federal chancellor, Gerhard Schröder, asked why Parma, the Italian prime minister replied, "Because of the prosciutto, of course!" Based on that logic a host of other cities were eligible: Naples, the world's capital of pizza; Cremona, the city of mustard; Turin, the center of risotto and *vitello tonnato*. Just about every Italian village could house the headquarters of the European Food Safety Agency.

Ultimately, we were unable to reach a consensus. Berlusconi and Finnish prime minister Matti Van Hanen continued to squabble. The whole seat issue was withdrawn from the agenda.

Regrettably, the argument between Finland and Italy was "resolved" much like all European problems. The European Food Safety Agency received not one but two headquarters: one in Parma that conducts "European supervision" and one in Helsinki that handles "coordination between the national food agencies." This solution is absurd and highly ill-advised because these two tasks are inseparable. We might as well have let Finland monitor the safety of the cold dishes and Italy the warm ones.

But the European heads of government have no creativity when it comes to untying knots. Ultimately, these various agencies are a pure waste of money for the glory of the member states, which, incidentally, believe that Europe costs them too much.

✳ ✳ ✳

EQUALLY ABSURD IS the fact that the European Parliament still meets in two places, while the commission, the council, and the parliament are a stone's throw from one another in Brussels. The consultations between the three institutions form the most important link in European legislative work. And yet for one week every month, we in the European

Parliament leave Brussels for Strasbourg, simply because the European Treaties say so. This costly and pointless mass migration entails a herd of parliamentarians, staff, and administrative personnel who rumble across the cobblestone streets of Strasbourg with their trolleys. The almost endless truckloads of suitcases and documents each year produce 19,000 tons of carbon dioxide emissions and necessitate an additional 180 million in taxes.

PATENT ABSURDITY

Those who think these are exceptions are dead wrong. Across Europe, rather than making hard decisions, we kick problems down the road due to conflicting national agendas.

The latest example comes by way of the European patent, which decades of haggling could only iron out once the three largest member states—France, Germany, and the United Kingdom—had each secured the use of its own language. A European patent that only existed in English was unthinkable for the French and Germans. The Netherlands and Austria were kept sweet with the promise of a European Patent Office seat, and two more were established in Germany: one in Munich and one in Berlin. This was not the end of the European patent ordeal, however.

For decades, companies and universities have proclaimed, in unison, that if Europe wishes to become the "the most competitive, knowledge-based economy in the world," a European patent is essential. After all, a European patent guarantees uniform protection for an invention throughout the union: one ownership, one jurisdiction, one payment for the renewal of the patent, and one asset, not twenty-eight different sets of rules and procedures, whereby inventors simply have to hope that their patent stands up in court.

As a result of this single European patent, costs for the applicant have dropped dramatically from an average of €32,000 to €6,500, largely due to the avoidance of exorbitant translation fees.

You would think that a European patent would be a no-brainer and a piece of cake to implement. Its introduction in Europe degenerated into procedural wrangling, however. Italy and Spain went to the European Court, where they sought annulment and then lodged an appeal. That dual endeavor failed. Their objection was as old as the hills: the patent would only exist in French, English, and German and thus not in Spanish or Italian—as if inventors and entrepreneurs give a damn about the language in which their intellectual property is protected. In any event, the idea of a European patent has now haunted the corridors of the European institutions in Brussels for over forty years.

PATCHWORK UNION

The difference between plan and outcome, between theory and reality, is ever growing in the European Union. In principle, all twenty-eight member states make up the internal market, which allows the free movement of goods, persons, and capital. At the same time the free movement of people is restricted between those member states that have not become part of Schengen, the agreement between a number of European states to abolish checks at their borders. Some member states, such as Bulgaria and Romania, want to participate in Schengen but are not permitted to do so; others do not wish to be a part, such as the United Kingdom. And then there are countries outside the union, such as Switzerland, that despite their isolationist reputation, actually do belong to the Schengen area. Meanwhile, the internal market includes countries such as Switzerland, Norway, and Iceland, which are not part of the union but do participate in Schengen. Thus identity checks and customs formalities still impede the border crossing points between some countries. Truly free movement throughout the internal market is therefore still not a reality.

Nor do we cooperate cleanly in the realm of security and policing. A good illustration comes by way of the so-called Prüm Convention, an agreement among a number of member states to combat international crime and illegal migration through the exchange of DNA, fingerprint, and license plate data. The United Kingdom opted out but reserved the right to reconsider its position and participate in the future. Other member states, such as Sweden, Italy, Portugal, and Poland, have one foot in and one foot out of Prüm. Although formally bound by agreements, they have not yet ratified this "enhanced cooperation."

Ultimately, nobody knows who is or isn't participating in Prüm. Besides, "enhanced cooperation" is a euphemism for each member state ultimately doing its own thing. Neither citizens nor companies know where they stand or what exactly to expect from the European authorities. Such vague lawmaking generates a complete lack of legal security.

In short, the union has become a patchwork, divided and fragmented by a seemingly endless series of opt-ins, opt-outs, enhanced cooperation agreements, and intergovernmental arrangements. Cohesion is not a priority; individual member state needs come first.

Perhaps this was more practicable in the early years, with six, ten, or twelve representatives sitting around the table, but it only leads to chaos when there are twenty-eight members.

We consequently create, from within, opposition to the union that undermines its stated goal: unity. Even prior to the Treaty of Lisbon (2009), the *Economist* wrote that the European Union is "a lake that has many deep parts (areas in which countries are similar) and many shallow parts (areas in which countries have major differences)." Nearly ten years and a treaty change later, we have to conclude that it has degenerated into a veritable mud pool. The fundamental rule—namely, one union for all member states—has been violated so much that there is now just one shallow layer of sludge through which the member states trudge in their boots as they see fit.

Anyone who has lost the plot in the meantime should try to imagine the United States operating in the same way as the European Union. The fifty US states would each be able to choose whether or not to use the dollar or to introduce their own, separate currency. They could also reintroduce border controls at their own discretion or opt out of cooperating with the Federal Bureau of Investigation or participating in US Coast Guard operations. Instead of having just one immigration system based on the green card, they would have fifty regimes and fifty cards.

Rather than one license and one patent, they would have fifty different patent regulations. It would be chaos. It would never work.

TOO MANY COOKS IN THE KITCHEN

Were the United States to emulate the European Union, the greatest change would of course involve replacing the president of the United States with at least two excellencies, the president of the commission and the president of the council. After all, nowhere is the disorder greater than at the top of our institutions.

Ultimately, neither the president of the People's Republic of China nor the president of the United States knows whom to contact in the event of an international crisis. The German chancellor in Berlin? The French president in Paris? The prime minister in London? The permanent president of the European Council? Or maybe the president of the European Commission? Perhaps all five?

When, during Barack Obama's visit to Europe in the spring of 2014, press photographers tried to capture a traditional handshake between the president and his European counterpart, they ended up creating an iconic albeit pitiful image. Both José-Manuel Barroso and Herman Van Rompuy had turned up as "president of Europe," leaving President Obama with no option other than to place his hand over their clasped hands, like a priest solemnizing a marriage. It was as if he were trying to say, "Now, now boys, don't make a scene. You can both be in the photo."

Even more amusing was the situation that arose some years later when the European Union received the Nobel Peace Prize. Three presidents made the journey to Oslo to receive it: the president of the European Council, the president of the European Commission, and the president of the European Parliament. Fortunately, the Norwegian Nobel Committee had organized the event in a way that allowed the winners to express their gratitude at the reception beforehand and during the dinner that followed rather than just during the presentation itself. This meant that all three representatives were able to say a few words. Two or three presidents heading up the union, with an additional twenty-eight headstrong heads of state and government, is too much of a good thing, and differences of opinion immediately result in a gargantuan political challenge.

The fragmentation of the European institutions and colossal lack of cohesion are only augmenting, not least because the president of the European Council is being saddled with a national EU presidency that rotates on a semiannual basis. Every six months, he or she faces a new president or prime minister who has waited patiently for fourteen years for the chance to excel at the European level, only then to fall just as quickly back into obscurity—and I should know. This merry-go-round may have been useful when there were only six member states, but with twenty-eight, it causes nothing but trouble.

* * *

ONE WITNESSES THE same chaotic dynamics with the "management" of the eurocrisis by not just two or three spokespeople but ten in an area where unity and cohesion are especially crucial.

First and foremost is the permanent president of the Eurogroup, who chairs the meeting of the ministers of finance of the euro area. Then there is the president of the Council of the Ministers for Finance of the entire union. According to custom, that is the finance minister of the country holding the rotating presidency. In the European Commission, no fewer than three commissioners are responsible for the rules of the stability pact, which forms the basis of the common currency. In addition, there is obviously also the president of the European Central Bank, Mario Draghi, assisted by an executive board of five directors and a board consisting of the nineteen governors of the national banks of the eurozone countries. And when it comes to the euro, the finance ministers of the large countries are never shy when it involves giving their unvarnished opinions, from Germany's Wolfgang Schäuble to France's Arthur Sapin.

The situation is hardly any better in the field of foreign policy. Who actually represents the European Union on the global stage? The high representative and vice president of the European Commission, Federica Mogherini, who also chairs the union's Council of the Ministers for Foreign Affairs? Or the permanent president of the European Council, Donald Tusk? And then you have the German chancellor and the French president vying for attention, for example, during the crisis in Ukraine. Angela Merkel and François Hollande, not Tusk and Mogherini, flew to Minsk in Belarus to conclude an agreement with Vladimir Putin.

Moreover, most European institutions are far too large because power in the union must be shared between twenty-eight member states. Thus we remain saddled with a European Commission of twenty-eight members—one for each member state. Anyone conducting an honest and serious audit would find that too many by far. Every time an expansion of the union is on the table and a new commissioner is sent to Brussels, a chorus of sighs breaks out. What new portfolio can we invent for him or her?

ELITE BETRAYAL

Why are we unable to create transparent European institutions? The answer is that we have spent decades beating around the bush, avoiding the creation of a full-fledged federal union. We slammed on the brakes halfway through the process of doing so and are now ensnared in an unparalleled institutional tangle.

The union has expanded from six, to nine, to ten, to twelve, to fifteen, to twenty-five, to twenty-seven, to twenty-eight member states. It has assumed further duties, not least the administration of a currency without a solid foundation. And perhaps most important of all: more than ever, the union is bearing the burden of its citizens' aspirations.

But when it comes down to it, our national political elites are overcome by fear: fear of surrendering power, existential angst over relinquishing sovereignty. Ultimately, more member states, more powers, and more aspirations have led not to more unity, more strength, and more resources but to more opt-outs, more exceptions, and more division.

This deadly fragmentation is particularly obvious at the executive level. Only the European Commission has the right of initiative. In principle, it also has to supervise the correct application of any measures introduced. However, the member states actually play the dominant role. They determine which actions are taken, how, and with what means. They also implement the decisions taken. But if the member states fail, they are never held to account; everyone points the finger at Europe. Many citizens feel that the union is therefore out of control, that action is only taken when the house goes up in flames, that only then is the European Council jolted awake.

Is it any wonder that in such circumstances citizens' erstwhile confidence in Europe has now gone? Europe has come to look, to them, like a proverbial top-heavy army, in which the generals outnumber the soldiers and would thoroughly trample each other to claim even the smallest victory.

PART IV

PANIC

CHAPTER SIXTEEN

THE BREXIT

GIVEN THE IMMENSE FINANCIAL TROUBLES IN EUROPE—THE strangled economy, the squabbling over scraps, the lack of problem solving—it is shocking to realize just how badly the continent has handled its recent political dilemmas. At every turn, rather than doubling down on the union—on finishing the federal project so as to create a rising tide that lifts all boats—we've seen member states desperate to eject their neighbors for the sake of "safety" or frantic to escape in pursuit of a dubious "freedom." The most arresting example of this is, of course, the vote of the British people to leave the union.

On June 24, 2016, after that referendum, Europe and Great Britain woke up with a serious hangover. For the first time in the union's history, a member state had decided to quit. The impact was instant: a dramatic 30 percent drop in the pound sterling, a multi-billion-dollar slide in stock markets worldwide, and a freeze on UK investments. Many economists estimate that the long-term damage will be even more severe. Before its EU membership, the United Kingdom had the slowest growth of the seven biggest economies in the world; it has had the fastest growth since it joined the union. So, the EU has not been bad at all for Britain. Moreover, the United Kingdom had carved out a special status within the EU thanks to its rebate and its opt-outs from Schengen, the euro, and Justice and Home Affairs policies. As a member of the union, the country had largely concentrated its focus on the internal market, the main driver behind its good economic performance. That is exactly what Britain risks losing.

The "Brexiters" campaigned with emotion, not rationality. After the vote, reality hit. Suddenly British workers saw the value of their pension funds cut or their dreams of living in Spain curtailed. Young people and the students in the counties around Oxford and Cambridge, who massively voted "remain," will be excluded from Erasmus, the European academic exchange program, from low tuition fees at European universities, and from hundreds of millions in European research grants from which UK universities profited disproportionately. But more than just "the happy few" are affected. The inhabitants of the poorest cities in the southwest and the northeast of England will no longer receive aid. Suddenly, all these EU membership benefits were headline news, whereas the tabloid press had never mentioned them previously, even in the heat of the campaign.

But the negative economic fallout was hardly the most surprising outcome of the Brexit vote. The complete absence of euphoria in the winning camp struck me most, as did the tepid, almost timid, reactions of politicians like former London mayor Boris Johnson, the most prominent "Brexiter." During his press conference the day after the referendum, he sounded diffident, which was completely out of character, and declared the outcome of the referendum would change nothing—an absurd message after months of bitter campaigning. Another prominent "Brexiter," UK Independence Party (UKIP) chairman Nigel Farage, added insult to injury by announcing he had been "wrong" in promising that the £350 million per week contributed by the United Kingdom to the EU would be diverted to the British National Health Service. It was a pretty unique sight: winners shying away from their own "victory."

The murmurs of the "leave" camp contrasted sharply with the harsh messages from Scotland and Europe. Scottish first minister Nicola Sturgeon announced a possible second referendum on the secession of Scotland, as "the Scottish people have voted overwhelmingly to remain in the EU." Political leaders in Northern Ireland started pipe-dreaming out loud about a reunited Ireland. The rest of the European member states almost unanimously said Britain should leave the union quickly and in an orderly manner.

The day after the referendum the Brits woke up feeling eerie in a divided country. Had they voted for the end of a united Europe or for the end of the United Kingdom? Racism and xenophobia had been let loose. The Polish community was bullyragged as "vermin"; schoolkids of color were told "go back to their country"—the results of a merciless leave campaign that had focused in the nastiest way imaginable on migration instead of whether to remain or leave. This campaign had reached its nadir when Nigel Farage unveiled a larger-than-life billboard of queuing refugees supposedly waiting to enter Britain, a ploy directly inspired by a Nazi propaganda film from the late 1930s that used exactly the same image with a voice-over describing refugees as "parasites undermining their host countries." Even the country's largest tabloid, the *Sun*, was shocked by the consequences of the campaign it had propagated all along: "We are appalled by the reports of racist abuse in the wake of last week's vote. Anyone caught inciting racial hatred must feel the full force of the law." Only a day earlier the very same newspaper had still been pushing the xenophobic agenda: "Streets full of Polish shops. Kids not speaking English. But the Union jack flying high again." This disgrace of a campaign had even motivated the murder of Labour member of Parliament Jo Cox, who was shot by a white supremacist while canvassing for the remain campaign.

A lot of people who voted "leave" were also in shock the day after the referendum. Many declared later that they had only wanted to get rid of David Cameron and his policies or that they would have voted differently had they known that a Brexit was really going to happen. Suddenly there were pro-European protests in the streets of London, and a petition for a second referendum received a massive number of signatures.

If the Brexit vote proved anything, it proved the "remain" camp right: the negative effects for the economy and society as a whole quickly set in. It has turned into a divorce that only a minority seems to have wanted. Normally, a victory has many fathers, while defeat is an orphan. This time, it was the other way around.

A CONSERVATIVE PLOY

Clearly the "leave" camp had not prepared a plan to make the Brexit happen in an orderly fashion. It didn't even have a contingency plan to mitigate the worst economic consequences, let alone clear a path forward.

So, how could the "leave" camp have been completely clueless about something they staged themselves? The answer is simple: the real driving force behind the Brexit had nothing to do with Europe. The referendum had been cooked up to paper over deep divisions within the British Conservative Party. It was a big show put on to ensure the unity of the party, whatever the cost; it was supposed to ensure peace and quiet at home. It did exactly the opposite: it deepened the division among Tories, split the whole country, and dragged the rest of the EU down with it.

❋ ❋ ❋

The British Conservative Party comprises three camps with regard to the European question. First, there are the many anti-European hard-liners who actually want the same thing as UKIP, namely, a complete withdrawal from the European Union and thus also from the single market, on the naive assumption that a UK-EU free trade agreement could be a done deal in a few weeks. Deep down, they are still "Little Englanders," clinging to the long-lost glory of the British Empire, nostalgic Tories often born and raised in the former colonies or in the defunct military bases that crisscross England.

Diametrically opposed to this group stand the pro-Europeans, a somewhat smaller group still counting a few dozen members in the House of Commons. They helped dream up the most basic concept of the European Treaties, the "ever closer union," together with the principle of subsidiarity, which prescribes that political issues should be dealt with at the most local level possible. Sadly, these pro-Europeans are a dying breed; some simply did not get reelected in the last general election. They are the dinosaurs of a moribund Tory tradition, disciples of Edward Heath, the Conservative prime minister who brought the United Kingdom into the union in the 1970s. Their number even included Margaret Thatcher in her early years, before she decided to score easy electoral points at Europe's expense.

But the majority of British Tories, including fading lights such as George Osborne and David Cameron, belongs to a third group within the Conservative Party that constantly oscillates between anti- and pro-Europeanism. They want mostly to participate in the single market and actually have few problems, if any, with the rest of the union—as long as things do not go too quickly or too far. They are archpragmatists. Boris Johnson actually belongs in this camp. He had never made more than a few bantering, ironic remarks against the EU until he saw that a Brexit could catapult him to 10 Downing Street.

OPPORTUNITY FOR CHANGE

Now that Cameron's bid to restore unity in his party has failed and even more damage has been done, it is important to understand that there is no way back. A second referendum or a reversal of the first one by the House of Commons is highly unlikely given that the Tory constituencies voted heavily in favor of the Brexit. The only way forward is to accept the outcome of the referendum and use it as an opportunity for reform. The biggest risk currently facing the EU is that Brexit negotiations will not start anytime soon, will drag on for years, and will join the long list of never-ending crises: the Greek crisis, the refugee crisis, an unresolved economic crisis, and the seemingly ever-present terrorist threat.

If we're soft now with Britain, giving it too much wiggle room to extract favors and deals, we will feed anti-European parties elsewhere in Europe and strengthen nationalists' and populists' belief that the European Union is a doormat. It is bad enough that Vladimir Putin is funneling Russian money to anti-European parties, from Marine Le Pen's National Front to Farage's UKIP.

The EU must take the outcome of the referendum seriously and move forward with an in-depth reform of its outdated institutions and policies. The British people were right to question the ability of this European Union to meet the challenges we Europeans face. For years in a row now, the EU's twenty-eight national leaders have gathered around the negotiating table, looked each other in the eye, and decided not to decide.

In a certain way, we should welcome the outcome and seize it with both hands by not only writing the United Kingdom out of the treaty but also making sure the other twenty-seven member states move forward. In other words we should undertake a fundamental redesign of the European Union. If the British—who have always dragged their feet every time we wanted to integrate further—actually want to re-invent themselves by leaving the union, we should not make an issue of it. We finally have an opportunity actually to get a grip on our challenges. The Brexit provides a golden opportunity to put an end to the politics of horse trading and papering over the cracks that has characterized Europe since the 1957 Treaty of Rome. If some countries, with the United Kingdom at the front of the queue, do not want full membership, so be it.

My proposal is not exactly original. It harkens back to what the union's founders had in mind back in 1953, when, under the leadership of Paul-Henri Spaak and Heinrich von Brentano, they drew up a first constitution for the European Union. Even at that early stage, they envisaged a two-tier form of membership: a country could have either full or associate status, either participating in all union policy areas or essentially joining only the internal market, a bit like Norway and Switzerland.

Full union membership would entail signing on to all policies, participation in the economic and monetary union (and thus the euro, provided the country in question satisfied all relevant criteria), and mandatory cooperation on home affairs in connection with defense and justice. A full member would have access to an "ever closer union" that would eventually end up as a federal union. No exceptions, no rebates. The ultimate aim would be the same for all. Any country becoming a full member would know that the train was heading to federation without further detours.

If that was just too much, or if a country could not or did not want to convince its people, it could sign on to associated status. This option would simply provide access to the internal market. However, it would come with an obligation to comply with all the conditions attached to that internal market. In that regard, the British need to realize that many of the rules they vilify, such as setting noise levels for vacuum cleaners or minimum quality levels for fruit, are part and parcel of a functional free market. If the EU did not lay down rules of this kind, we would get overregulation at the national level, as in the past, with twenty-eight different sizes and weights.

The United Kingdom has declared that it wants "to remain close to its European neighbors," but it will have to decide what that new relationship will look like. Does it want a trade deal with the EU, like Canada or Japan? Or does it want to go a step further and have access to the internal market or the European Economic Area, like Iceland and Norway—under the condition, of course, that it also accepts the free movement of people. After all, Britain and Europe remain close geographically and are major trading partners. There are goods and services to be sold on both sides of the English Channel. But remaining in the internal market would entail Britain's complete acceptance of EU rules without having a seat at the table while paying a hefty membership fee for that access. That will be a hard sell for British politicians who vowed "to take our country back." In any case, we have to end the current situation in which British representatives in the council and the parliament can vote on issues they have opted out of.

A NEW PATH FOR THE EUROPEAN PROJECT

Is this two-tier form of membership the solution to our British problem? I do not know, but from my contact with leading Tories before the referendum, including the former British foreign secretary, Philip Hammond, it would appear to be a serious option. It might present a way out of the stalemate the Brexit vote has created in British politics. For Europe, too, it would be a blessing. It would mean that countries uncomfortable with an ever-closer union no longer need hold us back. It could speed up the further integration needed to stabilize the euro. The same applies to the strengthening of our foreign policy, a necessity if Europe is to play a significant geopolitical role.

This two-tier form of membership would also mean we could draw a line under the enormous complexity of the EU and the quagmire of European institutions. The à la carte Europe that we currently know, with its opt-ins, opt-outs, rebates, earmarks, enhanced cooperation, and concentric circles, ultimately satisfies no one. It does not satisfy the Euroskeptics or the European federalists, as it makes Europe inexplicable and unsellable to broader public opinion. The British referendum should lead to exactly that clear choice—between full membership, associated status, or no relationship at all.

CHAPTER SEVENTEEN

THE GREXIT

Tʜᴇ sᴜʀʀᴇᴀʟ ɪɴᴠᴇʀsᴇ ᴏғ Bʀɪᴛᴀɪɴ's ᴇxɪᴛ ᴠᴏᴛᴇ ᴡᴀs ᴛʜᴇ sᴛʀᴀɴɢᴇ struggle to boot Greece out of the eurozone.

I've never met a more exuberant bunch of Greeks than those on the flight from Brussels to Athens on April 24, 2015. They were part of a government delegation, led by Prime Minister Alexis Tsipras, on their way back to Greece after yet another European summit in Brussels. They were in business class—not something you would immediately expect from members of the extreme left-wing party Syriza.

They were constantly joking and roaring with laughter. They didn't seem worried about anything: certainly not that Greece was on the verge of collapse and barely able to scrape the money together to pay for pensions and civil servants' wages. Or that the impending fiscal crisis might soon metastasize into a continent-wide conflagration threatening political dissolution of the union itself.

I was flying to Athens for a public meeting with my friend Stavros Theodorakis, a former journalist and the founder and leader of To Potami (The River), a new Greek political party that hadn't achieved any real results in the last elections but emerged as the country's fifth party, very close to Golden Dawn, the far-right anti-immigration party.

Before departure, I had bumped into Tsipras himself in the airport's VIP area. I knew him from the debates in which we had crossed swords in the run-up to the European elections. In the short time I had known him, I had developed a great deal of sympathy for him. He had an engaging smile and seemed like a very nice man. We had a brief conversation. He wanted to know whom I was meeting in Athens. He told me briefly about the mess they had found when Syriza came to power in February 2015.

A BLIND EYE

That mess has a long history. As in any Greek tragedy, several protagonists have played a decisive role. There is more than one explanation for why it all went wrong for Greece. The argument that the Greeks were admitted to the euro much too early is still the most popular. Their application was refused in 1999, and they were put on a strict diet. To everyone's surprise, two years later, all the objections evaporated.

On January 1, 2001, the country was admitted to the euro to triumphant cheering from the entire Greek establishment. The finance minister, Yiannos Papantoniou, declared solemnly that the Greek accession was "an historic day that would place Greece firmly at the heart of Europe." The Greek prime minister, Kostas Simitis, added that the Greek economy was already experiencing "euro conditions." Only Wim Duisenberg, then president of the European Central Bank (ECB), put a small damper on the Greek cheer. He said that Greece still had a lot of work to do to improve its economy and bring inflation under control. Two-thirds of the Greek population welcomed the accession.

Whether that early entry caused today's debacle is still up for debate. Would Greece have accumulated less debt if it had joined the eurozone a few years later? I strongly doubt it. Maybe the opposite would have happened. Who or what would have stopped it during those years from creating even more debt? Some say that the real and credible prospect of joining the eurozone gave Greeks access to low interest rates, which lulled the country to sleep, as if sedated. That observation is certainly not unjustified. But if Greece and Greek companies hadn't enjoyed the advantage of those low interest rates for so many years, the government deficits and private debt in the country could have been much higher, and Greece's bankruptcy might have been a fact much earlier.

One thing is certain: the Greeks have been distorting their financial figures and results for years. To do this, it hired Goldman Sachs, which used various derivatives to embellish Greek budget figures and keep the national debt artificially low. The US investment bank also used "cross-currency swaps," whereby government debt entered into in yen or dollars was temporarily expressed in euros or vice versa, depending on the position of the exchange rates. It even managed to come up with a virtual exchange rate, which allowed the Greek government to take out additional loans unnoticed, behind Europe's back, without increasing the debt on its books.

✳ ✳ ✳

ALTHOUGH ALL OF this is now indisputable, the outrage rings false. Even though we didn't know all the details, it had long been common knowledge that the official data provided by the Greek Ministry of Finance had to be taken with a huge pinch of salt. After all, there was a reason why the union corrected Greece's government deficit every other minute.

Moreover, the rules allowed the use of all those swaps and derivatives. Italy had already performed the same juggling act with the knowledge of the European bodies. For purely political reasons, all governments had simply looked away. If France and Germany had been allowed to ignore the stability pact in 2003, why make a fuss about Greece or Italy? Furthermore, it wasn't the first time this had happened in Greece. As early as 1975, Greece had applied to join the European Union, and even then the request was rejected on the main ground that "Greece was unable to meet the obligations of the monetary union." Six years later, in

1981, Greece was suddenly able to pull it off. Even then, the Greek government worked some financial wizardry on its budget, and the rest of Europe accepted it without much protest.

We made exactly the same mistake twenty years later, this time with much greater fallout. Because of the single currency, not just Greece but the entire eurozone has shouldered the consequences.

❋ ❋ ❋

THE GREEK CRISIS erupted in December 2009, precisely when the European Central Bank thought the worst of the financial crisis was over. As part of its "exit strategy," the ECB decided to stop accepting bonds and triple-B-rated certificates as collateral for providing the banks with liquidity. But most of the credit rating agencies had just downgraded Greek government bonds to triple B.

The ECB's decision was a match in a haystack on a hot, dry summer day. Greek bonds became an unwelcome hot potato in anyone's portfolio, and they certainly weren't an attractive purchase proposition. Overnight Greece's government debt could no longer be refinanced.

Yet, up until autumn 2009, there hadn't been a cloud in the sky. Greece paid only slightly more interest on its loans than other euro countries. Everything changed dramatically after the ECB's decision. Once it was made, long-term interest rates on Greek government debt soared. In just under two years, rates increased from 4.5 percent to 30 percent. That meant that, for every euro that Greece wanted to borrow, it had to pay thirty cents in costs and interest—an impossible situation. The country was heading toward bankruptcy at top speed. This Greek tragedy had dragged on for seven years, with new acts added daily.

The "rescue" of Greece started slowly—much too slowly. Instead of immediately taking the bull by the horns and raising a cordon around Greece, as well as imposing far-reaching reforms, political leaders began Greece "bashing," with some even suggesting kicking the country out of the eurozone or the EU without further ado. It was easier to blame

Greece for the euro crisis than to recognize the structural problems with the monetary union itself. This pushed interest rates even higher and Greece even further into the depths.

* * *

OUTSIDE EUROPE, THERE was bewilderment. This was supposed to be the single European currency. And yet, at the first sign of trouble, the monetary union was falling to pieces and throwing solidarity overboard. The total Greek government debt represented only a small percentage of the total wealth created in Europe every year—several hundred billion compared to a European gross domestic product of 15 trillion. That's 1.7 percent. What on earth were those Europeans fighting over?

The charade didn't end until May 2010. It began to dawn on everyone that this masochism had to stop, as it did nothing but undermine the monetary union. Meanwhile, the financial markets also had other weak euro countries in their sights, such as Portugal and Ireland.

In great haste, an emergency loan of €110 billion was cobbled together, linked with cuts and privatization. But that wasn't the end of it. Because the situation deteriorated, a new package of €130 billion had to be agreed upon barely a year later. Approval was then granted for a third package, this time consisting of more than €80 billion.

For Greece, these loans have gradually become a poisoned chalice, because they go hand in hand with conditions laid down by the bureaucrats of the European Commission and the International Monetary Fund (IMF): reorganizations and cuts. Only the financial outcome matters. That these measures damage the Greek economy and empty the pockets of ordinary Greeks is irrelevant. Only the bottom line counts.

This is how the euro has gone from being a blessing to a curse for Hellas. In the *Aeneid*, Virgil gives the Trojan priest Laocoön the famous line "Beware of Greeks bearing gifts." With those words, he tries to warn his fellow citizens about the huge wooden horse outside the city gates. For the Greeks, the opposite is now true: "Beware of Europeans bearing aid packages." Even the IMF, which together with

the ECB and the European Commission forms part of the rescue effort, has recognized this fact and issued a "mea culpa" for the economic
downturn that ensued.

Meanwhile, Ireland, Portugal, Spain, and even Cyprus have no further need of financial assistance, either from the IMF or from the European Union. But a Greek revival is nowhere in sight.

In late 2014, the Greek economy grew by just 0.8 percent, and unemployment remained at an unacceptably high level of 27 percent. Greece
remains a closed economy, exporting only 29 percent of its gross domestic product, while the average in the eurozone is 46 percent. Foreign
investments grew by 0.7 percent, whereas in the rest of the monetary
union they have grown by 3.5 percent (i.e., five times more). Even more
dramatic is the devastation at the bottom of the social ladder. Today,
more than 300,000 people live on food stamps and aid packages from the
government. Around 10,000 Greeks have committed suicide in recent
years, seeing no way out and having absolutely no idea how to make
ends meet.

ANTIQUATED CORRUPTION

Ordinary Greeks, along with European taxpayers, are footing the bill.
Yet one cannot ignore the fact that the responsibility for this catastrophic situation lies not just with the hesitancy of our heads of state
and government but also—even mainly—with the Greek political caste.
Seven years after the outbreak of the crisis, Greece only slowly began
the profound reforms necessary if the country wants to return to the path
of prosperity.

Greece remains a thoroughly corrupt society, based on a clientelistic system firmly entrenched by what were once the two largest political factions, Nea Demokratia and Pasok, in an effort to consolidate
power. Their "clients" may have differed, but the system both lived off
was identical. Anyone who wanted to obtain a job in administration, to
receive a benefit, or to win a government tender had to buy into the
system. Money was exchanged for votes. Almost all European countries

left these practices behind in the twentieth century, but they are still rife in Hellas.

According to Transparency International, each year €800 million is paid in bribes in Greece, and that amount increases every year. The beneficiaries are particularly civil servants responsible for urban development and the collection of taxes. Even for a doctor's appointment, there are "additional payments" that are never declared.

* * *

THIS CORRUPTION HAS its origin in a clientelistic system dating back to the mid-nineteenth century. Greece was a rural society without a proper free market and had hardly industrialized. Everything revolved around the relationship between patrons and their clients, who were economically and morally dependent on them. This system not only survived every political change but was strengthened in the 1920s when Greece, having lost a war against Turkey, faced an enormous influx of Greeks from Anatolia. Following coup after coup, an oligarchy came to power in the 1930s that entrenched the system even more. Some reforms were implemented by Charilaos Trikoupis (1875–1895) and Eleftherios Venizelos (1910–1933). The educational standards improved, and the administration was modernized, but not enough to completely eradicate clientelism and its associated corruption. On the contrary, the military regime (1967–1974) consolidated it, transmitting it to the more or less stable liberal democracy of today.

Rather than abolishing patronage, the two largest political parties developed a more sophisticated version: no longer a rural system, it now involves the mass mobilization of voters by well-oiled organizations. This inspired the American political scientist Francis Fukuyama to compare the current Greek political system with that in the United States in the 1800s. That system also featured intense clan formation, whereby votes and party loyalty were enforced, if necessary, by physical violence. But whereas in the United States and many other countries the middle classes and professions managed to break and abolish this system, this has never happened in Greece. Hence its suffocating public sector and domination of its financial sector by public banks whose main mission is to keep political parties alive with generous loans. Private banks and a smooth flow of credit to small and medium-size enterprises hardly exist in Greece.

For the same reasons, entry to certain professions is still closed off, and access is tightly controlled by the major political parties. For instance, in the 1990s, Pasok ensured that teachers were appointed no longer on the basis of objective criteria but according to party loyalty. Pasok party members were dropped en masse into almost every Greek school, while many nonsocialist directors and inspectors were simply dismissed or demoted. Like the Cultural Revolution in China, this coup was justified by the "antielitist" winds that swept through Greece. The same happened at the Greek National Bank, traditionally known for the high quality of its recruitment through a strict examination system until Pasok interfered. The bank's payroll was expanded by half, so that it eventually had 16,000 employees, creating an avalanche of new civil servants who were obviously exempted from any examination. At a certain point, virtually the whole of the bank's infrastructure consisted of political creatures.

Regardless of who won an election, each party afterward tried to purge the acolytes of the opposition. But because this is virtually impossible, every new government simply added new civil servants. Their number increased fivefold in forty years. When the Greek crisis erupted, the public sector employed nearly 800,000 civil servants earning nearly one and a half times as much as their colleagues in the private sector.

❊ ❊ ❊

DESPITE THE INVOLVEMENT of Europe, the IMF, and the European Central Bank, little or nothing has changed in recent years. That shouldn't surprise us. The "troika"—the tripartite coalition consisting of the ECB, the IMF, and the European Commission—follows simple accounting logic: the figures must tally. It doesn't seem to care much about how that happens.

The leaders of Nea Demokratia and Pasok, Antonis Samaras and Evangelos Venizelos, who were partners in a coalition government from 2012 to 2015, both went out of their way to safeguard the clientelistic system. Rather than implementing structural reforms, they let ordinary Greeks foot the bill by moderating minimum wages, reducing the lowest benefits, and imposing massive tax increases, which particularly hit the middle classes. Those at the core of clientelism, an inefficient, overblown bureaucracy and a corrupt government, remained unaffected.

Ordinary Greeks have therefore been the victims of a dilapidated democracy based solely on the purchase of votes rather than on party manifestos or political principles. The results of this system are downright catastrophic. The purchasing power of the average Greek citizen has been reduced by almost a fifth. Poverty and unemployment rates have tripled, and bankruptcies of small and medium-size enterprises are higher than ever.

It is therefore not surprising that the Greek electorate wanted a clean slate. The two traditional parties were massacred. Pasok almost disappeared, and a coalition of several smaller left-wing parties led by Alexis Tsipras won big. He entered the elections under the name Syriza, with the firm promise that his party's approach would be totally different—with regard to Europe and particularly with regard to Greece itself. Syriza promised to do nothing less than dismantle the corrupt Greek social system. Expectations were high.

After almost two years, few traces of the great revolution remained. The Greek government and the European Union sat locked in trench warfare for five months. Was it all a sham? It is difficult to say. The troika insisted on implementation of the measures negotiated with the previous government, whereas the Greek administrators had promised their voters the exact opposite. Both sides hurled reproaches. Europe accused the Greeks of breaking their promises; in turn, the Greeks demanded reparations for World War II, which really displeased the Germans.

Meanwhile, the European leaders continued to dither on a daily basis—one day, Greece had to pack its bags and pay back every penny; the next day, the eurozone could not survive a "Grexit." Domestic electoral concerns mainly drove this volatility. The most striking example was the German president of the European Parliament's saying in spring 2015 that he thought Angela Merkel's speculation about a Grexit was "irresponsible." A few months later, when he was on an election campaign in Germany, he said that Greece should "introduce a parallel currency," a thinly veiled code for a "Grexit." Less than a week later, under pressure from the European Parliament and European public opinion, he switched back to his previous statement: "Never a Grexit." European taxpayers are observing all of this and ultimately don't know whom or what to believe.

Anyone under the illusion that a new government with a radically different approach had taken office and would actually reform Greek society must be sorely disappointed. Even worse, it looks as if Syriza, like Pasok forty years ago, will not denounce clientelism and has simply tried to bend it to its advantage. Just like Pasok and Nea Demokratia previously, Syriza is now appointing party members to high government positions. It recruits previously dismissed civil servants, perhaps after they have first bought a Syriza party membership card. It has no plans to modernize Greek society or the economy and has scaled back on planned privatizations. Only in the fight against fraud and tax evasion has the Tsipras government taken steps in the right direction from the outset, but not enough so to speak of a new wind. The big cleanup has not materialized.

A "COUP"?

Only after the Greek treasury had been drained of every single penny in mid-2015 did Tsipras change course. He was forced to accept a new package of measures—some of them geared toward remediation and some toward restructuring—after a marathon session of the European Council that lasted no less than seventeen hours. A little after 8 a.m. he reluctantly approved the new package.

A lot has been written on that agreement already. Some, including prominent economists like Paul Krugman and his colleague Paul De Grauwe, have labeled it an outright coup by the callous finance ministers of the other eighteen other euro countries, particularly German's Wolfgang Schäuble. This is a gross exaggeration.

This agreement differs from previous ones largely in that Europe obtained a number of guarantees to ensure that the promise of reforms would not remain hollow. It defined, for the first time, a clear legislative agenda with clear instructions and definite deadlines. Although it includes many classic austerity measures, for the first time, it also involves structural interventions: addressing the clientelistic system and abolishing the privileges enjoyed by, for instance, the Greek islands and Greek shipowners. It also revives a number of privatizations that Tsipras had frozen on his appointment.

The press spoke of total humiliation, perhaps with good reason, given the outcome of a referendum—on whether to accept the troika's bailout conditions—organized by the Greek government a few days before. But humiliation for whom? The Greek government? Tsipras? The Greek population? The bailout agreement indeed represents a defeat for the entire Greek political caste but not for the Greek people. The Greeks need exactly those reforms and many more, which is what ultimately led so many to vote "no" en masse in the referendum: they have had enough of always footing the bill for a faulty political system.

✷ ✷ ✷

THAT NEED MOTIVATED my appeal in the European Parliament three days after the Greek referendum and a few days before the "cursed" agreement was concluded. Tsipras seemed rooted to the spot when I confronted him with the reality that his country was stuck, and though perhaps it did not need more austerity, it was definitely yearning for reform. He barely reacted, anyway. To defend himself, he referred to one or two minor measures taken by the government and tax authorities against tax fraud. But that was about it. He said not a word about the revolution that his country needed or the enormity of the Greek state apparatus. He barely even mentioned corruption and clientelism. He kept repeating that the Greek people had done more than enough. I, however, was referring not to the Greek people but the Greek political class, which hasn't lifted a finger to change—let alone reform—the system it lives off.

I challenged him to make a choice: he could go down in history as an "electoral accident" or as a "revolutionary reformer," a statesman who had not only saved his country but above all brought it into the modern age. "What are you?" I asked him outright, "a real leader or a false prophet?"

* * *

WHATEVER THE DEPTH of the planned reforms, anything is better than the alternative on the table: a temporary or definitive Grexit, an option that has gained resonance not only within Greece itself but even outside its borders. A Grexit, however, offers anything but a solution: it won't reduce the corruption, clientelism, and lawlessness; it will do the opposite.

A Greek exit from the euro—and the consequent reintroduction of the drachma—will lead only to the continued existence of this corrupt social system. Only pressure from the European Union, together with the voice of Greek voters, can force the political caste in Greece to make the necessary change. If that doesn't happen and Greek politicians continue to abdicate their responsibility, the Greek economy will never get off the ground, and the crisis will never end.

In *Why Nations Fail*, Daron Acemoglu and James Robinson make crystal clear that you can't build a successful economy without a solid rule of law. Citizens who have to bribe doctors to receive decent treatment, government officials to obtain a building permit, or local head teachers to get their children into school will, in the long term, lose their very sense of justice. Eventually, they will become infected themselves. Leaving the eurozone will not solve this towering problem; rather, it will result in less oversight and less external pressure, further isolating the Greeks.

For purely financial reasons, reintroduction of the drachma would also be an enormous disaster. The new currency would immediately devalue by 30 to 40 percent. This would certainly boost Greek exports but also increase the price of all imports. And because the Greek economy imports several billion euros' worth of goods and barely exports anything at all, the overall outcome would be negative. It's not for nothing that the country has experienced a trade deficit in the past fifteen years.

In any case, the net effect of a devaluation would be extremely detrimental to average Greeks, who have already given up enough in recent years. They have relinquished no less than 20 percent of their purchasing power. According to Adam Slater, an economist at Oxford Economics with a specialty in calculating the cost of breaking up monetary unions, the Greeks would lose about 10 percent of their overall wealth (gross domestic product) in one fell swoop upon leaving the EU—a new loss on top of their strenuous efforts in recent years.

But even for the eurozone, a Grexit would be the worst-case scenario, potentially contaminating other euro countries such as Portugal, Spain, and Italy and reawakening the crisis. Most of all, a Grexit would demonstrate that the eurozone is not a solid monetary union but an edifice of sand.

Greece and the eurozone need not a Grexit but a Grevo, a Greek revolution: a new, comprehensive agreement that provides the country with the necessary financial breathing space in exchange for a thorough change within the political culture and social institutions. That entails something quite different from moderating minimum wages or cutting the most basic benefits or pensions. Clientelism has to go. Corruption must be eradicated and the tax system drastically reformed. The Greek state must quickly dismantle and privatize banks and other state-owned enterprises and must liberalize the economic sectors, currently closed to newcomers, immediately. Finally, access to public office must once again be objectified: fair entrance exams for civil servants have to be reintroduced. Maybe the agreement reached in early July 2015 can serve as a gentle push in the right direction. But whether it is itself enough to spark decisive change is highly questionable.

DEMOCRACY OR DROWN

Even though it seems the worst of the Greek crisis has passed, the structural problems of the euro are not over and done with yet. On the contrary. What is to prevent Italy or another euro country from continuing to take on massive debt, asking for money from the EU, and then organizing a referendum and risking the future of the eurozone? A second Greece would deliver a killing blow to the euro, especially in a country the size of Spain or Italy.

Above all, it is madness to continue to require a unanimous vote to decide on the fortunes of the euro during a tête-à-tête between nineteen heads of state and government or nineteen finance ministers. This means that the fate of the single currency rests in the hands of a few dissidents in the extreme-left Syriza or the extreme-right True Finns, smaller coalition partners in Greece and Finland. Even worse, the eurozone remains subject to the whims of a few individuals who abuse the unanimity rule to prove that they are "right," or worse, to boost their own egos.

By governing the eurozone as a group of countries that have voluntarily chosen to use the same payment method, rather than as a solid block constituting one of the fundamental pillars of our unified continent, we have painted ourselves into a corner. The selfish aspirations of the member states have once again become more important than the common interest of the EU and its internal market. Instead of a well-functioning whole, the eurozone has become the mere sum of irreconcilable national interests and camps, creditors and debtors, hard-liners and laxists, all strengthened by their ability and willingness to use their veto.

Because of that faulty structure, we go from one clash to the next: North against South, large against small, France against Germany. In order to survive, the euro has to navigate safely between a Greek referendum and a Finnish or Dutch veto. A solid monetary union can't stand on such unstable ground. Such circumstances render creating a healthy economic climate totally impossible. The eurozone can function properly only if, in addition to monetary union, we also establish an economic and political union with all that implies: a government, a treasury, democratic control, and decisions taken by majority.

* * *

IMAGINE IF THE federal government and the US Central Bank didn't control the dollar and each governor of the fifty American states had to give his or her blessing on every decision. The dollar would be long gone. Or imagine if the European Central Bank proceeded in the same way as the Eurogroup or our heads of state and government during a European summit meeting—in other words, that a suffocating unanimity rule had a stranglehold on the ECB. Mario Draghi could never have carried out the emergency measures vital to keeping the single currency alive. The euro and the European economy would have long since perished.

Perhaps the Greek crisis provides one positive. It sheds a harsh light on a massive failure that we have completely ignored until now: the absence of a full-fledged European democracy within a real European political space.

The challenge the euro poses is existential. Technical trickery, such as a banking union, a stability mechanism, or a "fiscal compact," can no longer camouflage it. The eurozone needs institutions of its own that will manage it properly: a government, a budget, lending capacity, and a single external representation, all democratically controlled and monitored. That means a new transfer of sovereignty to democratic and representative institutions at the European level. It's democracy or drown.

CHAPTER EIGHTEEN

THE N-EURO AND S-EURO

A FEW DAYS BEFORE THE START OF THE EUROPEAN PARLIAMENT'S 2011 summer recess, the *Economist* contacted me to ask whether I wished to take part in a debate with Hans-Olaf Henkel.

I didn't know Henkel personally, though I had heard of him. He had a formidable reputation. Having previously worked as a manager at IBM and served as a former director of the Federation of German Industry, he had emerged during the previous few months as the foremost voice among Euroskeptics in Germany. Thus, unsurprisingly, he had become one of the most important members of the Alternative für Deutschland, a new party wishing to break up the eurozone and eject most of the southern European member states.

When the *Economist* contacted us both, the crisis in the eurozone had reached a crescendo, and the world was hearing one "by any means necessary" statement after another. Rather than formulating specific rescue plans, government leaders hoped to convince the markets that the political will to do whatever it took, regardless of the cost, was still intact. The European Council had held its final meeting on July 21, 2016, before its members, along with all other European politicians, went off on holiday, presumably to the beaches of southern Europe. The euro ship was under the sole command of technocrats from the International Monetary Fund and the European Central Bank.

Henkel and I were the only figures the *Economist* could find who, in the heat of summer, were prepared to take part in a debate about the euro.

NORTH AND SOUTH

Henkel started off the discussion, conducted via the *Economist*'s Internet forum, with the assertion that the eurozone ought to be subdivided into a northern and a southern zone, each with its own currency—a sort of "N-euro" and "S-euro." In his view, the economies of northern and southern Europe differ too starkly to continue operating a shared currency. Germany, the Netherlands, Austria, and Finland would belong to the "N-euro." Full stop. The "S-euro" would include all of the other eurozone member states, centered on France and Italy.

I asserted, on the other hand, that while Henkel's analysis may have had merit—especially when he stated that member states were riding roughshod over the rules and that the economic foundation of the euro was much too weak—his suggestion that breaking up the eurozone would solve this problem betrayed a complete misunderstanding of the situation.

❊ ❊ ❊

THOUGH HE WOULD never admit to it, Henkel may recall one lesson from history: the Zollverein, a German customs union formed in the second half of the nineteenth century. This in turn developed into an economic union, which ultimately led to the foundation of the first German state of the modern era.

According to Henkel's standards, German union and the introduction of the gold mark in 1873 would have been a particularly bad idea. The economies of the member states differed enormously. There was even potential for a schism between the agrarian societies in the old parts of Prussia and Bavaria, on the one hand, and the "new" industrialized areas in the Ruhr region and Baden, on the other. At one point, Hannover, Hesse, and Saxony even set up a separate southern customs union in order to neutralize the one dominated by Prussia. German historian Jürgen Angelow describes how that initial union, founded only as a means of monitoring the status quo and not to respond to the problems that the customs union itself generated, was doomed to fail. In the aftermath of the Austro-Prussian War, a unified and better organized customs union was set up in 1876. A full-fledged economic code was produced, and the right of veto enjoyed by each individual member state was abolished. This turned Germany into an economic powerhouse for the first time. The achievement of this union, not Otto von Bismarck's ascent to power, marked a revolution in German history.

Henkel, and with him all of Germany's Euro-haters, would love to return to a strong and independent Germany with its own currency, which never would have existed had their ideas been let loose on the Zollverein. Then, as now, opponents of union saw irreconcilable differences among members and predicted that intractable problems would arise. Then, as now, some defended the interests of a particular region over those of the country as a whole and stirred emotions with references to beer-swilling factory owners in southern Germany profiting from workers in the sweatshops of the Ruhr region.

We do not achieve progress, however, by reverting to old solutions every time we suffer a setback. We generate progress by finding new approaches or adapting and improving old ones. To use a modern-day analogy, a beta version serves to detect problems in order to fix them before launch of the final version. In the case of Germany, the customs union and the country's economic unification formed a radical shift that had a positive effect on its history. In one fell swoop, Germany had managed to reposition itself vis-à-vis the power bloc formed by France and the Austro-Hungarian Empire.

✳ ✳ ✳

TODAY, IN EUROPE, we risk becoming trapped between the United States, with its ever-increasing protectionism, and China, which is becoming ever more aggressive. The solution is right at hand. We already have a beta version of economic and monetary union. To abolish or split up the union would be an act of folly. Instead we must fundamentally improve and strengthen it so that we can move forward and produce the final version. As it turned out, the vast majority of *Economist* readers agreed: almost two-thirds of those who followed the debate on the website supported my view favoring further integration.

If we are to save the euro, we actually need greater political and economic integration. The common currency, the internal market, and the fiscal union are all irrevocably linked. If we strengthen one, we also strengthen the others. In that way, we could reverse the downward spiral that the euro finds itself in. Doing the reverse and abolishing the euro risks driving the internal market into the ground.

If we consistently follow Henkel's logic, we will inevitably find ourselves returning to a system of "national currencies." After all, each country differs as greatly from the others as the European North does from the South. France's economy is nothing like Italy's and is definitely unlike that of Portugal or Greece. The differences between the Dutch and the German economies are also not exactly small.

The tensions within the eurozone would simply get transplanted onto each of the two unified currencies proposed by Henkel—certainly in the case of the "S-euro." Ultimately, there would be no alternative but to subdivide that currency even further, ultimately culminating in the national currencies that we once had: the lira, the peseta, and the drachma. Competitive devaluations and demonetizations would become the order of the day, and monetary instability would again become the norm. And how viable would an "N-euro" be? In addition to Germany, the EU's largest member state, it would include only three members, all of them smaller countries.

And while we're on the subject of imbalances, splitting up the eurozone into northern and southern hemispheres would immediately put an end to the benefits that the euro represents: lower interest rates and streamlined trading between member states due to the lack of exchange rate differences. It would therefore represent a step backward on the journey toward the internal market.

***

THE STRANGEST ASPECT of Henkel's position was his blithe refusal to acknowledge that the underlying problem of the euro consisted of our diverging national economies. He seemed to believe that currency and an internal market have no effect on each other whatsoever. A currency is a means of payment associated with exchange rate risks and other transaction costs. The use of several different currencies within the same territory therefore gives rise to more exchange rate risks and higher transaction costs.

Introduction of an "N-euro" would not only make life more difficult for Germany's exporters but cut the German economy off brutally from two of its foremost customers: Italy and France. Together with the other southern European countries, these represent 200 million consumers who altogether account for 28 percent of German exports and 9 percent of Germany's gross domestic product. Or what if we take Greece as our example? Following the introduction of the euro, German exports to Greece tripled, from approximately €4 billion in 2002 to almost €12 billion in 2008, the year in which the crisis erupted. And that is no coincidence: the euro was introduced in 2002, engendering a spectacular export boost for Germany.

Euroskeptics dismiss the observation that the United States, with the US dollar as its currency, has to overcome internal economic differences of a similar magnitude to those faced by the European states. They argue that the United States has been a union for two hundred years, whereas we have not—as though we must wait patiently for a specified period before introducing a common currency. They also shamelessly advance the myth that the American federal authorities have never had to intervene in order to rescue one of the states—when everyone knows that California and Florida were virtually bankrupt in around 2012 and could no longer pay civil servants' salaries. This certainly presented no small challenge in view of the fact that the two states and their economies formed two of the largest in the American federal system. The Greek debt crisis, on the other hand, represented less than 2 percent of the prosperity generated each year in Europe. As a result of doubts being spread about Greece, the euro was shaken to its foundations. Yet no one entertained the slightest doubts regarding the stability of the dollar despite the impending bankruptcy of those two states. Why? Because California and Florida were backed by a strong, federal state that acted with solidarity. Apart from the troika, Greece had the backing of no one.

HISTORY REPEATS ITSELF

Henkel may well be a successful businessman, but that doesn't mean his view of the common currency rests on a rational foundation. He eagerly set out to illuminate various examples of the good old days before the European Union existed, larding them with rhetoric like "a Europe of fatherlands," as opposed to "Europe as our fatherland." His text radiated a lot of nostalgia but did not contain the beginning of a vision for the future of our continent, let alone a clear blueprint. Despite this, he reproached me as a Euro-romantic, a label given to many pro-Europe politicians.

But we "romantics" don't wish to fundamentally overhaul the European union or create a new European project from scratch. The true romantics are those who wish to return to the past, who hanker after the old nation-states established by the Congress of Vienna or who, like Henkel, look back longingly at the good old deutschmark. Anyone can invoke lessons from history in support of a cause and then deny or forget those events that do not fit into the made-up story line. I would never claim that the "Zollverein" is hard proof of anything. I merely wish to point out that every example from history can be countered with another, often one not so far-fetched, in defense of the exact opposite position.

* * *

ANY FAULTS THE currency union displays are due neither to the euro itself nor to attempts to achieve a larger monetary union in Europe. They stem from mistakes made when the euro was introduced, and we must rectify those shortcomings. That would be a much more sensible step than throwing the baby out with the bathwater. Relieving the euro of its deficiencies is my project for the next chapter.

PART V

REBIRTH

CHAPTER NINETEEN

A GOVERNMENT FOR THE EURO

ALMOST FIFTEEN YEARS AFTER THE EVENT, IT REMAINS A PUZZLE how the people of Europe managed to set up a currency union and introduce the euro without first laying a firm political and economic foundation. The economic integration of Europe in the absence of political unification has had tremendous negative consequences for us all: failure to keep us safe, failure to quell old nationalisms, failure to provide Europeans with tools to address the global problems of today.

In July 1997, the European member states hastily agreed on the financial stability pact. Various rules were set down, but no government, no treasury, no budget, and no bonds were ever created. From the start, it quickly became clear that the pact actually contained vague guidelines rather than firm agreements.

This currency union came to resemble a vast train station to which all countries could proceed, regardless of the state of their economic or budgetary health. The accession of Greece in 2001, without doubt, exemplified this most flagrantly, but actually, the admissions tests for more or less every country were faked back in 1998. As politicians, we had agreed to introduce a common currency on January 1, 2001. This had to take place, whatever the cost, even though we didn't have all of the institutions and regulations in order—we actually had no idea how to enforce these—and even though many member states did not entirely fulfill the conditions.

POLITICS BEFORE ECONOMICS

It was as if we had learned nothing from the Americans, who only introduced the dollar after a decade-long process of integration. The United States started out as a confederation of thirteen states within which decisions could only be taken unanimously. The majority of those states quickly concluded, however, that this system was not working as intended. During the 1787 Constitutional Convention in Philadelphia, the American confederation was converted into a federation, meaning that a government structure existed over and above the original member states. Decisions could now be made on the basis of a qualified majority.

Next the United States set up a common treasury as a means of collecting revenues and making payments. After that came the introduction of so-called treasury certificates, the American version of eurobonds. This did not happen without a struggle, however. Alexander Hamilton favored the plan, while Thomas Jefferson radically opposed it. In the end, they compromised: Hamilton got the go-ahead to introduce a system of bonds, and Jefferson got his choice of a capital city: Washington in the South. Only after they had put all this in place did the Americans introduce the dollar on April 2, 1792, with the entry into force of the Coinage Act.

* * *

IN EUROPE, EXACTLY the opposite occurred. We started out with a common currency—the euro—only later wondering whether any difficulties would arise and which pieces of the jigsaw puzzle might be missing.

We introduced the currency in a rush because the euro was primarily a political project: it represented the ultimate reconciliation between Germany and France. François Mitterrand and Helmut Kohl were members of the last generation of European politicians to have lived through World War II. Mitterrand was twenty-nine when the war came to an end; Kohl was fifteen. For them, the euro symbolized the final end of 1,000 years of European disputes and divisions and the permanent unification of the old continent.

But a second, less noble motive lay behind the introduction of the common currency, though this was never publicly admitted: the euro was the concession that Mitterrand extorted from Kohl in order to secure his agreement to the reunification of Germany. In other words, Kohl exchanged the deutschmark for the merger of the Federal Republic of Germany and the defunct German Democratic Republic. In one fell swoop, the reunified Germany would become the largest and most prosperous member state in the European Union—an acceptable situation only if the Germans shared the symbol of that prosperity, the strong deutschmark, with France and the rest of Europe.

✷ ✷ ✷

THE WELL-PUBLICIZED OBJECTIONS to this fiscal union are ill founded. Milton Friedman's analysis, for example, never dug any deeper than stating, "In Europe, we speak different languages and have different customs," as if that constituted an obstacle to the use of a common currency.

Dozens of countries, cultures, and peoples, both inside and outside the United States, use the dollar, and all of them are different. For 2,000 years, the currency of India, the rupee, has been the respected legal tender on a continent that is home to 2,000 ethnic groups, twenty languages, and four major religions.

The euro did not find itself in difficulty simply because the Greeks speak Greek and the Germans speak German. Quite the contrary. All reputable studies conclude that the eurozone represents the ideal type of currency union. Not only has the euro drastically reduced banks' and investors' exposure to exchange rate risk but, most of all, it has ensured that nowadays we can manage liquidities much more efficiently than was the case before.

As a result, our economy can put precisely the correct amount of money into circulation so that it functions as it should. Thus, the euro was a blessing as far as Europe's economy is concerned, placing it on a much firmer footing and reducing risk. In other words, the euro fell victim to the irresponsible behavior of the banks and not the other way around.

* * *

WHAT IS MORE—AND this is the most important point—the common currency actually created stability during the financial crisis and its aftermath. That was no mean feat. Speculators have pushed weak currencies further into oblivion by investing money when rates are falling. The Europeans of today can state with pride that their currency offers the same level of certainty and security as the US dollar. Whereas at the start of the financial crisis, currencies such as the Hungarian forint and the Danish krone lost a lot of value, the euro remained a beacon of stability.

Exporting nations in particular reaped the rewards of this. Germany still benefits daily from the blessings of the euro. Based as it is on the cooperation of countries from northern and southern Europe, the European common currency is in fact relatively undervalued by German standards, providing a sustained and long-term boost to German exports. Conversely, we could also say that the countries of southern Europe are footing the bill for this boost. They are saddled with a relatively expensive euro, which artificially slows down their exports. That does not immediately benefit brands like Alfa Romeo, Maserati, Gucci, Armani, and many other creative southern Europe companies that serve the global market. This is useful to consider whenever we discuss the issue of "solidarity" within the eurozone.

In the same spirit, we need to move away from false clichés about the strong, hardworking North and the lazy South. The list is long of strong companies from France, Spain, and Italy, from a small specialist company in Bologna to major companies such as Peugeot, Danone, or Total. Following the outbreak of the euro crisis, the Spanish and Portuguese put their public finances in order. They have saved more and carried out more fundamental reforms than either Belgium or the United Kingdom. We must incorporate this crucial information into our political understanding.

A NEW PLAN FOR THE EURO

In order to deal with the euro crisis, we need to resolve two specific shortcomings. First and foremost, we need to forge a close and genuine economic union, with all that this implies.

This means that the euro urgently requires a treasury, something every national or supranational state institution or organization in the world already has. The revenues for such a treasury would come from taxation in Europe and would be deducted from the taxes levied by the national member states. Together with any loans entered into, the revenues thus obtained would enable us to draw up a European budget considerably larger than the paltry 1 percent that applies at present. The budget would also ensure that our national economies keep pace with one another and gradually grow together.

The euro actually requires a treasury like that of the United States that can convince the markets of its ability to achieve two objectives. First, it must be able to rescue countries or states that have gotten into difficulties as a result of their banks or their public finances. Second, it must be capable of implementing a stimulus policy that encourages the economies of the various states and regions to converge.

The US federal budget totals just under 25 percent of the country's gross domestic product. If, in order produce a viable comparison with Europe, we remove social security expenses from that amount (as in Europe the member states pay these), or if we look at the amount paid out by the US federal government before the New Deal, we arrive at a figure equivalent to around 10 percent of the US gross domestic product. We must then add another $600 billion, or 3.5 percent, to finance the system of interstate solidarity. The federal government then redistributes that amount to the less prosperous states with relatively low development potential or to those that have gotten into financial difficulties. Overall, this budget is thirteen times larger than that of the European Union.

* * *

An integrated currency requires an integrated economy. Achieving this, however, will involve more than having a European Central Bank (ECB) that sets the short-term interest rate and controls the amount of money within the economy.

The euro requires a government of its own, under the leadership of a European minister of finance, made up of members of the European Commission who manage the portfolios relating directly to the eurozone. That government would determine the success of the currency itself and of the European economy as a whole. Under the leadership of the European minister of finance, it would manage the treasury, collect taxes, and issue permitted loans. The ministry would have direct responsibility for the expenses that form part of the European budget and for enabling the various economies within the currency union to grow together. The minister would also be responsible for developing a convergence code for the euro.

Alongside the stability pact, this code would formulate objectives and criteria that the member states would be required to obey in all policy areas of essential importance to the strength of the economy and the well-being of the euro: the labor market, taxation, the pension system, innovation, and scientific research. Finally, the euro government would be given full powers to enforce the rules laid down in the stability pact and the criteria that form part of the convergence code; the current practice, in which member states supervise one another, is not working.

* * *

No currency union in the world is governed as superficially as is the euro. This why, in the eurozone, we are always talking about "governance" when we actually need a "government"—not endless meetings that ultimately lead nowhere but a full-fledged government with sufficient powers to make all of the decisions necessary to ensure currency stability, economic growth, and prosperity; a government that sketches out the route for the reforms that are needed within the member states, obliges them to adhere to the rules, and actually applies sanctions if they fail to do so.

We need a government that is also fully accountable to Europe's elected representatives. Some people regard this idea as a transfer of democratic control from the member states to the European level and thus as an attack on the sovereignty of the member states. But that flawed idea is based on the misconception that member states themselves would be accountable and democratic, which is certainly not the case. Once national leaders assemble in the council in Brussels and close the doors behind them, they are accountable to no one. That is anything but democratic and the very problem here. A fully accountable government for the euro would not replace national democracy or take away power from the member states. It would fill a void and strengthen democracy throughout our union. The euro government would sketch out the route, subject to European democratic control, but the member states would decide how, within the specified framework, to achieve the agreed objectives and established criteria, under the supervision of their national parliaments, in their capacity as national democratic bodies.

The responsibilities are clear: the objectives and strategic framework of the monetary union and the European economy as a whole would be irrevocably determined on a European level. This would require a non-discriminatory tax system that promotes growth, a mobile labor market that creates jobs, an affordable pension system that guarantees substantial payouts, and an effective health-care system that takes everyone on board. Member states would have exclusive responsibility for determining precisely how to achieve this, whether the tax system would be progressive or not, whether the labor market would encourage precarious employment or part-time jobs, whether the pension system would be based on redistribution or capitalization, and whether private or public hospitals would provide health care.

DEMOCRACY FOR THE EURO

Nowadays, the political epicenter of Europe is not located at the European Parliament, or in the national parliaments, or at the European Commission. Member states make all important decisions in the European Council. The controls exercised by national parliaments with regard to the European policy of their respective governments are minimal. In some member states, they do not exist at all. The national governments arrange everything by mutual consultation, without any involvement from the other European institutions: the amount they will contribute to the European budget, the rescue mechanisms they will put in place for the euro or the banks, and the agreements they will negotiate and conclude with Greece. Not only is there no accountability—there is no transparency either.

It is extremely important that we not allow this situation to continue. We could stop it by tasking the directly elected European Parliament with verifying the application of budgetary rules and the implementation of necessary reforms. Negotiations with "the Greeks" have now been under way for years, first with Antonis Samaras, now with Alexis Tsipras, tomorrow with some other prime minister of Greece. But all of this takes place in back rooms, at secret meetings between the Greek government, the European Central Bank, the European Commission, the Eurogroup (which unites the nineteen ministers of finance), and the International Monetary Fund (IMF).

How is democratic legitimacy maintained? What democratic controls are exercised on a national or European level? Members of the European Parliament, the government of Greece, and the government of Germany can only guess what is going to happen. Once the deal has been done, they need only give formal approval.

For example, the Greek parliament had only six hours in which to work through and approve the most recent package of legislation, which ran to 977 pages. Not a single member of the Greek parliament could have read through the entire text in such a short period. The situation in the other national parliaments was hardly any better. The Lower House in the Netherlands and the Bundestag in Germany could only accept what was on the table. Everyone knew that saying no was not an option. This was a classic example of "rubber stamping," in which the government puts the proposals before parliament at the very last minute in order to maintain an appearance of democracy. Such a practice doesn't exactly make Europe more popular, even though the member states—Germany, Italy, and France—not the European Union, were responsible in this instance.

The reproaches on social media came in thick and fast. Many people were scandalized, dubbing "that type of Europe" a disgrace. On Twitter, the hashtag #thisisacoup was trending shortly. The needed European revolution should restore not only European democracy but national democracy at the same time. Those who staff the barricades to uphold "national sovereignty" and the "superiority of national democracy" are either slavish adherents of this backroom brand of politics or have failed to grasp that today the true power lies with the heads of state and government and no longer with the people or their elected representatives.

At present, Europe has a very large number of extremely weak institutions. You typically find that in developing countries or emerging economies, and it is a disgrace. For centuries, Europe has set the standard due to the superiority of its democratic institutions—from the Magna Carta and habeas corpus, to the Renaissance development of banks, to the enforcement of intellectual property rights in the seventeenth and eighteenth centuries, to the introduction of parliamentary democracy and human rights in the two centuries that followed. Each time, these institutional innovations paved the way for new levels of prosperity. The time has come for Europe to set a new standard once again.

CONVERGENCE IS KEY

Alongside the financial stability pact, a convergence code, drawn up and promulgated by the euro government, would form the cornerstone of the eurozone. This would put an end to the "open coordination" method, whereby a random group of member states work together on a voluntary basis, which has functioned as biblical writ in the area of economic policy in Europe until now. The method has been a complete failure. Instead of growing together, the economies of the eurozone countries have grown apart, and it is not difficult to discover why.

Whether we are talking about the Lisbon Strategy, the 2020 agenda, the fiscal compact, or the European semester, the open coordination that serves as their basis has failed to move the member states to implement structural changes. Objectives and recommendations are formulated, and nothing more. Here too, we can say that there is much governance but little government.

A convergence code would operate very differently, however. It would not aim to harmonize the member states, as the differences between them are, in some cases, simply too large, but would set out to oblige the eurozone countries to take steps in the same direction in crucial areas of economic policy. To that end, the European Commission would establish minimum and maximum levels in each of those domains, forming a range that individual member states must respect.

Pensions are a good example. In view of the aging population in Europe, the pension system will, in the near future, exert a substantial strain on the public finances of all member states and therefore also upon the stability of the eurozone as a whole. The convergence code would stipulate the precise conditions that the individual member state pension systems must fulfill. This would prevent creation of new imbalances in one country that only another country's involvement could resolve. One Greek tragedy is enough. The convergence code would therefore establish the level of financial support necessary. It would determine demographic sustainability and the social minimum, a level designed to ensure that each retired person in Europe receives a reasonable income.

How member states adapted their pension system in order to fulfill those criteria would be up to them. In Europe, clearly some countries have systems able to fulfill those conditions fairly easily; others will face a long reform process. A comparison of the pension systems in Germany and the Netherlands provides an effective illustration. The Dutch system is largely based on collective capitalization, while Germany operates a system based on redistribution. This enables the people of the Netherlands to receive higher pensions at a lower retirement age than is the case in Germany. It also enables them to ensure that the system continues to operate effectively, both from a financial and from a demographic point of view. The convergence code would aim to enable the German system to converge with the Dutch one, not the other way around. It would be a matter not of "cut and paste" but of adopting principles and mechanisms that have proved their value. In that way, the convergence code would guarantee that the economies of the eurozone do not grow so far apart that the common currency is no longer tenable.

A NEW EUROBOND

What if countries refused to adhere to the code? The fines imposed under the stability pact do not work. No one would contemplate imposing an additional punishment on a country already in financial difficulties.

A much more sensible solution would be to create joint debt management within the currency union. Until the early 1990s, the market for government bonds was relatively straightforward. Countries largely borrowed money from their own populations. Many people bought bank bonds from their governments. On the bonds' maturity, governments would then repay that debt with interest.

Since the 1990s, however, the financial markets have gained the upper hand. Ever since, banks and institutional investors have supplied the bulk of loans to countries and therefore dictated the associated lending terms. In good times, these types of loan are available at attractively low interest rates, but when the economic climate is poor, those same markets respond aggressively, and base rates can shoot through the roof, with consequences for the interest burden and therefore the budget of the country concerned.

Nowadays, each member state in the eurozone offers government bonds on the bond market as a means of covering its national debt. Nineteen different treasuries seeking capital are therefore assigned separate credit ratings and interest rates. In times of budgetary restriction, this pushes the interest rates of each of the member states, the spread, apart, putting the currency union under extreme pressure.

We can only combat this by issuing eurobonds to mutualize debt management. It goes without saying that we would then obtain better terms and lower interest rates than if Dutch, Belgian, French, Greek, and Italian bonds were placed on the market separately. But eurobonds too will come at a cost: they will involve harmonizing budgetary and economic policy much more than we do now. Otherwise, a eurobond would simply amount to a premium for poor and undisciplined policies, a "moral hazard." In order to escape this and still enjoy the benefit of lower base rates, a convergence code will be essential. Only those who adhered to the code could enter the system of eurobonds. Any country that flouted the code would not therefore be approved.

Those that adhered to the code would enjoy reduced interest rates, which at present are reserved for major economic blocs such as the United States and Japan or for countries like Germany that obediently follow the rules. Eurobonds, linked to a convergence code, would therefore lead not to a "moral hazard" but to greater discipline and a greater urgency for reforms. They would reward good behavior and prevent "lazy" member states from requesting aid from the European Union at the drop of a hat. And most of all, they would prevent taxpayers from the wealthiest member states from having to cough up even more.

Eurobonds are available in many shapes and sizes, however. Probably the most attractive are those issued by a European debt repayment fund, an entity proposed by the Sachverständigenrat, a panel of economic experts that advises the German government. Entry to the fund would be linked to structural reforms. But the fund would be specific, in the sense that it would not set out to address all European debt but would bring together the debt that exists over and above the Maastricht standard of 60 percent and would offer it to the financial markets. The fund volume would be around €2.3 trillion. It would therefore offer substantial liquidity and could guarantee low interest rates. It could bring pressure to bear upon the markets, instead of markets' exerting pressure on member states, as happens today. It would also remove the immense pressure on the ECB, which is still obliged to buy up unlimited quantities of dubious government bonds in order to operate as a lender of last resort, throwing off its own balance sheet.

It is extremely surprising to hear that eurobonds and a European debt repayment fund would encourage irresponsible behavior, when such behavior is already taking place in the form of requiring the ECB to buy up unlimited quantities of Greek and other dubious bonds in order to keep the eurozone afloat. Eurobonds have the potential to prevent that very problem.

A EUROPEAN BANKING UNION

If we strengthen the public finances in the eurozone by introducing eurobonds, we must also make sure private money lenders are trustworthy. To that end we need to establish a European Banking Union not only in name but also in deed. This is the only way to break through the lack of credit acting as a millstone around our necks. After much discussion, we took banking supervision away from the member states and transferred it to the European Central Bank. Rather than turning the European Banking Union into a separate legal entity, we decided to entrust its supervisory tasks to the European Central Bank. Fortunately, for once, we avoided the common error of institutional fragmentation. But the job is not yet finished. The most important part of the banking union—a robust rescue fund—has yet to be established. The size of the current fund is not sufficient to enable us to withstand the domino effect caused by failing financial institutions.

To be effective, a rescue fund must at least be capable of rescuing two of our largest banks at the same time. At the moment, the fund barely covers 1 percent of all deposits in Europe. This equates to €55 billion, which represents barely half of the Hypo Alpe-Adria-Bank, a small Austrian financial institution that failed. We could swell the fund by requiring the banks posing the greatest risk to make larger contributions. At present, the basic contribution is the same for every bank. After that, a risk weighting is applied, which varies from a factor of 0.8 to a factor of 1.5. Contributions are meant to rise on an exponential basis, in line with the risk profile presented by each bank. Finally, national partitions must be removed so that European banks can be rescued using European funds and the mobilization of those funds no longer depends upon approval from all member states. It is simply too risky for a bank rescue to require the unanimous approval of twenty-eight member states. Though the majority of Europe's banks are historically based in one member state, every single one of them is nowadays a European bank. ING is no longer a Dutch bank, in the same way that BNP-Paribas is no longer French.

ONE VOICE FOR THE EURO

Despite its importance in the global economy—only the dollar precedes it as a reserve currency—the euro is currently underrepresented in international forums, such as the International Monetary Fund, the World Bank, the Group of Eight (G8), and the Group of Twenty. That is the case even among informal bodies, such as the Basel Committee, the Financial Stability Board, and the International Accounting Standards Board. This is because the eurozone is still not speaking with a single voice.

This disunited resistance to the euro is still extremely significant. I myself grossly underestimated it when, in collaboration with the late Tommaso Padoa-Schioppa, then Italian minister of finance, I hatched a mad plan to merge our "constituencies" in the IMF as the first step toward a single representation of the eurozone. A "euro constituency" would, in one fell swoop, acquire greater voting rights on the IMF's executive board than that of the dollar.

But we got a rude awakening. When we presented the plan to our respective government colleagues, we were almost laughed out of the council room. I had imagined that my Belgian colleagues, the most prominent being the minister of finance, would applaud the idea; instead they deemed it naive. Why would we relinquish our position as chair of a constituency, to which countries such as Turkey, Luxembourg, Austria, and Hungary also belonged, in order to fulfill a European dream? I called Tommaso, he told me of his similar experience, and we put our dream on ice. Whatever else we may do, instituting a single government with a single treasury headed up by a minister of finance would, in one stroke, end the absence of the euro on an international platform.

NO WAY BUT FORWARD

Projections of Europe as an all-dominating and all-devouring leviathan are a farce. One of the most popular slogans and associated memes circulating on social media is the so-called EUSSR, a contamination of the English abbreviations for the European Union and the former Soviet Union. It not very subtly implies that the European Union is no better than the Soviet-era Communist dictatorship.

Though sensible people recognize the grotesque hyperbole, such a comparison nevertheless hits a sore spot. We must face the fact that in the lack of transparency with which they make their decisions, the European Commission and especially the heads of state and government display many of the same characteristics as the Soviet government and the Politburo of the former Communist Party, respectively.

In all other aspects, however, this comparison does not apply. The Soviet Union controlled the Russian economy and the lives of its citizens from A to Z. Its institutions served one goal: implementing the Communists' perverted logic. In that regard, the European Union is actually the opposite. It has no perverted logic. It simply has no logic at all.

The European Union barely controls 1 percent of prosperity, 1 percent of the economy, and 1 percent of Europe's revenues. In the Soviet Union, the state controlled 100 percent of official prosperity, 100 percent of the legal economy, and 100 percent of national income.

Citizens' frustration has nothing to do with the existence of a European USSR or superstate; it has to do with the inability of European institutions to address the challenges confronting Europe as a whole. We already have a European government in the form of the European Commission and a European Parliament; yet we are still incapable of gaining control over the crisis on our continent. Citizens are asking themselves what purpose those institutions serve if the national elites ultimately make all the decisions. Even that 1 percent is then too much. The powerlessness of European institutions is the source of European citizens' aggravation, not the fact that Europe is playing too big a role.

* * *

A GOVERNMENT FOR the euro, with a European treasury that issues eurobonds, accompanied by a convergence code that dictates a new economic strategy, would represent a gigantic step in the right direction. It represents our only opportunity to survive in a world where the United States is stronger than ever and China's advance is unstoppable.

On an economic level, we have no choice but to accelerate and complete our integration. We need to set about creating an economic and a political union to stand alongside the monetary union in place since February 1992.

The alternative is to throw in the towel and make a final break with the project we initiated sixty years ago. That, however, would entail immediately forgoing the economic benefits that it brought—ease of doing business, freedom of movement, abolition of customs posts, and removal of the need to convert currency—not to mention relinquishing our hopes of ever again playing a strong geopolitical role on the world stage. The choice is ours.

* * *

WE NEED WHAT Henry Kissinger describes in *On China*. An elderly, retired Deng Xiaoping's successors asked him for advice about growing unrest during the switch from China's tightly controlled planned economy to a free market: "Now the aged leader of an ancient people was giving a last instruction to his society, feeling besieged as it attempted to reform itself. Deng sought to rally his people not by appealing to its emotions or to Chinese nationalism, as he easily could have. Instead, he invoked its ancient virtues: calm in the face of adversity; high analytical ability to be put in service of duty; discipline in pursuit of a common purpose. . . . The deepest challenge, he saw, was to prepare for the future when the immediate danger had been overcome."

Maybe Europe will take a lesson from China's approach to the greatest economic shift that civilization has ever experienced. Here too, the immediate danger has passed. We too now face a choice: to take the easy course and revert to nationalism, to whip up emotions and parrot the posts we read on Internet forums and social media, or to adopt a political approach that combines insight with understanding and to bring about greater integration within the European Union that it may remain a source of prosperity for the generations to come.

CHAPTER TWENTY

A EUROPEAN ARMY

T HE DISCORD OVER THE AMERICAN INVASION OF IRAQ AND Europe's fatal indecisiveness in the face of Russian provocation in
Ukraine have taught me that we will never play a significant geopolitical
role if we do not first succeed in establishing a European defense community, and soon.

That is not exactly a new idea. European leaders tried to set up such
a community as early as 1954. The governments and representatives of
the six founding members of the European Coal and Steel Community
reached an agreement, but a few months later the French National
Assembly withheld its consent. And so we ended up merely with the
customs union subsequently established under the Treaty of Rome.

A UNIFIED COMMAND

Almost half a century later, in July 2002, I wrote to my French and British colleagues in the European Council, Tony Blair and Jacques Chirac,
as they represented the two member states with the strongest military

capabilities and resources. Four years previously, in Saint-Malo, both had agreed to provide the European Union with an autonomous and credible military force.

My letter was actually an act of desperation. I was scandalized by Europe's negligible role in Operation Allied Harmony in Macedonia. For months the North Atlantic Treaty Organization (NATO) had been urging Europe to take over its military operations in the Balkans, but no matter how much European Union high representative Javier Solana exhorted them to do so, the majority of member states refused to commit itself. This was only the latest conflict in the Balkans that I feared the Americans would end up having to deal with, as in the case of Kosovo. I suggested that the European Union should finally take control of the situation.

The silence from London was deafening. I heard, informally, through my diplomatic advisor, that the letter was the worst initiative I had ever taken. My relationship with Tony Blair had sunk to new depths since informal discussions about a possible invasion of Iraq had started. The letter received a far better reception in Paris. One of the French president's senior advisors was dispatched immediately by high-speed train to my office in Brussels. His proposal to put paid to Europe's indecisiveness in the future was music to my ears.

An article under negotiation for insertion into the European constitution would lay the foundations for the establishment of a European General Staff, which would plan and carry out military operations autonomously. Each of the three "major" states—Germany, France, and the United Kingdom—already had its own operational headquarters. Three other countries—Italy, Spain, and Greece—had plans to establish one. This not only represented a terrible waste of money but reinforced disagreements about the European order of battle. Which headquarters should take the lead, when, and in which operations? Instead of three dogs fighting for the bone, we would now have six. A single European headquarters was the only solution. Belgium would provide buildings and infrastructure, and the European General Staff itself would comprise high-ranking army officers from the countries that wished to participate.

Germany was also enthusiastic. Jacques Chirac, Gerhard Schröder, and I decided to strike while the iron was hot and set to work immediately. Our main concern at this stage entailed preventing the plan from being watered down. We decided to offer it to the other member states as a fait accompli, on a take-it-or-leave-it basis. To give momentum to the plans and policy, we held several high-level meetings in rapid succession. We also presented our proposal immediately to the group of politicians and experts writing the European constitution. This group, under the leadership of former French president Valéry Giscard d'Estaing, took inspiration from the 1787 Constitutional Convention in Philadelphia. It aimed to replace the endlessly complex treaties with a simple but appealing constitution that would make the EU more transparent, democratic, and efficient. (Years later, their text was rejected in the 2005 French and Dutch referenda.)

✻ ✻ ✻

ALTHOUGH THE GERMAN press wrote scathingly about the defense discussions, Chirac and Schröder were undeterred. In the spring of 2003, we decided to hold a defense mini-summit to set the seal on the whole business. The press labelled it the "Chocolate Summit," expecting very little more from it than some Belgian chocolates and sweets with the coffee.

Yet the announcement still caused a huge stir. There was great resistance to the plan in the United Kingdom, Denmark, and the Netherlands, but far more important than the protests were the many quiet expressions of support that flooded in, and not only from minor personalities. Javier Solana and Romano Prodi, for example, expressed their solidarity. Greece, Portugal, and Hungary were keen to participate, although under enormous pressure from London not to do so. We saw clearly that we could do only one thing: hold to our purpose. Although ambitious, the plan was also entirely reasonable. In Europe, however, that is no guarantee of acceptance.

The defense mini-summit was an important step in the expansion of European defense after Saint-Malo. Everyone who took part agreed that the European General Staff had to play its part within NATO and should therefore strengthen the transatlantic alliance. The participants also agreed that membership should be an open cooperative arrangement. Anyone who wished to join should be able to do so at any time. The general staff should ultimately include all European member states.

Otherwise we kept the mini-summit's conclusions as concrete as possible. The crippling unanimity rule should be scrapped. Countries wishing to enter into military cooperation should do so within the new structure of the European General Staff. This staff would be responsible for planning and carrying out autonomous European operations. A real European intervention force should also be set up by integrating troops from Belgium and Luxembourg into the existing French/German brigade. We should also create a European high command for strategic air transport and a European protection force to combat nuclear, bacteriological, and chemical weapons. Finally we agreed on establishment of a European weapons agency to procure military equipment, among other things. In the end, this summit of European heads of government produced rather more than just hot air.

I lost no time in acting on the decisions, proposing to the Belgian government that it house the European General Staff in the Panquin barracks, an impressive building, dating from 1750 and situated in Tervuren Park, that still formed part of the ducal palace. The Panquin barracks would become a tangible symbol of a new European defense, something opponents under the leadership of Tony Blair would do everything in their power to prevent. By then, Blair had realized that there was no way back and—after getting the green light from the Americans—had expressed a willingness to cooperate on an "if you can't beat them, join them" basis. But he had an ulterior motive, as soon became clear.

As ever, the British tried to weaken and torpedo the whole enterprise. In the end, the Panquin barracks building was rejected as a home for the general staff. We had to change the words "staff" and "headquarters" to "strategic civil/military planning cell," a mouthful that boiled down to the same thing. Eighteen months after I sent the letter on the Macedonian question, we had finally made some progress on European defense.

By no means as ambitious as I had hoped, it was still, I thought, a step in the right direction. In the end, the victory turned out to be pyrrhic. To keep Blair and the British on board, Schröder and Chirac had to make one final concession: retention of the unanimity rule on a vote related to using the strategic civil/military planning cell to lead a military operation.

This mistaken concession actually handed the British a veto on every decision regarding the assignment of operation leadership to the European headquarters, a veto they have since used constantly. The planning cell, now housed in a barracks of the Military Academy on the Kortenberglaan in Brussels, a stone's throw from the European institutions, has led not one European operation. As before, the operational headquarters of a major member state always takes over operational leadership and supplies the majority of the forces. There still exists no real European operation or intervention.

❋ ❋ ❋

WITH OUR UNIFIED command in place in 2002, we could have prevented so much woe. Since then, the world has changed dramatically. Europe faces cyberattacks on military and civil targets, especially by Russia in the Baltic states, for example. In recent years, Vladimir Putin has made incursions into two sovereign states: Georgia and Ukraine. More than 9,000 people have perished since the beginning of the conflict in the closest of these states. More than 2 million people have left their homes and fled to West Ukraine, Russia, or Europe. Putin has literally shot the Ukrainian economy to pieces. He armed Russian troops on Ukrainian territory, provided them with intelligence, and gave them strategic support.

The European Union contented itself with imposing a few "targeted sanctions" and, as during the Balkan conflicts, left the initiative to the United States—but Ukraine is in our backyard, not theirs. In 2003 the European Union security strategy (drafted by Javier Solana) still spoke of Europe's being surrounded by "a ring of friends." Now, it is more like "a ring of fire," with Putin attempting to redraw the map of Europe by force.

On our southern borders too, in the Middle East, sectarian violence has broken out, and a dictator is using chemical weapons against his own people. More and more states in the region are on the brink of failure, leaving the door open to terrorism and extremism. Jihadis and terrorist organizations are using tactics that completely blur the lines between external and internal threats. In short, now is not the time to show disunity or to bury our heads in the sand in the hope that these threats will blow over by themselves. It is time to recognize that we need our own military force—a defense community that goes much further than the creation of an informal general-staff-that-cannot-be-called-by-that-name or a list of European battle groups that only exist on paper. We must devise and establish structures that go far beyond what we envisaged at the Chocolate Summit. We must create a true European Defense Union.

WASTEFUL AND MISGUIDED

Europe's military weakness is legendary. The twenty-eight member states together spend more than €250 billion on defense. The United States spends around €560 billion. Despite the picture France and England would like to paint, in military terms they simply are not in the same league. The combined European effort amounts to less than half of America's. The most dramatic fact is that, with half the resources, we cannot even develop 15 percent of America's military capability and expand operations into conflict zones outside Europe. In concrete terms, that means we are three to four times less efficient than the Americans.

This is not so much because we spend too little but because we waste far too much by buying everything twenty-eight times over. We have twenty-eight navies, air forces, and armies. We maintain twenty-eight medical and intelligence services. We procure twenty-eight lots of ships, tanks, and aircraft. Now and again we do agree to joint procurement or joint development of military equipment, but never to the point of fully integrating combat forces. Indeed, each member state continues—with a few exceptions—to maintain specialist battalions, whether for minesweeping, strategic air transport, or special intervention.

How big a waste of money this is really only becomes clear when you look at Europe's military expenses in detail. The United States spends 30 percent of its annual budget on personnel; Europe spends 50 percent. The Americans can set up more military operations, faster, with fewer soldiers. Currently 2.1 million Americans work in the US armed forces, while the EU member state armies have 2.4 million soldiers. With roughly the same number of military personnel, Europe is able to develop scarcely one-seventh the interventions of which the United States is capable.

The gap is widening all the time. Six years ago the Americans had more service personnel than the Europeans. So our personnel numbers have risen faster than those of the United States. We are even playing catch-up in how we deploy our military personnel. The United States has twice as many civilian personnel as Europe and also ensures that its military personnel have better logistical support. It has more modern weapons and more innovative equipment. American soldiers have at their disposal a budget three times that of their European colleagues.

Of course the number of soldiers and how they are equipped is not everything. These days, wars and conflicts are controlled and fought not with boots on the ground but with technology. In this area, Europe is stuck in the 1930s, as the lack of European cooperation means we have few resources to spare for innovative investment. Europe spends a fifth of its defense budget on technology, research, and development; America spends half as much again. The Americans also pool their resources in one large pot, while Europe spreads resources and capital-intensive investments over twenty-eight member states.

The solution is obvious. We must move toward a single European Defense Union, with European armed forces composed of soldiers wearing the same uniform. In the light of past experience, I propose that we do not start from scratch but expand the Eurocorps, established in May 1992 and operational since 1995, into a full European army. With a French/German brigade at its core, symbolizing peace on the continent of Europe, it currently includes troops from five member states: Belgium, France, Germany, Luxembourg, and Spain. Poland will also join soon, at which point Eurocorps will consist of soldiers from countries that make up half the population of Europe. At the moment, its core force of several thousand soldiers can be expanded into a combat force of 65,000 for deployment.

But we have to aim higher. We must turn Eurocorps into a full-scale European army comprising both land troops and air and naval capabilities. In addition to a rapid response team, the conventional army units will include special forces (for chemical warfare, for example), a logistics corps, and medical capability. All twenty-eight member states should run a single joint budget for these and for personnel, military equipment, research, and development.

To achieve this, we must first integrate the existing regional and bilateral cooperative arrangements into Eurocorps. In the short term, this will allow us to set up a European army capable of conducting, simultaneously, a single large military operation and three smaller interventions on land, at sea, or in the air. The soldiers of the European army will wear the same uniform with the same EU insignia. The army will be under the command of a general who, together with the rest of the general staff, will be responsible for all operations, procurement, and communication, much like the head of NATO in Europe. Troops will be stationed on European territory in line with Europe's strategic and military interests, not under a crazy distribution system dreamt up in some private back room or other. This will require the full cooperation of all twenty-eight member states and, in particular, harmonization of their different national defense plans.

❋ ❋ ❋

THE END RESULT will be a single joint European defense strategy, which will provide the framework for all military decisions. The high command will be based close to the institutions to which it reports. A short line of communication with European diplomats will be vital. It may seem paradoxical, but without a credible military capability of this kind, it is often impossible to achieve diplomatic success or enforce solutions to conflicts. "Hard power" is needed to achieve good results with "soft power."

We can no longer afford to show the disunity we displayed when America invaded Iraq. That is why the EU high representative for foreign affairs must cooperate closely with the European Defense Union and should preferably occupy the same building as the European General Staff. European defense policy must however fit seamlessly into the union's general security concept and strategic vision for foreign affairs. The diplomatic priorities and the actions of the European army must run in parallel. The member states will continue to maintain their own armed forces, but besides guarding their own territory, they will primarily be integrated into the broader European strategy and must be ready for rapid, efficient deployment. The internal procedures of the various ministries of defense will also have to be integrated seamlessly.

This will require an amendment to the European Treaty. Among other things we will have to abolish the unanimity rule so that in the future the European Council can make its decisions with a qualified majority. The council and the European Parliament will exercise the democratic supervision of the European Defense Union, whose services, along with the External Action Service, will be integrated into the European Commission, which will manage the budget and personnel. It will be financed from general EU resources, supplemented, if necessary, by compulsory contributions from the member states. Procuring military equipment and managing large parts of the armed forces jointly will save a huge amount of money. It will also create budgetary scope to relieve the burden on national budgets or, conversely, to provide additional resources for the procurement of military equipment or to boost our military research and technological development efforts.

The European army will make our continent both safer and more prosperous. The European Defense Union will not only stave off a wide range of threats but create a single European defense market in place of the twenty-eight different ones we have now. A single such market will create enormous economies of scale, particularly for development and innovation. We will be able to manufacture logistical equipment, satellites, communication systems, surveillance technology, advanced ammunition, and any other defensive or offensive weapon you can think of, from the simplest rifle to the largest aircraft carrier, in Europe.

Shortly after the 1999 Balkan crisis, the European states and their government leaders stated, "The European Union must create a force that can act autonomously, consists of credible military units, has resources and the power to decide to use them, and is ready to do so, so that it can react to international crises without waiting for a decision from NATO." Europe must indeed realize that playtime is over. We cannot keep outsourcing our defense to the Americans.

STANDING ON OUR OWN TWO FEET

I am by no means suggesting that we should cease to work closely with the Americans within NATO. We simply must not be so dependent on this alliance that we no longer have any say in what happens on our own continent or in our immediate neighborhood. NATO was not established as a security blanket for Europeans. And yet that is exactly what it has become, as we rely far too heavily on American support, not to mention American leadership, for our territorial integrity. Washington gave the Baltic states moral and military support immediately after Putin's invasion of Ukraine. Washington guarded their airspace and then supplied military equipment to most of the countries of eastern Europe. Washington then launched large-scale military exercises to ward off a potential Russian invasion.

It might have been the first time I have seen a nervous—or at least wavering—Putin. His reaction to the Italian newspaper *Il Corriera della Sera* was telling: "Only a lunatic would believe that Russia would attack NATO." For once, Putin's words were not a provocation. The speed and decisiveness with which he branded this scenario as ridiculous betrayed the extent of his uneasiness. We had not seen a nervous Putin since the conflict over Ukraine. Before that, we had only faced a self-assured Putin who boasted of the Russian army's "unrivalled" power—showing once again that only a credible defensive force can enforce peace and security, a fact that still escapes many self-proclaimed pacifists.

American politicians on both the right and the left have repeatedly expressed the view that Europe should be more militarily independent. And rightly so. Operation Atalanta, conducted to rid the Somali coast of pirates, shows that, if we really want to, we can also help to build a safer and more prosperous world and demonstrate global leadership as Europe. But we will have to expand these operations to other zones of conflict close to our borders. What we are doing for the Somali coast, we must also do in Mali, Libya, Syria, and Ukraine.

Thanks to the free movement of people, goods, and capital in Europe, the union forms a single economic area with a single currency. We must therefore defend and safeguard the project and the continent as a whole. If the Estonians or Latvians are threatened, so are the Portuguese or Spanish, and vice versa. A single European defense force to defend our territorial integrity and our values is an essential pillar of our free European society. It will make our continent safer. It will swallow fewer resources and strengthen our military power. It will make us a more reliable ally within NATO. What embodies the sovereignty of a people better than the defense of its citizens and their freedoms?

Thus, in the end, a joint defense program will contribute to sovereignty in the true sense of the word—not the sovereignty of countries or nations, which themselves are no more than lines on a map, often determined by historical accident or geographical obstacles, but the sovereignty of its peoples, the freedom of men and women who know they are protected to choose how they wish to lead their lives. Only a unified Europe—and no nation alone—can guarantee its citizens this sovereignty.

CHAPTER TWENTY-ONE

THE UNITED STATES
OF EUROPE

IT IS TIME TO REBUILD THE EUROPEAN UNION—TO GIVE IT THE powers and the means to tackle the crises it faces. Fortunately we already have a blueprint for this new and stronger union: the original Brentano constitution of 1952.

Heinrich von Brentano's constitution is a fine starting point, but it is not suited perfectly to today's world. It rested on three institutions: a parliament, a senate, and an executive council. So far so good. But his proposal also included a European court of justice and a council of national ministers. By fusing this proposed council of ministers with the senate—thereby forming a single institution representing the member states—we arrive at the perfect framework for the European federation that we need to establish.

Europe does not need a classical bicameral system, familiar from centralized states, where the upper house or senate reviews the legislation produced by the lower house or national assembly. One strong parliament and one council of ministers is enough, with the latter best transformed into a senate of member states. As envisaged in the text of that first European constitution, the parliament should not merely act as a control on the other branches of government but instead have all the sovereignty and authority befitting such a continental democratic body. It should approve the budgets and finances of the federation—in other words, make decisions about both income and expenditure—and thus fully exercise its democratic control over all executive bodies, not least the European government.

The representatives of the people would be elected in accordance with rules laid down in the law. These should enable the creation of transnational voting lists. Today, each candidate for parliament is currently elected only by voters from his home state. This means Germans can only vote for German politicians, French only for French ones, and so on. Since the European Council nominates the commission president and must "take the election results into account" in doing so, the commission president is elected only in his or her own country. Thus the majority of European voters never has the opportunity to speak out in favor of or against the commission president. If we used transnational lists, the lead candidates of each European political party would stand in all twenty-eight member states simultaneously. As in any democracy, parliament should also be able to change the electoral law on its own, by a simple majority, and should no longer be subject to unanimous consent in the council, as is the case today.

Alongside a parliament, the 1952 constitution also provided for a European government. At present, we still call that government the European Commission. Under Brentano's proposals, the president of this executive council would be nominated by one of the two legislative chambers. That was groundbreaking, as more than half a century would transpire before it effectively happened. At the 2014 European elections, each European political party nominated a lead candidate for the first time, and those candidates campaigned in virtually all twenty-eight member states. For the European People's Party, that candidate was Jean-Claude Juncker; for the Socialists, it was Martin Schulz; for the Communists, it was Alexis Tsipras; for the Greens, it was Ska Keller; and for the Liberals, it was me. Whoever won the most seats in the European Parliament had the right to make the first attempt to gather a majority behind his or her nomination. Whoever managed to do that would automatically be appointed president of the European Commission. In this way, the appointment of the head of the commission was no longer accomplished through backroom deals in the European Council but in the full glare of transparency. The European electorate determined, for the first time, not only the composition of the European Parliament but also who would lead the European government. It must be said, though, that all of this is built on extremely shaky ground. After all, in contrast to Brentano's text, nowhere do the current treaties stipulate that the president of the commission will be nominated in this way. They merely mention that the appointment of the president of the commission must "tak[e] into account the elections to the European Parliament." The lead candidate of the largest party in the parliament's being given a fair chance to form a majority had more to do with bumbled maneuvers on the part of David Cameron and the fact that Angela Merkel was under pressure from the German press. Ultimately, a pro-European coalition was formed between the Christian Democrats, the Socialists, and the Liberals. Many politicians and commentators are convinced that the appointment of Jean-Claude Juncker as president of the European Commission set a democratic precedent that the European Council can never overturn. Personally, I am not so sure. In the worst-case scenario, we may see another power struggle next time around, with the European Parliament and not the European Council coming off worse this time. In a well-functioning democracy, matters like this are not left to chance; they are laid down in a treaty or constitution, as proposed by Brentano. He also called European commissioners what they really are: ministers of the European community.

The members of the European government or executive council are chosen by the president—an important federalist starting point. After all, the European government and its president now derive their legitimacy from a majority in the European Parliament and not from the European Council. Today's European Commission, however, has become a mishmash of appointments from all those member states. A lottery, rather than voters, decides its composition, and its size—twenty-eight commissioners—is grotesque. There are simply not enough portfolios to go round. The 1952 European constitution, on the other hand, set the maximum number of members of the European government at twelve. A member state could have a maximum of two ministers. Moreover, it made no stipulations about the composition, in terms of either nationality or political affiliation.

To reiterate: the key notion is that the president, appointed by the parliament, puts together his or her own government team, which can then rely on a sustainable majority in the European Parliament. Under this arrangement, the European government, like its president, is installed by the parliament, to which it must also be accountable on a permanent basis. As in any democracy, the parliament can bring down the European government by means of a vote of no confidence, which required a three-fifths majority in the Brentano constitution.

In the same spirit, the European government must have the ability to lay down requirements for the member states. In so doing, it should state precise objectives, not how the member states must meet them. So, the member states could receive instructions, but in contrast to the current situation, such instructions would be democratically created, amended, and passed in the European Parliament rather than in the back rooms of the council building.

The conversion of the council into a senate to represent the member states provides the third institution of the future European federation, next to the European government and the European Parliament, as laid out in the Brentano constitution. Some serious thought must go into its composition. We need to put an end to the current chaos—whereby the member states are sometimes represented by the relevant national ministers, sometimes by their heads of state or government, and sometimes by their ambassadors in a system of meetings known as Coreper. Total confusion results whenever the heads of state or government take a different view from their foreign ministers on existential issues, as happened in relation to sanctions against Russia.

In its current form, the council, in which the majority of decisions still requires unanimity, has gradually become a graveyard for any legislative initiative taken at the European level. Each proposal either becomes stillborn—as the ministers or ambassadors cannot reach a decision—or, through amendment, becomes a completely watered-down, scarcely recognizable pastiche of the commission's original proposal. It is then crushed, pulverized, and stripped of its essence in what is known as the "trialogue," a euphemism for the countless rounds of negotiations between the commission, the council, and parliament, which squeeze out every last drop of the initial proposal's ambition and vision. This happens not with a view to the interests of European citizens but always with an eye on domestic electoral agendas.

We must replace this council with a senate that operates within the strict limits of a revising legislative body. The national parliaments could elect its members. Every upper and/or lower house in every member state could delegate its representatives for a term identical to that of the European Parliament, namely, five years. Unlike the current council, the European senate would have a fixed membership, and the dual capacities of ministers or heads of state or government would disappear for good. Recent years have delivered more than ample proof that a system in which national political leaders wear two hats is not functional. Every time, we see the subordination of European interests to national, regional, or local concerns.

If each national parliament delegated its own representatives at the European level, this problem would disappear. We would, in fact, be copying the Belgian federal system, where the state parliaments nominate the senate delegates from among their members. Other approaches are possible though, including the German model, where the state governments provide the delegates, or the US model, in which senators are directly elected.

A number of different solutions are also conceivable when it comes to the number of senators per member state. One option is to impose strict equality for all member states, as in the United States, or to take into account population size, which may be represented absolutely or within an agreed range. In the Brentano constitution, the number of senators ranged from twelve (for Luxembourg) to twenty-one (for Germany). That is roughly a factor of two. In Germany, the number of senators that each *Land* sends to the Bundesrat varies from three to six. That, again, is a factor of two. This seems to me a fair ratio for a Europe with twenty-eight member states, from small countries like the Baltics, to mid-range countries including Benelux and lots of eastern European countries, to large member states with populations in the tens of millions. I would keep the size of the senate as small as possible: one representative for the small and mid-range member states and two for the big ones: Germany, France, Italy, Poland, and Spain. This would bring the total number of members to thirty-two.

The more equality among the member states in terms of the number of representatives they get in the senate, the more we must adhere to strict proportionality when it comes to assigning the seats in the European Parliament, which represents the people. In other words, you cannot give the smaller member states more seats in the European Parliament than they would actually deserve on the basis of their population size and at the same time plead for a strict equality of all member states in the composition of the new senate. That would be unfair. It is one or the other: either full equality in the senate plus full proportionality in the parliament, or diluted proportionality in both chambers. In any case, we must limit the number of senators.

The European senate's job is not to form a second legislative tier and redo the work of the parliament, which directly represents the people of Europe. Nor is it to bring forward legislative initiatives. Its role is to act as a crucial second set of eyes on every piece of legislation adopted by the European Parliament. First of all, the senate must investigate whether each law is in contravention of the European constitution. Then it must check whether there is any conflict of interests—in other words, that no country will suffer a disproportionately negative effect. This was also the idea behind Brentano's proposals, which granted larger member states only a limited number of seats in parliament to prevent a coalition of a couple of countries from blocking the rest of the member states—a risk that the establishment of a senate would put a definitive end to. The senate would only veto and must have cause to do so. Once adopted by the parliament and approved by the senate, a law would be signed by the president of the European government. Without this being my explicit aim, we thus find ourselves with the American system, where the president is the head of state and leads the government, while the vice president takes up the role of president of the senate.

The Brentano constitution aptly separated the powers between the various bodies of government. It provided for a detailed division of competences, something our union has struggled with for decades now. Those competences that are currently the exclusive domain of the European Union are particularly limited: the customs union, competition policy, trade policy, and monetary policy for those countries that have adopted the euro as their common currency. Only in these areas can Europe make autonomous decisions and negotiate international treaties. All in all, they represent a limited range that we urgently need to expand.

First of all, we need a truly common foreign and defense policy in addition to congruence in the economic policy areas necessary to maintain a currency union. This can take the shape of "convergence rules" that bring the economies of the member states closer together rather than allowing them to grow apart. As stated above, in practical terms, this means that the union must lay down social and fiscal standards and the corresponding tolerances within which the member states must operate. When it comes to pensions, Europe must set the criteria that ensure financial and demographic sustainability for each of the national pension systems, along with the minimum guaranteed income needed to prevent ever larger groups of pensioners from falling into poverty. The same should apply when it comes to unemployment benefits, which should guarantee a minimum level of subsistence across Europe but also encourage people to work. Health care must also satisfy common standards while remaining financially viable. Finally, in the area of taxation, Europe must lay down the tolerances and manage common definitions for the tax base. This way, tax competition between member states would be much more up front than at present, and scandals such as LuxLeaks, which exposed unfair fiscal competition between member states through nontransparent tax rulings, could be eliminated.

Thus Europe would not determine how the pension system or the labor market or the tax system of each member state should look. That would be up to the member states themselves. Europe would, however, define the financial and social boundaries within which each of those systems must fall. This would not represent some kind of diktat from Europe but a guarantee of the vital cohesion and convergence without which an economic and monetary union is doomed to fail.

＊＊

How SHOULD WE fund this new Europe? The Brentano constitution delivers a crystal clear answer to this question too: by voting annually in the parliament on "the total receipts and expenditure." This happens in every true democracy, but in today's Europe it would be a revolution. The revenue in question would derive primarily from "own receipts," obtained from levies—from taxation, in other words. Yet a European federation could also borrow in order to pay for necessary investments.

The new Europe must, in any event, be able to function with financial independence, like any other democratic state in the world. With what levies exactly? What rates? Generating how much income? These highly ideological questions would be answered differently depending on the political majority in control in the European Parliament—and thus also in the European government—at the time. Ideally, of course, the levies in question would directly relate to Europe or the internal market, as is the case with customs duties, charges on carbon dioxide emissions, and indirect taxes such as the value-added tax. Both in Canada and the United States, a portion of the "sales tax" is an important source of revenue for the federal government. Every receipt indicates what percentage, and what actual amount, goes to Washington or Ottawa and what portion stays in local state or provincial coffers. This provides full transparency about the funding of the union or federation. In Europe it would provide a direct link between citizens and their political institutions at the European level and allow member states' contributions to fall. Europe's citizens would pay directly for its operation; they would thus take a much greater interest in where their money was going and, if necessary, call their elected representatives for an account.

⁂

IF YOU FAMILIARIZE yourself with the Brentano constitution, you will see straight away that a democratic and efficient union on the model of the United States—with clearly defined competences and transparent institutions—is no pipedream. It shows that we need less bloated, more effective institutions; a small, efficient European government whose members stand up for all European citizens, not just for those who belong to their own national support base; a government that, like in any democracy, is accountable to a directly elected, fully authorized parliament able to generate proposals and initiatives itself.

Anyone who sees in this the creation of a superstate is either acting in bad faith or willfully blind. The new union, as a federation, would acquire more competences only where they would generate effective added value. A federation would also put an end to the à la carte Europe, in which each member state picks and chooses its own form of European Union via opt-ins, opt-outs, earmarks, and enhanced cooperation. This kind of cherry-picking would be a thing of the past because it not only weakens the union as a whole but makes it unworkable. It is no longer acceptable to participate in a thriving internal market but refuse to assume the basic tasks necessary for its operation.

This leads to the idea—also found in the Brentano constitution—of introducing a two-tier form of membership: full and associated. This would allow Great Britain to abandon its current "full" membership and perhaps exchange it for an "associated" version. More generally, it would end the many inefficiencies and injustices that result from the arbitrary situation in which we find ourselves after so many decades of European compromises. A two-tier form of membership would give all member states the same option.

The Brentano constitution is simpler, more transparent, more democratic, and more efficient than the institutional makeup we have today. We like to think of the European Union as a great achievement, a step forward in civilization, and a sophisticated political enterprise. The Brentano constitution bears witness that this was certainly the ambition of our founding fathers, but we threw it in the garbage. We thought we were smarter than our predecessors, and instead of establishing a federal Europe at once, we opted for a "step-by-step" Europe. This led to an à la carte Europe, which culminated in an undemocratic, inefficient, and wasteful European Union.

The good news is that what human hands have wrought they can unmake. We can dig up the first constitution again, dust it off, and execute it. It is never too late to recognize our mistake. The political class in Europe is excessively late. We are running out of time. But, no, it is not too late.

EPILOGUE

THE UNITED STATES IS—IN ITS OWN WORDS—"FREAKED OUT" by the Brexit, but even before that vote, Americans were wondering out loud whether Europe still had any life. Simon Tisdall wrote an article provocatively titled "Is Europe Dead?" in response to the Greek crisis and the latent conflict with Vladimir Putin. It expressed great concern about events on the other side of the Atlantic and concluded, "Europe is not over, yet. But it is in deep trouble."

From an American perspective, that's a harsh but fair take on reality. The long list of problems and unresolved issues discussed in this book show that Europe is dangerously ill. And the disease afflicting Europe knows no borders, so it can no longer be treated independently by each of the nation-states. Only by working together and making a new leap forward in European integration can we cure the malady.

Our forefathers already knew this. They had to find out the hard way that we must resolve economic and political differences not on the battlefield but in conference rooms—in other words, we need to cooperate rather than draw our daggers. But the further away we get from the two world wars of the previous century, the more we lose sight of this fact.

Even though as a group of twenty-eight nations we have a great deal in common in terms of our history and culture, we are failing as a collective. We are no longer able to perceive the European project as a force for good. We fail to realize that today's world order—one dominated not by nation-states but by wealthy "empires" like China and Russia, multicultural federations like India and the United States, and subregional blocs like Mercosur and the Association of Southeast Asian Nations—compels us to adopt a new, positive, joint approach. In contrast to what Francis Fukuyama believes, no social model has had the upper hand in this process. Liberal democracy and the free market economy have not emerged from the ideological arena as the all-out victors. Today's world more closely resembles the "clash of civilizations" described by Samuel Huntington than the "end of history" predicted by Fukuyama. In a world of power struggles and shifting alliances, we can only hold our own by forming a European federation so as to stand alongside other superpowers. No single European nation-state can do that alone—not even Germany or the United Kingdom and certainly not France. We need to form a close-knit economic bloc to vie with China or the United States, especially if we want to safeguard our ecological norms and social standards. We can only hold our ground against an authoritarian Russia, whose leaders no longer believe in liberal freedoms or human rights, by also becoming a political and military superpower.

For too long now, we have tinkered on the margins. It is time, to paraphrase Neil Armstrong, to take a giant leap. And we must make that leap in full awareness that we will sometimes have to set aside our national interests in favor of a greater European good. We must realize that each time we make a sacrifice, twenty-seven occasions will follow in which others sacrifice something to our advantage. The benefits of a European federation would far outweigh the burdens or efforts it would entail. The paradox currently trapping European politics is this: we look to Europe to solve many social problems, but no one is prepared to equip Europe with the resources it needs to solve them. Behind closed doors, many politicians acknowledge the need for a United States of Europe but claim that their voters would not support pursuit of this goal.

That is a misrepresentation of the facts, to put it mildly. Yes, the anti-European lobby is vociferous. But it by no means speaks for the majority. However loud their voices, Euroskeptics from left and right nowhere represent more than a quarter of the population. What's more, European leaders underestimate pro-European feelings among their citizens. The most recent Eurobarometer, which polled public opinion when the euro crisis was rocking Europe, shows that the majority of Europeans wants more, not less European integration. Most voters—on both sides of the political spectrum—have had enough of today's malfunctioning union, but they certainly don't want to ditch the European project. The average European wants a thoroughly reformed union that is more efficient, more democratic, more multifaceted, and more transparent. Institutions that functioned well in the days of Robert Schuman and Jean Monnet or Helmut Kohl and François Mitterrand have ceased to meet the needs of today's globalized, digitized world.

So for a long time now, pro-European politicians have been in an awkward predicament. They have to defend a project that urgently needs reform. At the same time they know that reform of this scale will not happen automatically because heads of state and government must unanimously approve it. This inevitably results in tiny steps forward—in a few meaningless compromises that do little or nothing to solve the enormous challenges we face.

Instead we need vision and politicians who take the lead, who are inspired by an ambitious project that spans the entire continent, who are guided by what people really want. Two-thirds want a common economic policy drawn up so that the euro can remain a strong, stable currency. Of those polled 60 percent say they identify as both a European and a national of their own member state. That goes up to almost 70 percent in countries like Germany, Sweden, and the Netherlands. Contrary to popular belief, a feeling of Europeanness is least pronounced in eastern and southern Europe. And it's no coincidence that those member states have the most reason to doubt European sol-idarity. Italy, once the bastion of Eurofederalism, is turning its back on Europe—not because Europe is taking on too much but because it is insufficiently European. Take the way Italy was left to tackle the refugee crisis virtually on its own.

The postwar years were marked by optimism. They were followed by a period of unemployment, economic problems, and slow enlarge-ment—dubbed euro-sclerosis—but we overcame these difficulties thanks to the pioneering vision and unbridled enthusiasm of a new generation of politicians. They launched the common market, enabling Europe to grow once again and look confidently to the future. Today we confront a much graver crisis, a truly knotted dilemma with moral, political, and economic dimensions.

To resolve that dilemma, we will need to find a new path, one that breaks with populism and the exploitation of superficial national differ-ences. We must concentrate once again on that which binds us, on the challenges we face jointly. We must be led by the following question: How can we strengthen our position in a constantly changing world? We must be guided not by our prejudices or fears but by our ambition to play a meaningful role in the world of the future.

A federal Europe is the only option. It is both logical and inevitable. But that federal Europe will not create itself. We will have to fight for it. We will have to forge it with all the strength we possess.

ACKNOWLEDGMENTS

I AM MOST grateful for the help I got from Bram Delen with the research and the ample drafts he provided me. Also special thanks to Ben Platt, whose editorial skills made this book faster-paced and even more politically charged than I envisioned it.

NOTES

1. DIVIDED WE FALL

16   **Jamal Zougam, who carried out:** Eric Pelletier, Jean-Marie Pontau-tavec Laurent Chabrun, and Cécile Thibaud, "Les nouveaux objectifs d'Al Qaeda," *L'Express*, March 22, 2004, http://www.lexpress.fr/actualite /monde/les-nouveaux-objectifs-d-al-qaeda_490269.html.

17   **The British parliamentary committee:** Kim Howells, MP, "Could 7/7 Have Been Prevented? Review of the Intelligence in the London Terrorist Attacks on 7 July 2005," Gov.uk, May 2009, https://www.gov.uk /government/uploads/system/uploads/attachment_data/file/224542/7-7 _attacks_intelligence.pdf.

17   **In 2014, Mehdi Nemmouche:** Laurent Borredon and Soren Seelow, "Nemmouche est repassé en France avant la tuerie à Bruxelles, selon un porche," *Le Monde*, June 7, 2014.

17   **The same pattern crops up:** "Who Were the Charlie Hebdo Killers?" Radio France International, January 10, 2015.

3. AMNESIA

40   **"We are working to implement"**: Robert Schuman, speech on the establishment of a European Community, Strasbourg, May 16, 1949.

41   **"United States of Europa"**: Speech by Winston Churchill, Zürich, September 19, 1946.

44   **"not stressful enough"**: Wolfgang Munchau, Eurointelligence, October 24, 2014.

4. THE EUROPEAN DWARF I: THE MIDDLE EAST

57   **"freedom and democracy for all Syrians"**: Koert Debeuf, "What Does the Free Syrian Army Want?" Fikra Forum, March 28, 2013, http://fikraforum.org/?p=3161#.V5S6co9OLRk.

57   **Meanwhile, small brigades**: Koert Debeuf, *Has the Arab Revolution Ended? A European Perspective* (Dar el Badael, 2015).

58   **The longer Europe remained inactive**: Erin Banco, "The Free Syrian Army Has Collapsed," *International Business Times*, March 14, 2015.

5. THE EUROPEAN DWARF II: RUSSIA

66   **"I have just had the French"**: Condoleezza Rice on *Fox News Sunday with Chris Wallace*, August 17, 2008.

72   **"It sounds like a chapter"**: Luke Harding, "We Should Beware Russia's Links with Europe's Right," *Guardian*, December 8, 2014, https://www.theguardian.com/commentisfree/2014/dec/08/russia-europe-right-putin-front-national-eu.

73   **"most admired"**: Ibid."

73   **"more honest than the British"**: Ibid.

73   **"a phenomenon that is seen"**: Ibid.

74   **"weak, permeable and susceptible"**: Ibid.

6. THE CHRONIC CONDITION OF NATIONALISM

76   **"a radical Christian party"**: MTI, "Jobbik Confident of Winning EP Seat, Party Leader Says," politics.hu, May 13, 2009, http://www.politics.hu/20090513/jobbik-confident-of-winning-ep-seat-party-leader-says.

76 **"global capitalism and Zionism":** Gregg Morgan, "Hungary's Jobbik Party Hold Anti-Semitic Rally in Budapest After Ban Attempts Fail," *Telegraph*, May 4, 2013, http://www.telegraph.co.uk/news/worldnews /europe/hungary/10037377/Hungarys-Jobbik-party-hold-anti-semitic -rally-in-Budapest-after-ban-attempts-fail.html.

77 **"multikulti had utterly failed":** "Integration: Merkel erklärt Multikulti für gescheitert," *Der Spiegel*, October 16, 2010.

81 **"A nation presupposes a past":** Ernest Renan, *Qu'est-ce qu'une nation?* (Paris: Calmann Lévy, 1882), chap. 3, iii.

7. "QUICK FIX" POLITICS

95 **"the euro can only be saved":** Tina Kaiser, "Nur eine politische Union kann den Euro retten," *Die Welt*, November 10, 2013, http://www.welt .de/wirtschaft/article121721097/Nur-eine-politische-Union-kann-den -Euro-retten.html.

95 **"Because monetary union wasn't":** Paul Krugman, "The Macroeconomics of European Disunion," *New York Times*, June 3, 2013.

96 **"Granting federal aid to Spain":** Paul Krugman, *New York Times*, June 2, 2012.

96 **"The crisis has exposed":** "Towards a Fiscal Union for the Euro Area," IMF Staff Discussion Note, September 2013.

96 **"fiscal union for the euro area":** Ibid.

97 **"the most advanced knowledge-based":** Conclusions of the European Council, March 23 and 24, 2000.

8. THE HUNGARIAN DISGRACE

109 **"The details are yet to be hammered out":** Dennis Lynch, "Putin and Hungary's Orbán Agree to Gas Deal," *International Business Times*, February 17, 2015.

109 **"tyrannizing the Hungarian people":** Neil Clark, "Taking on the Big Six Energy Giants Is Not a Leftwing Delusion—Ask Hungary," *Guardian*, October 29, 2013.

110 **Of greater concern:** Nils Muiznieks, report of the commissioner for human rights following his visit to Hungary from July 1 to 4, 2014.

111   **"RTL is threatening the country"**: "Government Throttles Media with New Tax on Advertising," Reporters without Borders, June 12, 2014.

113   **"I don't think that our European Union"**: Zoltan Simon, "Orbán Says He Seeks to Eliminate Liberal Democracy in Hungary," *Bloomberg*, July 28, 2014.

113   **"A once-promising democracy"**: Kati Marton, "Hungary's Authoritarian Descent," *New York Times*, November 3, 2014.

114   **"While limitations may be"**: Plenary debate, European Parliament, April 17, 2013.

114   **"The implementation of this provision"**: Ibid.

114   **"How can you [Orbán] sleep"**: Andrew Rettman, "US Diplomat Lashes Out at Hungary's Orbán," *EU Observer*, October 3, 2013.

116   **"They're a weak lot"**: "Margaret Thatcher About the Weakness of European Countries," video posted to YouTube by ybn on October 14, 2011, https://www.youtube.com/watch?v=RBzAwro8M90.

9. THE MASS GRAVE OF THE MEDITERRANEAN: MIGRATION AND SECURITY

121   **"That image of hundreds of coffins"**: "Barroso Visits Lampedusa in Wake of 'European Tragedy,'" *Euronews*, October 9, 2013.

121   **"I don't care if he comes here or not"**: Ibid.

121   **"What are they"**: Ibid.

124   **Tens of thousands of Syrians**: United Nations High Commissioner for Refugees, Syria Regional Refugee Response, July 15, 2015.

11. THE DECLINE OF EUROPEAN INDUSTRY

144   **From a third of the global economy**: Maarten Schinkel, "China grijpt financiële wereldmacht tegen 2050," *De Standaard*, April 9, 2015. Figures from IMF and HSBC.

144   **"the balance in the global economy"**: Ibid.

152   **A truly unified airspace**: Figures: European Commission, *DG MOVE Statistical Pocketbook* 2012, 120–133.

12. THE CREDIT CRUNCH

162   **"The banking sector and"**: Speech by Mario Draghi, conference for the

twentieth anniversary of the establishment of the European Monetary Institute, Brussels, February 12, 2014.

162   **"If we don't solve the problem":** Ibid.

15. THE QUAGMIRE OF EUROPEAN INSTITUTIONS

185   **Equally absurd is the fact:** See the Single Seat campaign website (http://www.singleseat.eu).

188   **"a lake that has many deep parts":** "Coalitions for the Willing," *Economist*, February 1, 2007.

16. THE BREXIT

195   **On June 24, after that referendum:** Chris Giles, "Brexit in Seven Charts—the Economic Impact," *Financial Times*, https://next.ft.com /content/0260242c-370b-11e6-9a05-82a9b15a8ee7.

197   **"parasites undermining their host countries":** James O' Brien, London Broadcasting Company, June 28, 2016.

17. THE GREXIT

204   **"an historic day that would place Greece":** "Greece Joins Eurozone," *BBC News*, January 1, 2001.

204   **Only Wim Duisenberg:** Ibid.

209   **Rather than abolishing patronage:** Francis Fukuyama, *Political Order and Political Decay: From the Industrial Revolution to the Globalization of Democracy* (London: Profile Books, 2014).

19. A GOVERNMENT FOR THE EURO

245   **"Now the aged leader of an ancient people":** Henry Kissinger, *On China* (New York: Penguin, 2011).

20. A EUROPEAN ARMY

256   **"The European Union must create":** "About the CSPD—the Cologne European Council," European External Action Service, http://eeas.europa .eu/csdp/about-csdp/cologne_council/index_en.htm.

EPILOGUE

269 **"freaked out":** Nicola Gaouette and Stephen Nicollson, "Why the U.S. Is Freaked Out by Brexit," CNN, June 25, 2016.

269 **Americans were wondering out loud:** Simon Tisdall, "Is Europe Dead?" CNN, June 2, 2015.

INDEX

GUY VERHOFSTADT was prime minister of Belgium from 1999 to 2008 and has served in the European Parliament as president of the Alliance of Liberals and Democrats for Europe since 2009.